The Oxford Introductions to U.S. Law

Family Law

D1607482

The Oxford Introductions to U.S. Law

Family Law

BRIAN H. BIX

OXFORD
UNIVERSITY PRESS

OXFORD
UNIVERSITY PRESS

Oxford University Press is a department of the University of Oxford. It furthers the University's objective of excellence in research, scholarship, and education by publishing worldwide.

Oxford   New York
Auckland   Cape Town   Dar es Salaam   Hong Kong   Karachi   Kuala Lumpur   Madrid
Melbourne   Mexico City   Nairobi   New Delhi   Shanghai   Taipei   Toronto

With offices in
Argentina   Austria   Brazil   Chile   Czech Republic   France   Greece   Guatemala   Hungary
Italy   Japan   Poland   Portugal   Singapore   South Korea   Switzerland   Thailand
Turkey   Ukraine   Vietnam

Oxford is a registered trade mark of Oxford University Press in the UK and certain other countries.

Published in the United States of America by
Oxford University Press
198 Madison Avenue, New York, NY 10016

Library of Congress Cataloging-in-Publication Data
Bix, Brian.
The Oxford introductions to U.S. law. Family law / Brian H. Bix.
    p. cm.—(Oxford introductions to U.S. law)
  Includes bibliographical references and index.
  ISBN 978–0–19–998959–1 ((pbk.) : alk. paper)
1. Domestic relations—United States. I. Title. II. Title: Family law.
  KF505.B59 2013
  346.7301'5—dc23

                 2012041150

9 8 7 6 5 4 3 2 1

Printed in the United States of America on acid-free paper

Note to Readers
This publication is designed to provide accurate and authoritative information in regard to the subject matter covered. It is based upon sources believed to be accurate and reliable and is intended to be current as of the time it was written. It is sold with the understanding that the publisher is not engaged in rendering legal, accounting, or other professional services. If legal advice or other expert assistance is required, the services of a competent professional person should be sought. Also, to confirm that the information has not been affected or changed by recent developments, traditional legal research techniques should be used, including checking primary sources where appropriate.

(Based on the Declaration of Principles jointly adopted by a Committee of the
American Bar Association and a Committee of Publishers and Associations.)

You may order this or any other Oxford University Press publication
by visiting the Oxford University Press website at www.oup.com

Contents

About the Editor

DENNIS PATTERSON HOLDS the chair in Legal Philosophy and Legal Theory at the European University Institute in Florence, Italy. He is also Board of Governors Professor of Law and Philosophy at Rutgers University School of Law, Camden, New Jersey, and Chair in Jurisprudence and International Trade at Swansea University, UK. Patterson is the author of *Law and Truth* (Oxford University Press 1996) and *The New Global Trading Order* with Ari Afilalo (2008). He is general editor of *The Blackwell Companion to the Philosophy of Law and Legal Theory*. He has published widely in commercial law, trade law, and legal philosophy.

About the Author

BRIAN H. BIX is the Frederick W. Thomas Professor of Law and Philosophy at the University of Minnesota, where he teaches and writes in the areas of family law, jurisprudence, and contract law. He received his law degree from Harvard Law School and his doctorate from Oxford University. He is a member of the Bars of Minnesota, Massachusetts, and Connecticut, and a member of the prestigious American Law Institute. Professor Bix has published fifteen books and over one hundred articles; his work has been translated into eight languages.

Preface

A BOOK ABOUT family law is necessarily a book both about family life and the role law (and government generally) can and should take in regulating family life. Individually and together, these are vast topics, and the limits of both space and expertise mean that only a small part of what could be written on these topics will be discussed in this book.

This book aims to offer a critical introduction to family law, for the use of law students and scholars equally: offering not only an overview of the basic rules of American family law but also the history behind those rules and the principles underlying them. That is a large task, and there is no doubt that it can be done only very imperfectly in the space available. However, if the text succeeds in portraying even a portion of the richness and complexity of family law, it will have been worth doing.

An additional, and more specific, caveat: because American family law is primarily a matter of state law, the rules that govern inevitably vary from one jurisdiction to the next. This text does not purport exhaustively to detail every state-by-state variation, but rather to discuss the general principles that currently dominate legislation and case law in the area, and to mark any trends for change.

Also, American family law is ever-changing (and this is likely true of the family law for most countries in modern times). A significant number of important family law decisions and legislation came down just during the period in which this text was written (and, inevitably, many more will appear during the production process;

books on this subject are doomed to be at least somewhat out of date the day they appear!).

Inevitably, this book will not discuss many issues that have some connection with family law (and covered in many family law courses). Among the excluded topics are many will and estate issues relating to families, abortion, the ethics of representation (including the ethics of collaborative law practice), the rights of gay and transgender individuals (beyond the same-sex marriage and parenting issues the book does discuss), family-related immigration and asylum issues,[1] the interaction of family law and criminal law,[2] and many issues relating to procedure and representation in family law proceedings.

I am grateful for the help and support of Dennis Patterson, Dedi Felman, Lori Wood, and Jennifer Gong, and in general for all the assistance (and patience) of the editors and staff of Oxford University Press. I am also grateful to Barbara Ann Atwood, Beverly Balos, Karen Helfand Bix, Jill Hasday, Joel A. Nichols, and Robin West for their comments and suggestions, and for the research assistance of the University of Minnesota Law Library.

---

1. *See, e.g.,* Nicole Lawrence Ezer, "The Intersection of Immigration Law and Family Law," *Family Law Quarterly,* vol. 40, pp. 339–366 (2006).
2. *See, e.g.,* Dan Markel, Ethan J. Leib, & Jennifer Collins, "Rethinking Criminal Law and Family Status," *Yale Law Journal,* vol. 119, pp. 1864–1903 (2010).

PART ONE

General Principles

ONE

The Principles of American Family Law

IN STUDYING OTHER areas of law, it is common to come across theories that purport to make sense of the whole field, or to offer guidance for reform across the entire doctrinal area. Thus, one sees theories of property, theories of tort law, theories of contract law, and so forth, in which an area of law is claimed to be entirely or primarily about corrective justice, autonomy, efficiency, or the like.[1] Whatever the merits of this view in other doctrinal areas,[2] I do not think that a comparable claim can be made about (American) family law. However, even if there is no single overarching theory of family law, there are persistent themes that pervade its various issues, though the relative strength of each theme will usually vary from topic to topic.[3]

This chapter will outline and briefly explain certain basic themes and principles that recur within family law. The basic themes and

---

1. *See, e.g.,* Stephen R. Munzer, *A Theory of Property* (Cambridge: Cambridge University Press, 1990); Gerald J. Postema (ed.), *Philosophy and the Law of Torts* (Cambridge: Cambridge University Press, 2001); Peter Benson (ed.), *The Theory of Contract Law* (Cambridge: Cambridge University Press, 2001).
2. I raised doubts about there being a general or universal theory of contract law in Brian H. Bix, *Contract Law: Rules, Theory and Context* (Cambridge: Cambridge University Press, 2012).
3. In a recent work, Vivian Hamilton offered a list of family law principles that varies from the one offered in this text. Her list has four "important concepts"—conjugality, privacy, contract, and *parens patriae*—which in turn are said to embody "two distinct underlying principles"—biblical naturalism and liberal individualism. Vivian Hamilton, "Principles of U.S. Family Law," *Fordham Law Review*, vol. 75, pp. 31–73 (2006). For a different, lengthier list of the themes of family law, see Carl E. Schneider & Margaret F. Brinig, *An Invitation to Family Law* (3rd ed., St. Paul: West, 2006), pp. 179–223.

principles discussed below are (1) federalism, (2) ex ante versus ex post decision making, (3) discretionary versus nondiscretionary decisions, (4) contract versus status, (5) bright-line rules versus functional standards, (6) the proper level of deference for traditional or conventional views and practices, (7) family privacy, (8) the problem of inadequate data, (9) using or ignoring existing categories, and (10) the nature and role of "family." Many of these themes are not exclusive to American family law and appear in other legal areas (and other countries), but they still take a distinct form in American family law. For example, issues relating to federalism affect many areas of American law (and federalism or subsidiarity affects the law in many other countries), but there is a special spin in American family law, where many judges and commentators claim that family law is a matter exclusively of state law, but in fact federal law is pervasive and increasingly important. These themes will be outlined in this chapter and revisited later in the text as they are exemplified in rules and principles within different family law topics.

⅋ A. Federalism

Federalism describes the complicated interaction of states and the federal government in the U.S. governmental system, in which powers are distributed between the federal government and the individual state governments.[4] Family law has traditionally been a matter of plenary state power, but in recent years state power has been constrained on one hand by federal congressional action, and on the other hand by judicial readings of constitutional provisions (including the Full Faith and Credit Clause of the U.S. Constitution,[5] which requires states to recognize sister states' judgments in

---

4. Many other countries have federalist governmental structures, and while those countries may distribute powers between the levels of government in different ways, certain basic issues will arise however power is distributed.

5. U.S. Const., art. IV, § 1.

family law (and other) matters, and the Due Process Clause, which has been held to protect both marriage[6] and parental rights[7]).

Congressional interventions on the regulation of domestic relations have sometimes been direct (e.g., the Indian Child Welfare Act[8] and the Parental Kidnapping Prevention Act[9]). Equally significant have been the conditioning of significant block grants to the states on their passing certain legislation (e.g., relating to child support guidelines[10]).

Significant federal (judicial) intervention in the name of constitutional rights have included decisions regarding when states can grant nonparents rights to seek visitation,[11] when states can cut off parental rights,[12] and limits on what legal disabilities can be visited on nonmarital (illegitimate) children.[13] There have also been significant refusals of the U.S. Supreme Court to intervene in the name of the Constitution: holding that states have wide power to exclude from adoption proceedings biological fathers who had played no role in their children's lives;[14] to create (or fail to create) a conclusive presumption of a husband's paternity of a child born to his wife;[15] to allow parents to place their children in institutions with only minimal procedural review; and to allow state agencies to act against the interests of long-term foster parents in child placement decisions.[16]

---

6. *E.g.*, Zablocki v. Redhail, 434 U.S. 374 (1978).

7. *E.g.*, Troxel v. Granville, 530 U.S. 57 (2000).

8. 25 U.S.C. § 1901, *et seq.*

9. 28 U.S.C. § 1738A.

10. Child Support Enforcement Amendment (SCEA) of 1984, Pub. L. No. 98-378, 98 Stat. 1305.

11. Troxel v. Granville, 530 U.S. 57 (2000).

12. Santosky v. Kramer, 455 U.S. 745 (1982).

13. *See* Levy v. Louisiana, 391 U.S. 68 (1968); Clark v. Jeter, 486 U.S. 456 (1988).

14. *See* Lehr v. Robertson, 463 U.S. 248 (1982).

15. Michael H. v. Gerald D., 491 U.S. 110 (1989).

16. Smith v. Organization of Foster Families For Equality and Reform, 431 U.S. 816 (1977). More precisely, *Smith* strongly questioned whether foster parents had constitutional rights in continued contact with their children and held that whatever modest rights they might have had been met by the state procedural protections challenged in the case.

The federalist aspects of American family law involve not only the federal constraints on state action but also the differences from state to state. Because family law is primarily a matter of state law, there is a great deal of variety within the United States, from one state to the next, in the rules and principles governing many of the family law topics we will be considering. In part, this is a celebrated benefit of federalism: that the states can, and do, serve as "laboratories" for different family law experiments,[17] as states in the 1970s could have learned from California what the effects might be of no-fault divorce, and as states are now learning from Louisiana and other states what the effects are of covenant marriage and from Massachusetts and other states about the effects of recognizing same-sex marriages.

The variety of rules and principles across states also, of course, reflects the different cultures and norms of the different parts of this large country: how California will be predictably different from Utah, and New York different from Texas, and so on. There are obvious benefits to allowing communities to structure their legal system to reflect their own values, though there are also costs—for those who do not share the values of the majorities in their communities, and the problems caused in a mobile society by the absence of legal uniformity when one travels (even if just for a vacation) from one state to another. In the following chapters, we will see how marital and parental rights can alter for some people as they cross state lines.[18]

---

17. New State Ice Co. v. Liebmann, 285 U.S. 262, 311 (1932) (Brandeis, J., dissenting) ("It is one of the happy incidents of the federal system that a single courageous State may, if its citizens choose, serve as a laboratory; and try novel social and economic experiments without risk to the rest of the country.").

18. Barbara Atwood reports that there is also a rich range of cultural differences across Indian tribes (which have significant autonomy in family law matters). Barbara Ann Atwood, "Tribal Jurisprudence and Cultural Meanings of Family," *Nebraska Law Journal*, vol. 79, pp. 577–656 (2000).

✹ B. Ex Ante vs. Ex Post Decision Making

As the United States has a common law legal system (the same
system one finds in England, Canada, and Australia, among other
places, but contrasted with the "civil law" or "code-based" legal systems one finds in continental Europe, and elsewhere), the resolution of particular legal disputes frequently creates new law binding
on future cases decided by the same court and lower-level courts.
This, broadly speaking, is the idea of "precedent" or "stare decisis."[19]

Because the decision of the present case can affect the outcome
of future cases—and, in turn, the way people act in the "shadow" of
the changed law—the rule that is the most just (or optimal) for this
case may be in tension with the best rule to apply to future cases (and
to guide future action). This tension is sometimes restated in terms
of whether we should focus primarily on "doing justice" between the
parties or, rather, on creating the proper incentives for future actors
(focusing on matters "ex ante" versus focusing on matters "ex post").

This is a general phenomenon, at least in common law countries. For family law, examples where a backward-looking focus
and a forward-looking focus may ground differing outcomes may
include the proper rules for alimony in "traditional" marriages, the
proper treatment of individuals in long-term nonmarital relationships, and the legal treatment of unmarried fathers. In these cases
and many more, the standard that seems best for the parties before
the court may not be the one that creates the incentives for optimal
behavior by other parties in the future. With long-term "traditional"
marriages, the wife has stayed at home throughout the marriage,
perhaps giving up a career, but in any event not increasing her earning capacity, while her work in the home likely facilitated her husband's ability to succeed in his career. Given those sacrifices and
contributions, to many it seems fair to award wives in these sorts of

---

19. *See, e.g.,* Frederick Schauer, "Precedent," *Stanford Law Review*, vol. 39, pp. 571–
    605 (1987).

marriages permanent (indefinite) alimony.[20] However, some commentators have argued that the availability of permanent alimony only encourages wives to be dependent and subservient in marriage, and that it would be better for women generally to get rid of permanent alimony, even if this worked a hardship or injustice in the divorces that arise from some existing (traditional) marriages.[21] One might similarly speculate on whether different rules regarding child support might make couples more or less likely to stay married, and then the question is whether the benefits of keeping some married couples married is worth the cost of erroneous levels of child support obligations for other couples.[22]

The argument about long-term unmarried cohabitants is similar (see chapter 3, section A). Often such cohabitation leaves one partner (usually the woman) with significantly less of the household resources (and also significantly less earning capacity) than the other partner. Justice seems to require some level of compensation or support for the disadvantaged partner, but the argument is that it may be better over the long run, both for society generally and for individuals entering romantic relationships in the future, to encourage marriage strongly, or to encourage express contractual arrangements, by making legal recourse unavailable to unmarried cohabitants, whatever the claims of justice arising from individual cases.

With unmarried fathers, current constitutional law and other case law (as will be discussed, see chapter 5, section B) appears to be grounded on a view of fathers as distinctly different from mothers in their commitment to parenting.[23] However, when the courts cite to the irresponsibility of fathers (however well statistically grounded this criticism) to uphold statutes that *assume* that fathers

---

20. As will be discussed in chapter 12, "permanent" alimony remains subject to court-ordered modification, if the court finds that this is justified by the changed circumstances of one or both former spouses.

21. The different possible justifications for alimony are discussed in chapter 12.

22. It is not mere speculation. There is empirical work on the subject. *See, e.g.,* Douglas W. Allen & Margaret F. Brinig, "Child Support Guidelines: The Good, the Bad and the Ugly," *Family Law Quarterly*, vol. 45, pp. 135–156 (2011).

23. *See* Lehr v. Robertson, 463 U.S. 248 (1982).

THE PRINCIPLES OF AMERICAN FAMILY LAW   9

are irresponsible (and may allow mothers to use the law to cut off even the fathers who are responsible), the law may be working to reinforce rather than fight those tendencies.[24] Perhaps more men would be more likely to take fatherhood seriously if the law treated them as though they did.

A similar type of analysis occurs when the courts must consider a general set of structures, processes, or formal rules that might be basically reasonable, but whose application to the particular case before the court appears to be unjust. In *Lehr v. Robertson*,[25] New York created a "putative father registry," such that all an unmarried father needed to do to make sure he had a right to be heard in a proposed adoption of his child was to send in a postcard to the appropriate government office.[26] The putative father in *Lehr* had in fact done a great deal to claim his rights,[27] including filing legal actions, but had not done any of the things offered under New York's scheme for dealing with putative fathers. The Court in *Lehr*, in rejecting the father's claim, focused on the adequacy of the state scheme, rather than assessing fairness through a focus of the particular facts of the case. The rules under scrutiny in *Lehr* were the product of wanting to encourage putative fathers to take certain actions to identify themselves, combined with a preference for a simple and predictable bright-line rule (as against a complex and unpredictable all-things-considered standard) for determining who needed to be contacted and who had a right to be heard before an adoption could go forward, and the resulting greater stability for the new family produced by the adoption. The *Lehr* Court held that the balance the state struck was constitutionally permissible.

---

24. Sylvia Law, "Rethinking Sex and the Constitution," *University of Pennsylvania Law Review*, vol. 132, pp. 955–1040 (1984), at pp. 988–998.
25. 463 U.S. 248 (1982).
26. The treatment of unmarried fathers in adoption cases is considered further in chapter 5, section B.
27. This is under the plaintiff's version of events, which was to be accepted as true, given the procedural posture of the case. *See Lehr*, 463 U.S. at 268–269 (White, J., dissenting).

The contrast between rules that create the best guidance for future behavior versus rules that do justice between the parties before the court also appeared in the Kansas Supreme Court decision of *In re* K.M.H.,[28] where the issue was a law that a sperm donor only obtained paternal rights and obligations when there had been a *written* agreement to that effect with the intended mother.[29] The plaintiff in *K.M.H.* claimed that there had been an *oral* agreement that he would have paternal rights,[30] but the Kansas court focused not on the fairness of denying the plaintiff paternal rights despite the oral agreement but rather on the reasonableness of the requirements of an agreement and that the agreement be in writing. Again, the underlying law expressed a preference for a bright-line rule in that factually and emotionally complex area, even where the standard's application might lead to unfortunate outcomes in individual cases.

One matter, though, that must be considered is that the effect of rules on behavior is always uncertain, especially for rules (like those relating to the financial consequences of divorce) whose application is uncertain (many people never divorce) and in the distant future. Individuals tend not to know what the law is, and even when they do know the law, they may be overly optimistic about the likelihood that they will ever face a negative event like divorce.[31] However, even if the effect of a legal rule is only on a small portion of those subject to the rule, and even if it only operates "on the margin," these are still consequences cumulatively worth taking into account.

As noted, the rules best for future parties are not always the best for parties currently before the court. And because family law disputes frequently involve heart-tugging questions involving the custody and care of children, courts will feel a strong pull to do justice (as the

---

28. 169 P.3d 1025 (Kan. 2007).

29. The topic of gamete donation and parental rights is considered further in chapter 6, section A.

30. Again, this was an allegation that was accepted as true because of the procedural posture of the case. *E.g.*, *id.* at 1038.

31. *See* Lynn A. Baker & Robert E. Emery, "When Every Relationship Is Above Average: Perceptions and Expectations of Divorce at the Time of Marriage," *Law and Human Behavior*, vol. 17, pp. 439–450 (1993).

court sees it) between the parties, regardless of the consequences for guiding other parties or resolving other disputes. Additionally, Meir Dan-Cohen has shown (in the context of discussions about criminal law) that the standards we want to apply to disputes may not be the standards we want people to use in guiding their lives.[32] In criminal law, the idea is exemplified by how wide knowledge of clemency rules for those who are insane or acting under duress might cause bad people to commit crimes with the hope of feigning insanity or duress. In family law, it may be that the rules that are fairest in the division of property upon divorce, for example, might work in some circumstances to create an unwelcome incentive to end marriages (e.g., where one has a rich spouse).

There is a related but somewhat different theme: to what extent can and should family law (or the law in other areas[33]) respond to the variety of fact situations? Should the law try to develop different standards that apply to the different contexts (in this case, including different family forms) in which disputes arise, or should there be a single set of standards that are to be consistently applied across different factual contexts?[34]

✳ C. Discretionary vs. Nondiscretionary Decisions

It is commonplace to report both that "best interests of the child" is the pervasive mantra of American family law—a standard that seems to pop up for almost every doctrinal question—and that

---

32. Meir Dan Cohen, "Decision Rules and Conduct Rules: An Acoustic Separation in Criminal Law," *Harvard Law Review*, vol. 97, pp. 625–677 (1984).

33. I discuss the issue in the context of contract law in Brian H. Bix, "The Role of Contract: Stewart Macaulay's Lessons from Practice," in Jean Braucher, John Kidwell, & William Whitford (eds.), *Revisiting the Contracts Scholarship of Stewart Macaulay: On the Empirical and the Lyrical* (Hart Publishing, 2013), pp. 241–255.

34. A good discussion of this and related topics can be found in Katharine K. Baker, "Homogenous Rules for Heterogeneous Families: The Standardization of Family Law When There Is No Standard Family," *University of Illinois Law Review*, vol. 2012, pp. 319–371.

this standard is amorphous, frequently leading to subjective and unpredictable results. "All things considered" judgments like "best interests of the child" may be more common and more strongly supported in family law than in any other area of law; later chapters will consider why this is, and whether it is justified.

There are, however, places within American family law where the law has moved toward the opposite extreme: relatively rigid rules and guidelines, or at least strong presumptions. The best example of this in current family law is child support guidelines (discussed in chapter 14), which deliver fairly predictable and consistent outcomes, at the cost, critics say, of failing to give the "right" or "best" decisions in many individual cases. The debate between the merits of predictability and the merits of discretionary decision making (already touched upon in the previous subsection) has been especially prominent in the area of child support and child custody decisions.

There are also, however, phenomena common to family law statutes, but that likely can be found in statutes in other areas of law as well: multiple-factor tests that give the appearance of guidance and constraint but likely only act to mask (or facilitate) broad discretion. A statute of this sort will direct a judge to consider a long list of factors before deciding (on property division, alimony, relocation of a custodial parent, or the like), but will say nothing about how the factors are to be prioritized or balanced. Such statutes create some constraint, as judicial decisions that fail to discuss the required standards are at risk of reversal on appeal. However, beyond the requirement to discuss the factors, it appears that judges can, with minimal creativity, reach a preferred conclusion with little fear of reversal.

⁂ D. Contract vs. Status

Family law has traditionally been a matter of status, not contract. That is, the terms and consequences of a legal category were set entirely by the state, with the parties having little or no power to waive or alter them. Entering a legal relationship might be voluntary (to a point). However, once one (for example) chose to marry, or chose to be a parent (or, at least, chose to do actions that put one at risk of becoming a parent), the rights and obligations that came with being a spouse or a parent were almost entirely selected by the state, with little to no opportunity for individuals to alter that package of rights and duties. Later chapters will show that "contract"— obligations undertaken, altered, or waived based on the individual choice of the participants—has made significant inroads on "status" in family law, but the extent to which individual choices will be recognized or enforced varies greatly.

The extent to which rights and responsibilities within a relationship, marriage, or family can or should be determined by party choice is most prominent in the question about whether and when to enforce surrogacy agreements, separation agreements, premarital agreements, cohabitation agreements, and same-sex parenting agreements, but is also present in many other debates (e.g., regarding "open adoption").

In modern academic debate, choice ("contract") seems to have all the advantages over antiquated lack of choice ("status"), but this is certainly too quick a conclusion. One basic problem with enforcing individual preference in family law matters is that there are often obvious, and not-so-obvious, third parties affected by the choices, but who have little to no say in making those choices. The obvious third parties are (minor) children, affected, for example, by parents whose union or lack thereof can affect the well-being of those born to that household. The less obvious third party is society generally, which, according to some, is harmed by unstable families and by children created or raised in unconventional ways.[35]

---

35. *See generally* Brian H. Bix, "Private Ordering and Family Law," *Journal of the American Academy of Matrimonial Lawyers*, vol. 23, pp. 249–285 (2010). For a comprehensive defense of status approaches to marriage, see Don S. Browning & John Witte, Jr., *Christian Marriage and Modern Marriage Law* (Cambridge: Cambridge University Press, forthcoming, 2013).

✻ E. Bright-Line Rules vs. Functional Standards

A standard distinction in legal analysis is that between rules and standards.[36] In this contrast, rules are clear, "bright-line" guidelines (mentioned earlier) that have the (purported) benefit of predictability and certainty while also having the (alleged) disadvantage of sometimes creating outcomes that are contrary to the reasons and purposes underlying the rules. Standards are more amorphous, giving only general direction, or offering a long list of factors that must somehow all be taken into account in decision making. At their best, standards are more just, because they can be tailored to the individual case, but this potential is gained only at the cost of greater uncertainty and unpredictability, and a greater risk of hidden bias and error.

In family law, this same tension often comes up in the context of legal status, in particular the status of parent. What makes someone a mother or a father? Traditionally and conventionally, the answer was easy: the mother was the person who gave birth to the child, and the father was the person married to the mother (and legally presumed[37] to be the biological parent of the child). The answer was a little more complicated if the mother was not married, or if the child was adopted, but still the rules tended to be relatively straightforward.

---

36. *See, e.g.*, Duncan Kennedy, "Form and Substance in Private Law Adjudication," *Harvard Law Review*, vol. 89, pp. 1685–1778 (1976) (rules vs. standards); Ronald Dworkin, *Taking Rights Seriously* (rev. ed., Cambridge, Mass.: Harvard University Press, 1978), pp. 24–28 (rules vs. principles).

37. In many jurisdictions, the presumption that the mother's husband is the biological ("legitimate") parent of the child is all but conclusive, at least if neither spouse challenges the conclusion and the father was not proven to be impotent or absent for the nine months prior to birth. A growing number of statutes, however, allow the use of DNA evidence to overcome the presumption, certainly if one or both spouses join the challenge, but in some cases even if they do not. On the presumption, see generally Jana Singer, "Marriage, Biology, and Paternity: The Case for Revitalizing the Marital Presumption," *Maryland Law Review*, vol. 65, pp. 246–270 (2006).

In the contemporary world of same-sex couples, gamete donation, in vitro fertilization (IVF), surrogacy agreements, and high rates of unmarried cohabitation and children being born and raised out of wedlock, many commentators and a growing number of courts have urged the use of a functional definition of who is a parent, rather than one based exclusively or primarily on some combination of genetic or gestational connection and marital status.

In considering those questions, and other areas where "functional" standards are proposed, one sees the usual concerns in this area: greater predictability and certainty on one side; potentially more optimal (or at least more reasonable) outcomes on the other side.

✹ F. The Proper Level of Deference for Traditional or Conventional Views and Practices

There are few areas of law which have changed faster or more pervasively in recent decades than has family law. At the same time, there are also few areas where public feelings run as high as they do in resisting change, because of attachment to the status quo (or a desire to return to the norms, rules, and practices of an earlier time, real or imagined). At times, this theme merges into a somewhat different argument: that certain arrangements are "natural" or (in a more scientific and apparently less value-laden parlance) "hardwired." It used to be common to think about opposite-sex marriage in those terms. It is still common to speak in those terms regarding parenthood (imposing significantly higher obligations on parents as regards their children, and giving the parents significantly higher rights and privileges), though even this may be undermined by the uncertainty of whom to call "parent" in a context of new reproductive technologies and new family structures. To what extent is it sufficient justification to ground judicial and legislative action in favor of the traditional rules and practices by simply saying, "this is the way it has always been"?

Justice Oliver Wendell Holmes, over one hundred years ago, gave a paradigmatic modern American response to such arguments: "It is revolting to have no better reason for a rule of law than that so it was laid down in the time of Henry IV. It is still more revolting if the grounds upon which it was laid down have vanished long since, and the rule simply persists from blind imitation of the past."[38]

At the same time, when we are speaking about social practices and institutions, and not (just) legal rules, the long duration of a practice or institution may say a great deal about the merits of that way of doing things, as both Edmund Burke and Friedrich Hayek famously argued.[39] Traditional ways of doing things may encode the wisdom gained by the experience of many generations learning which practices work and which do not.[40] And traditional or conventional ways of doing this are, at a minimum, practices (and outcomes) that we know. Change is always, by definition, a move to the unknown, where the outcomes of change might, we fear, be very bad.[41]

% G. Family Privacy

In thinking about family law, it is sometimes useful to divide one's inquiry into, first, what one believes the moral obligations of family members are to one another, and, second, which of these moral obligations should be translated into legal obligations. The idea of "family privacy"—not to be confused with the related but distinct

---

38. Oliver Wendell Holmes, Jr., "The Path of the Law," *Harvard Law Review*, vol. 10, pp., 457–478 (1897), at p. 469.

39. Edmund Burke, *Reflections on the Revolution in France* (New Haven: Yale University Press, 2003) (first published 1790); Friedrich Hayek, *Law, Legislation, and Liberty*, three vols. (Chicago: University of Chicago Press, 1973–1979).

40. For an example of an argument for reform that takes seriously the Burke/Hayek analysis of tradition, see Jonathan Rauch, "Objections to These Unions," *Reason*, June 2004, available at http://reason.com/archives/2004/06/01/objections-to-these-unions/singlepage.

41. This ties in with the discussion later in this chapter regarding how inadequate the social science data is for analyzing or predicting the effects of alternative rules and practices.

constitutional doctrine of privacy (which has often been applied to family law issues)[42]—is the notion that the state should not attempt to regulate certain matters internal to family affairs, like the relation between parents and children, and between spouses in an intact marriage, even in circumstances where one might believe that there are right and wrong answers about how to behave.

A standard case exemplifying the idea of family privacy is *McGuire v. McGuire*,[43] in which a court refused to order a husband to spend more money on his wife as part of his marital support obligation. The court noted that a support order could be given if either spouse sought a legal separation or divorce, but that the court would not interfere in the arrangements within an intact marriage.

As Carl Schneider has helpfully summarized, there are a variety of considerations that make governments reluctant to regulate ("intervene" in) such matters: (1) regulation might lead courts to become embroiled in every trivial dispute within the family; (2) it is hard to come up with standards that would apply across different sorts of situations and different sorts of families; (3) going to court may exacerbate rather than mitigate intrafamily problems; (4) harm may come from publicizing problems from the most private parts of people's lives; (5) there are enforcement problems in criminalizing actions that usually occur entirely in private; (6) enforcement efforts may lead the perpetrator to harm the victim more; and (7) the emotional nature of domestic ties may mean that law's persuasion and coercion may have little effect.[44]

On the other hand, many scholars have pointed out how "family privacy" often has the effect (if not the purpose) of protecting husbands' domination of, and sometimes abuse of, their wives and children.[45]

---

42. *See* Griswold v. Connecticut, 381 U.S. 479 (1965) (invalidating on privacy grounds a Connecticut statute forbidding the use of contraceptives).

43. 59 N.W.2d 336 (Neb. 1953).

44. Carl E. Schneider, "Moral Discourse and the Transformation of American Family Law," *Michigan Law Review*, vol. 83, pp. 1803–1879 (1985), at pp. 1835–1839.

45. *See, e.g.*, Reva B. Siegel, "'The Rule of Love': Wife Beating as Prerogative and Privacy," *Yale Law Journal*, vol. 105, pp. 2117–2207 (1996); Frances E. Olsen,

Nonintervention is a problem, not a benefit, when there are inequalities (of physical power and social opportunity) within the family, risks of exploitation and oppression in many households, and limited recourse for vulnerable parties.

H. The Problem of Inadequate Data

When courts, legislators, or commentators argue for legal change in family law—or when they argue for the status quo, for resisting change—they often do so on the basis of an express or implied claim about the effect a proposed change would have on human behavior. Perhaps we want one custody rule rather than another because we think it will be for the long-term benefit of (most) children. We may prefer one set of divorce rules over another because we believe that it will have the best overall consequence for social and individual well-being. We think same-sex marriage will have good consequences for same-sex couples and the children they raise, or perhaps we think that allowing such marriages will undermine marriage generally in society.

These are empirical claims about the world, and they are in principle subject to experimental support or refutation. However, the fact is that in family law (and likely in many other areas of law), the social science data relevant to law and law reform is scarce, and what data there is, is frequently controversial and subject to challenge.

Therefore, one theme of family law (though it is one less often noted and discussed than the other themes noted in this chapter) is how the courts and the legislatures do and should react to inadequate or conflicting social science data regarding the effects of various family practices and legal changes. On the whole, the answer seems to be that courts and legislatures fare little better in their

---

"The Myth of State Intervention in the Family," *University of Michigan Journal of Law Reform*, vol. 18, pp. 835–864 (1985).

dealings with social science data—its scarcity, its complexity, and its controversy—in family law matters than they do elsewhere. In principle, legislatures (and administrative agencies) should be better positioned than courts are to gather relevant empirical data, hear competing experts, and come to reasoned conclusions about difficult policy issues. However, in practice, both courts and legislatures seem unbothered when there is little (or conflicting) data to support (or refute) the justifications offered for legal change or for resisting such change, they are equally unbothered when what data there is opposes their conclusions,[46] and they are not very sophisticated in evaluating data when it is contested or controversial.[47]

There are also reasons to be skeptical about the claims of effects of, for example, different parenting structures and family forms on children, even if the studies are otherwise well done. First, there is a bias in the literature toward finding causal effects (studies that find no effects often are not sent for publication by their authors or accepted by journals). Second, correlations can sometimes be "created," or be made to seem more important than they actually are, by subdividing groups—introducing factors until some group appears to correlate in a statistically significant fashion with some effect.[48] And, of course, third, correlations *only sometimes* indicate

46. Sex education—in particular, the advocacy of "abstinence only" education—appears to be an area where government action has gone in the face of contrary social science data. *See, e.g.,* Linda C. McClain, *The Place of Families* (Cambridge, Mass.: Harvard University Press, 2006), pp. 256–289.

47. *See, e.g.,* Carol S. Bruch, "Sound Research or Wishful Thinking in Child Custody Cases? Lessons from Relocation Law," *Family Law Quarterly,* vol. 40, pp. 281–314 (2006); John Corvino, "Are Gay Parents Really Worse for Children? How a New Study Gets Everything Wrong," *The New Republic,* June 11, 2012, http://www.tnr.com; *see also* Sarah H. Ramsey & Robert F. Kelly, "Assessing Social Science Studies: Eleven Tips for Judges and Lawyers," *Family Law Quarterly,* vol. 40, pp. 367–380 (2006). On the related topic of the difficulty of using biological research in family law, see Elizabeth Mertz, "Translating Science into Family Law: An Overview," *DePaul Law Review,* vol. 56, pp. 799–821 (2007).

48. On these and other dangers in the social science research on families, see Judith Rich Harris, *The Nurture Assumption* (New York: Free Press, 1998), pp. 7–9, 14–32.

that there is an underlying causation, and there may also be doubts about the direction in which the causation goes.[49]

𝕸 I. Using or Ignoring Existing Categories

A basic aspect (and, perhaps, the basic purpose) of much of legal reasoning is the use of analogical reasoning to fit novel fact patterns and new legal issues into existing doctrinal rules and categories.[50] This sort of analogical reasoning is said to have the benefit of constraining judges and increasing principled consistency across cases. On the other hand, if the fit of the new item in the old category is poor, the outcome can be a bad rule with bad consequences.[51] One can find many examples in family law of such efforts to put new issues into "old boxes."[52]

At the same time, family law judges (and commentators) may be more willing than judges in other areas to seek entirely new responses, rather than trying to find analogies to existing categories, for cases of first impression. For example, new reproductive technologies have thrown a series of new legal questions at courts (sperm donation, egg donation, surrogacy, division of frozen embryos, posthumously conceived children, etc.), many of which will be discussed later in the book. Increasingly, efforts to put these new cases into old

---

49. One standard example in family law about the uncertainty of causation arises from consistent data showing that married individuals do better (are healthier, make more money, live longer, etc.) than single individuals. Even assuming a causal connection from this correlation, does it show that being married induces better habits or does it show that those who seem likely to be healthy and good providers are considered more attractive by those seeking marriage partners?

50. *See, e.g.,* Frederick Schauer, *Thinking Like a Lawyer: A New Introduction to Legal Reasoning* (Cambridge, Mass: Harvard University Press, 2009).

51. For a good discussion of the good and bad sides of this sort of analogical reasoning, see Richard A. Posner, *The Problems of Jurisprudence* (Cambridge, Mass.: Harvard University Press, 1990), pp. 86–98.

52. One of the best examples of the genre is Marsha Garrison, "Law Making for Baby Making: An Interpretive Approach to the Determination of Legal Parentage," *Harvard Law Review,* vol. 113, pp. 835–923 (2000).

categories (Is having a sperm-donor child like having an illegitimate child? Is surrogacy like baby-selling? Is division of frozen embryos at divorce like the division of property?) are being put aside, with courts instead facing the questions fresh—if not quite on a fresh slate (lawyers and judges are unaccustomed to thinking entirely on a fresh slate), then at least using only broad metaphors, while considering the consequences of different possible rules and principles. However, the tension between settled categories of analysis and trying to tackle new issues from first principles is one that recurs, if for no other reason than many people suspect that faulty analogies and analytical categories may still do less long-term harm than having current judges and legislators, most of them poorly trained in social science, biological sciences, and policy science, come up with new rules for themselves. (And there is also the issue of the incomplete and controversial empirical data, discussed in an earlier subsection.)

✹ J. The Nature and Role of "Family"

In a sense, all of family law is about what (and who) counts as "family," and what consequences follow from one's legal status as part of a family. Debates ranging from same-sex couples and polygamous groups wishing to marry to benefits debates regarding posthumously conceived children all turn on questions on how to define family and which connections should receive legal recognition. With more children being raised by unmarried couples (including same-sex couples), greater use of contact agreements between adopting parents and birth parents, the ongoing use of kinship care in many communities, and the repercussions of sperm donation, egg donation, and surrogacy, there are strong pressures for a definition of "family" (and especially "parent") that focuses more on function and less on marital status and genetic connection. This debate inevitably ties in with two other themes already discussed: rules versus standards, and the proper deference for traditional or conventional approaches.

✳ K. Conclusion

In the chapters that follow, all of these themes will be revisited and reconsidered. We will see how different legal rules and court decisions try to resolve the various tensions in different ways for particular topics. However, these themes and tensions are never entirely solved or resolved; whether hidden or expressed, they are always present.

Suggested Further Reading

John Eekelaar, *Family Law and Personal Life* (Oxford: Oxford University Press, 2006).

Lawrence M. Friedman, *Private Lives: Families, Individuals, and the Law* (Cambridge, Mass.: Harvard University Press, 2004).

Joanna L. Grossman & Lawrence M. Friedman, *Inside the Castle: Law and the Family in 20th Century America* (Princeton: Princeton University Press, 2011).

🌈 PART TWO

Marriage

THERE WAS A time, not that long ago, when marital status was far more important than it is today in both American life and American family law. In that earlier time, sex outside of marriage was considered shameful, and a great sin—at least for women; pregnancy and birth outside of marriage was subject to so great a social stigma that unmarried pregnant girls would go into hiding and would, in any case, be subject to summary dismissal from school or work; and divorce was both difficult to obtain and somewhat scandalous.[1] Children born out of wedlock were subject to significant legal as well as social sanctions. And unmarried parents (especially unmarried fathers) might have little or no legal obligations to their children, or rights in relation to them.

Today—for better or for worse—marriage does not bring the significant social and legal changes and benefits it once did; the questions of why one should marry, or why the state should encourage marriage or be involved in any way in the intimate relations of consenting adults, thereby become more prominent. More precisely, the issue is about civil marriage—marriage legally recognized by the state—putting aside the recognition or nonrecognition of marital status within religions, independent of the state. Particular religions may choose not to recognize divorce even when the state does; and may recognize same-sex unions or polygamous unions even when the state does not.

---

1. This was apparently true mostly of girls in white communities. *See* Rickie Solinger, *Wake Up Little Susie: Single Pregnancy and Race before Roe v. Wade* (New York: Routledge, 1992).

Of course, to many, the questions of why marry or why encourage marriage will seem strange: marriage is a long-standing institution that continues to have strong social and religious significance. However, a growing number individuals and couples (not just in the United States but also in many other countries) are choosing not to get married or are choosing to have children outside of marriage. Additionally, there are numerous proposals to change marriage in significant ways (some of which will be discussed in the following chapters).

It is useful to try to place current debates about the nature and the place of state-sanctioned marriage into some historical context. Marriage in Western societies has changed greatly over time—some of those changes are attributable to the rules of marriage itself; others are due to altered social circumstances.[2] If one goes back to biblical times, polygamy was once the norm; currently, most Western countries forbid polygamy, though under some interpretations of Islamic and Hindu law, a man may have multiple wives, and a number of countries authorize polygamy for members of those religious traditions (though the actual rate of polygamy in those countries tends to be low). And there are many more significant changes: for example, the diminished role of parents in choosing marital partners; the change in the role of marriage from being one focused on property and status (for the rich) or daily work (for the less well off) to now being more focused on love and happiness; and the vast changes in the social and legal gender constraints on roles within marriage. In Western Europe during the Middle Ages, marriages were sometimes informal (sometimes labeled "secret" or "clandestine" marriages), involving neither the state nor clergy but only an exchange of present declarations of marriage;[3] this is no longer an

---

2. On this topic, see, e.g., E. J. Graff, *What Is Marriage For? The Strange Social History of Our Most Intimate Institution* (Boston: Beacon Press, 1999).

3. *See, e.g.,* Charles Donahue, Jr., "'Clandestine' Marriage in the Later Middle Ages: A Reply," *Law & History Review,* vol. 10, pp. 315–322 (1992). Such marriages sometimes went under the term "*de presenti* marriages," indicating that they arose from a declaration of present marriage (*sponsalia per verba de presenti*), rather than a promise of future marriage (*sponsalia per verba de futuro*). Charles Donahue, Jr., *Law, Marriage, and Society in the Later Middle Ages* (Cambridge: Cambridge University Press, 2007), p. 600.

option in most countries, though American common-law marriage (discussed in chapter 2, section D) is related to that earlier informal form of marriage.

Divorce has become much easier to obtain and carries (in most places) less of a social stigma; greater equality in the division of property upon divorce and less discrimination against women in the workplace have also made it easier for women to exit unsatisfactory marriages. As will be discussed (chapter 4, section A), marital status is also no longer so closely tied to parental rights and responsibilities.

Marriage has become a focal point for cultural and political debate—especially concerning the terms of divorce, covenant marriage, and same-sex marriage. Some have gone so far as to recommend as a solution abolishing civil marriage, leaving marriage to regulation only by private choice or religious institutions.[4]

John Witte, Jr., offered what he described as the four perspectives on marriage "within the Western Christian Church," though the list (slightly modified) could be equally helpful for considering perspectives on marriage generally, secular or otherwise:

1. marriage as a religious or spiritual association;
2. marriage as a social estate, subject to societal expectations and serving social interests;
3. marriage as a contract, subject to the choices of the partners; and
4. marriage as a natural, prelegal, and perhaps presocial institution.[5]

---

4. *E.g.*, Edward Zelinsky, "Deregulating Marriage: The Pro-Marriage Case for Abolishing Civil Marriage," *Cardozo Law Review*, vol. 27, pp. 1161–1220 (2006); Martha Albertson Fineman, *The Neutered Mother, the Sexual Family, and Other Twentieth Century Tragedies* (New York: Routledge, 1995); Stephen B. Presser, "Marriage and the Law: Time for a Divorce?," in Joel A. Nichols (ed.), *Marriage and Divorce in a Multicultural Context* (Cambridge: Cambridge University Press, 2012), pp. 78–91.
5. The list is adapted from John Witte, Jr., *From Sacrament to Contract: Marriage, Religion, and Law in the Western Tradition* (Louisville: Westminster John Knox Press, 1997), p. 2.

The different perspectives will reappear repeatedly in the chapters that follow: for example, the contractual aspects of marriage, and their limits, come to the forefront in discussions of premarital agreements, marital agreements, and separation agreements. Discussions of the spiritual, religious, or traditional aspects of marriage are prominent (if often unstated) elements underlying the opposition to extending marriage to same-sex couples. The instrumental aspects of marriage come out in nearly every issue and controversial claim relating to marriage; for example: What are the effects on children of easier access to divorce? Will allowing the enforcement of premarital agreements lead to inequality within marriages which, in turn, will be bad for society? Will presumptions favoring mothers in custody decisions work to reinforce men's lack of commitment to parenting and their unwillingness to take equal responsibility in parenting? and Will presumptions favoring joint custody encourage greater sharing of parenting while marriages are intact?

The chapters that follow look at the basic legal outlines of civil marriage in the United States, and the legal treatment of some alternatives to marriage.

TWO

Marriage Eligibility, Marital Rules

THE QUESTION OF who can marry has become prominent in recent years as same-sex couples have sought the legal right to marry. Whatever else may be at stake in debates about who can marry, there are certain practical consequences for the couples involved. A recent publication advocating opening marriage to same-sex couples documented over 1,300 statutes and regulations under one state's law where marital status affected a party's rights or obligations.[6] This chapter will explore the debate about same-sex marriage, but will also consider more general (and less controversial) aspects of the civil marriage in American law.

The legal regulation of marriage raises special problems. Marriage is both a social and religious institution with a long history independent (or largely independent) of legal regulation, and an institution in part defined by its legal terms. This dual nature is what gives much of the power and intractability to recent debates about marriage (primarily, the argument about same-sex marriage but also debates surrounding rules for divorce and proposals for "covenant marriage").[7]

The rules for entry into marriage are relatively few. All American states limit marriage to couples—polygamy is not an option (nor

---

6. Empire State Pride Agenda Foundation & The New York City Bar Association, *1,324 Reasons for Marriage Equality in New York State* (2007), available at http://www.nycbar.org/pdf/report/marriage_v7d21.pdf.

7. *See, e.g.*, Joel A. Nichols, "Misunderstanding Marriage and Missing Religion," *Michigan State Law Review*, vol. 2011, pp. 195–208.

is bigamy—so if one was previously married, that prior marriage needs to have been dissolved through either a legal divorce or an annulment or the death of the other spouse before a second marriage can be entered). Most American states limit marriage to opposite-sex couples, though a growing number allow same-sex couples to marry; this will be discussed further in section D, below. Other less prominent legal rules of entry into marriage include ages of consent to marriage (and perhaps rules for parental consent for those under age) and rules concerning incest (regarding what family connections are too close for marriage; e.g., some states allowing the marriage of first cousins, while other states forbid such marriages[8]). Additionally, three American states now offer two forms of marriage—along with conventional marriage, something called "covenant marriage," that is meant to be a more binding form of marriage (in which the couple voluntarily accept certain limitations on their ability to leave the marriage). (I will return to covenant marriage in connection with the discussion of divorce in chapter 9.)

State rules that govern entry into marriage, the terms of marriage, and exit from marriage (the rules of divorce, discussed in chapters 8–13), all combine to express, intentionally or unintentionally, the state's view of what marriage should be, and what role marriage should play both within individual lives and within society. However, a further complication is that, within the American federal system, there are constitutional rules and federalist principles that effectively constrain states' abilities to effectively enact policies

---

8. Marriage between first cousins is not allowed in roughly half the states in the United States (but allowed in the other half). Sarah Kershaw, "Shaking Off the Shame," *New York Times*, Nov. 26, 2009. In many parts of the world, marriage between cousins is common. It is estimated that worldwide, over 10 percent of marriages are between people who are first or second cousins. *See id.* (also discussing the data that the risk of genetic defects in the children of such couples is only slightly higher than with other couples). On the genetics point, one scientist recently stated that genetic defects appear in 4–4.5 percent of marriages between first cousins, compared to 2–2.5 percent of the marriages *not* between first cousins. Anna Turner & Michael Field, "Cousins Marrying No Big Problems, Say NZ Geneticists," *Press* (New Zealand), July 10, 2012 (quoting Christchurch geneticist Alexa Kidd).

in this area. For example, most state rules regarding who can marry and when one can get divorced can be circumvented by simply going to another state to marry or moving to another state before divorcing. The complications of interjurisdictional enforcement of family law marriage and divorce rules will be considered at greater length later (chapter 2, section H, and chapter 9, section C).

❧ A. The History: Traditional, Gendered, Hierarchical Marriage

Historically,[9] the state set detailed rights and duties that varied by gender (e.g., it was common, under state statutory or case law for a husband to have a duty to support his wife but a right to set the family domicile; wives had a duty to care for their husbands[10]). Additionally, the legal outlines of the marriage were set by various intrafamily immunities and privileges, as well as legal disabilities imposed on wives (e.g., an inability to contract or own property).

In the nineteenth century and continuing well into the twentieth century, states passed Married Women's Property Laws that allowed women to keep their own property upon marriage and during marriage, and allowed married women to enter into legally binding contracts in their own name.[11] In recent decades, other

---

9. By "historically," the text refers to the modern period of significant legal regulation of marriage (which, in England, is marked by the Marriage Act of 1753). There were earlier periods of Western history, during which legal regulation was spotty at best, and informal (unrecorded) marriages were common. *See, e.g.,* Charles Donahue, Jr., *Law, Marriage, and Society in the Later Middle Ages: Arguments About Marriage in Five Courts* (Cambridge: Cambridge University Press, 2007), esp. pp. 600–603.

10. *E.g.,* Manby v. Scott, 1 Mod 124, 86 E.R. 781 (1663).

11. *See, e.g.,* Richard H. Chused, "Married Women's Property Law: 1800–1850," *Georgetown Law Journal,* vol. 71, pp. 1359–1425 (1983). The motivation and operation of the Married Women's Property Acts remain a matter of uncertainty and controversy. *See, e.g.,* Ellen Darrin, "Marriage and Law Reform: Lessons from Nineteenth Century Married Women's Property Acts," *Texas Journal of Women and the Law,* vol. 20, pp. 1–53 (2010). In England (but not

gendered legal differences have all but disappeared in the face of constitutional challenges and social reform movements. The state rules of marriage rights and obligations, such as they are, are now gender neutral. For example, both partners may have obligations to support their spouses (and pay spousal debts), and both spouses may have equal rights to manage and dispose of community property (the topic of marital property is covered in the next section).

B. Marital Property

Much of what is taught in family law courses about marital property is in fact the small but important subset of marital property rules concerning what happens to household property upon divorce.[12] Those rules will be the focus of chapter 10. The fact is that, at least in states that are not community property states (a label explained in a moment), there are usually few rules that regulate property within marriage, beyond the availability to married couples, but not to others, of certain forms of joint ownership.[13]

Marital property rules vary from state to state, but they can be grouped roughly into two large categories: those that follow common law property rules, and those that follow community property rules. Between eight and ten states have community property rules,[14] a property system that derived from certain continental European

---

in the United States), prior to those enactments, married women's property was protected through a special kind of trust called the "separate estate." *See* Allison Tait, "Unhappy Marriages and Unpaid Creditors: Chancery's Enforcement of a Wife's Right to Property Within Marriage in Seventeenth- and Eighteenth-Century England" (2012), http://ssrn.com/abstract=2007144.

12. On rights on the death of one's spouse, see generally Laura A. Rosenbury, "Two Ways to End a Marriage: Divorce or Death," *Utah Law Review*, vol. 2005, pp. 1227–1290.

13. For example, married couples can own real property under "tenancy by the entirety," whereby the couple jointly owns the property, and upon the death of either, the survivor gains ownership of the other spouse's share.

14. Eight states (Arizona, California, Louisiana, Idaho, Nevada, New Mexico, Texas, and Washington) have traditional community property regimes; a ninth,

countries and is generally associated with those parts of the country, in the Southwest, that had been under Spanish or Mexican rule prior to becoming part of the United States. Community property exemplifies a strong partnership theory of marriage. Under this system, all property brought to the household through earnings during the marriage, or property purchased through such earnings, belongs equally to *both* spouses, regardless of who the nominal wage-earner or investor was, and regardless of initial legal title.[15] Generally, states with community property either allow both spouses equal rights of control and management during the marriage, or require the consent of both spouses for some actions (e.g., sale of property or use as collateral).[16] Property acquired by either spouse prior to the marriage, or given to either spouse by gift or inheritance, remains "separate property."

The remaining states follow "common law" property rules, where the ownership and control of property follows title to the individual spouses. However, even in common law property states, the spouses may elect to own property together: through joint ownership of bank or stock accounts, or property ownership under the rubric of "joint tenancy," "tenancy in common," or "tenancy by the entirety."[17]

Wisconsin, effectively adopted community property through its enactment of the Uniform Marital Property Act. A tenth, Alaska, allows married couples to enter a "community property agreement," placing all, or specified portions, of their property under community property rules. *Alaska Stat.* §§34-7.010 to 34-7.995.

15. There are myriad issues of detail that affect the size of the community property estate (as against what gets characterized as "separate property"). Thomas Oldham shows how two community property states, California and Texas, treat many of these detailed matters in diametrically opposed ways, such that the community property estate is consistently larger in California and smaller in Texas. J. Thomas Oldham, "Everything Is Bigger in Texas, Except the Community Property Estate: Must Texas Remain a Divorce Haven for the Rich?," *Family Law Quarterly*, vol. 44, pp. 293–316 (2010).

16. An earlier Louisiana law, giving husbands exclusive control of community property, was struck down as unconstitutional. Kirchberg v. Feenstra, 450 U.S. 455 (1981).

17. The difference between "joint tenancy" and "tenancy in common" is that in the first, but not the second, upon the death of one owner, the other automatically gains the share of the deceased, and then owns the whole property. "Tenancy by the entirety" is similar to joint tenancy, but is only available to married couples.

Also, as will be seen in chapter 10, the two different regimes for property during marriage converge somewhat in the rules for division of property upon divorce.

✽ C. The Right to Marry

As noted, the regulation of marriage in the United States has historically been a matter primarily of state law, not federal law.[18] The first occasion on which a state regulation of marriage had been invalidated by the Supreme Court on the basis of the U.S. Constitution was *Loving v. Virginia*, where a state anti-miscegenation law (a law preventing marriage across racial lines) was invalidated.[19] The primary grounds for invalidating the law was that it made distinctions based on race, contrary to the Equal Protection Clause of the Fourteenth Amendment. However, the *Loving* Court also added that "[t]he freedom to marry has long been recognized as one of the vital personal rights essential to the orderly pursuit of happiness by free men," protected by the Due Process Clause of the Fourteenth Amendment.[20]

What is usually cited as the case first clearly declaring constitutional protection for the right to marry was *Zablocki v. Redhail*,[21] where the Supreme Court considered a state regulation that prohibited someone with child support obligations to marry unless that person could prove *both* that the obligations were fully paid off *and* that the children would not be on public benefit. The Court

---

18. Though it is easy to overstate the state-law focus of American family law, and many commentators and courts do. For a useful corrective, see Jill Hasday, "Federalism and the Family Reconstructed," *UCLA Law Review*, vol. 45, pp. 1297–1400 (1998).

19. 388 U.S. 1 (1967). Nearly twenty years earlier, the California Supreme Court had invalidated that state's anti-miscegenation laws on the same (federal) constitutional grounds. Perez v. Sharp, 32 Cal.2d 711, 198 P.2d 17 (1948).

20. *Loving*, 388 U.S. at 12.

21. 434 U.S. 374 (1978).

invalidated the legislation, focusing on the fact that some people were so poor that they would be unable to pay off their obligations, and/or so poor that their children would remain on benefit even if all support obligations were paid. The Court held that marriage is a fundamental right, and that direct barriers to marriage would be subject to "critical examination," a kind of intermediate scrutiny. Direct barriers were contrasted to the indirect barriers that occur, for example, when marital status is used to set or limit state benefits.[22]

𝄞 D. Common Law Marriage

While many American states at one time recognized common law marriage (marriage based on a present agreement between a man and a woman that they are married), most of those states abolished the status in the latter part of the nineteenth century or the early part of the twentieth century.[23] Such marriages are often thought to trace back to a time in the American colonial settlement or Western expansion, when many of the scattered settlers may not have had easy access to clergy, but the historical origins are far from certain.[24] Further back in Western history, common law marriage echoes a time when marriage was considered a matter of agreement between the partners, potentially secret from all, and where neither Church nor State need be involved.[25]

---

22. *See also* Turner v. Safley, 482 U.S. 78 (1987) (invalidating regulations that restricted the right of prisoners to marry).
23. On the history of common law marriage in the United States, see Cynthia Grant Bowman, "A Feminist Proposal to Bring Back Common Law Marriage," *Oregon Law Review*, vol. 75, pp. 709–780 (1996), at pp. 717–750.
24. While the colonial/settler story is commonly recited, the first published opinion clearly recognizing common law marriage appeared only in 1809. Fenton v. Reed, 4 Johns 52 (N.Y. 1809). A much earlier case, Cheseldine's Lessee v. Brewer, 1 H. & McH. 152 (Md. Prov. 1739), is sometimes cited, but its significance for common law marriage is disputed. *E.g.*, Rebecca Probert, "Common Misunderstandings," *Family Law Quarterly*, vol. 43, pp. 587–597 (2009), at pp. 590–594.
25. "It was not until 1563, … when the Council of Trent accepted marriage as a canonical sacrament, that the church made the liturgical priestly blessing of

Utah appears to be the only state (in 1987) to have established or revived recognition of common law marriages in the last one hundred years (by most accounts, this revival was motivated by a belief—likely mistaken—that recognition of common law marriage would prevent cohabiting individuals from obtaining greater government benefits).[26] Eleven states, the District of Columbia, and a few Indian tribes currently offer some form of recognition for common law marriages.[27] Such marriages, if entered into in a state

---

the couple a condition for the validity of the marriage." Don S. Browning & John Witte, Jr., *Christian Marriage and Modern Marriage Law*, ch. 7; *see also* Charles Donahue, Jr., "The Western Canon Law of Marriage: A Doctrinal Introduction," in Asifa Quraishi & Frank E. Vogel (eds.), *The Islamic Marriage Contract: Case Studies in Islamic Family Law* (Cambridge, Mass.: Harvard University Press, 2008), pp. 46–56, at p. 52 ("Although couples were strongly encouraged to have their marriages solemnized, no solemnity or ceremony was necessary for the validity of marriage [under Church law] at any time between Alexander III in the late twelfth century and the council of Trent in 1563.") However, the extent to which secret informal marriages (without Church ceremony) were ever recognized in England, even before Lord Hardwicke's Act 1753, has likely been overstated. Rebecca Probert, *Marriage Law and Practice in the Long Eighteenth Century* (Cambridge: Cambridge University Press, 2009), pp. 73-95.

There were such informal marriages further back, in ancient Roman law, though the connections between American common law marriages and the Roman law correlates are, at best, uncertain and unproven. *See* Rebecca Probert, "Common Misunderstandings," *Family Law Quarterly*, vol. 43, pp. 587–597 (2009), at pp. 588–589.

26. On Utah's legislation and its motivation, see, e.g., Bowman, "A Feminist Proposal to Bring Back Common Law Marriage," 749–750.

27. *See Colo. Rev. Stat.* § 14-2-104; Creel v. Creel, 763 So. 2d 943, 946 (Ala. 2000); *Kan. Stat. Ann.* §§ 23-2501, 2502; S.C. *Code Ann.* § 20-1-100; *Tex. Fam. Code* § 2.401; *In re* Marriage of Martin, 681 N.W.2d 612, 617 (Iowa 2004); Demelo v. Zompa, 844 A.2d 174, 177–78 (R.I. 2004); *In re* Estate of Ober, 62 P.3d 1114, 1115 (Mont. 2003); *N.H. Rev. Stat.* § 457:39; Stinchcomb v. Stinchcomb, 674 P.2d 26, 28–29 (Okla. 1983); *Utah Code Ann.* § 30-1-4.5; Johnson v. Young, 372 A.2d 992, 994 (D.C. 1977); *Navajo Nation Code* tit. 9, §4(E). The New Hampshire statute recognizes common law marriage only at death. *See also* Göran Lind, *Common Law Marriage* (Oxford: Oxford University Press, 2008), pp. 8–12 (listing jurisdictions and citing relevant case law and statutes). Additionally, four states will recognize common law marriages created before some earlier deadline: Georgia (before Jan. 1, 1997), Idaho (before Jan. 1, 1996), Ohio (before Oct. 10, 1991), and Pennsylvania (before Jan. 1, 2005). *See* Jennifer Thomas, Comment, "Common Law Marriage," *Journal of the American Academy of Matrimonial Lawyers*, vol. 22, pp. 151–167 (2009), at p. 151.

where they are valid, will be recognized in other states, even if those other states themselves do not allow marriages to be entered that way (the basic principles and limits of interjurisdictional recognition of marriages will be discussed in section H, below).

While common law marriage is nominally just a different way of entering marriage—through a present agreement to marry, with no license or ceremony required—in reality it is usually a means for long-term cohabitants to claim benefits after a partner has died, on the basis that the couple were in fact married. Most states that have common law marriage have statutory or court-decision-based evidence for determining whether a common law marriage had in fact occurred, criteria that usually include long-term cohabitation and the couple's having held themselves out as married (to friends and acquaintances and on official and business documents).[28]

🕮 E. Same-Sex Marriage

Few family law issues have created more controversy in recent years than that of same-sex marriage. It is a topic that has been the subject of whole books, but here can only be described in the barest outline.

At the time of writing: (1) nine states (Massachusetts, Connecticut, Iowa, Vermont, New Hampshire, New York, Maine, Maryland, and Washington) and the District of Columbia allow same-sex marriages;[29] (2) same-sex couples can enter civil unions or domestic partnerships

---

28. *See, e.g.*, Spitz v. T.O. Hass Tire Co., 815 N.W.2d 524 (Neb. 2012) (for purposes of woman's worker's compensation benefits claim regarding a male cohabitant, Nebraska court concludes that couple did not meet Colorado's standard for proving a common law marriage, because they did not hold themselves out as married).

29. *See* Goodridge v. Department of Public Health, 798 N.E.2d 941 (Mass. 2003); Opinions of the Justices to the Senate, 802 N.E.2d 565 (Mass. 2004) (opinion that legislative proposal to allow same-sex couples to enter civil unions would not satisfy the state constitutional requirement that they not be excluded from marriage); Kerrigan v. Commissioner of Public Health, 957 A.2d 407, 289

that will grant them all the state-law rights and obligations[30] of marriage (but under a different label) in California,[31] Delaware, Hawaii,[32] Illinois,[33] Nevada, New Jersey,[34] Oregon, Rhode Island,[35] and the District of Columbia;[36] and (3) Wisconsin and Colorado have an available legally recognized status that offers same-sex couples

---

Conn. 135 (2008); Varnum v. Brien, 763 N.W.2d 862 (Iowa 2009); *D.C. Code* § 64-401(a); *N.H. Rev. Stat. Ann.* § 457:1-a; *N.Y. Domestic Relations Law* § 10-a; *Vt. Stat. Ann.* tit. 15, § 8. In the November 2012 general elections, Maine by referendum authorized same-sex marriage, while Maryland and Washington by referendum approved legislation that had earlier authorized such marriages.

Additionally, at least two American Indian tribes have approved same-sex marriage. *See* William Yardley, "A Washington State Indian Tribe Approves Same-Sex Marriage," *New York Times*, Aug. 12, 2011.

A number of foreign jurisdictions, including Argentina, Canada, Belgium, Iceland, Mexico (Mexico City only), The Netherlands, Norway, Portugal, South Africa, Spain, and Sweden also allow same-sex marriages.

30. As long as Section 3 of the Federal Defense of Marriage Act (DOMA) remains law, states cannot grant same-sex couples the rights and obligations of marriage that derive from federal law. That section of DOMA is currently under constitutional challenge, as discussed in section H, *infra.*

31. The California Supreme Court had also authorized the inclusion of same-sex couples in marriage, *In re* Marriage Cases, 43 Cal.4th 757, 183 P.3d 384, 76 Cal. Rptr. 3d 683 (2008), but that decision was subsequently overturned by a 2008 state referendum ("Proposition 8"). However, the same-sex marriages celebrated between the time of the court decision and the time of the referendum remain valid. *See* Strauss v. Horton, 46 Cal.4th 364, 93 Cal. Rptr. 3d 591 (2009). Additionally, a federal appellate court subsequently ruled that Proposition 8 was unconstitutional; at the time of writing, the case is being reviewed by the U.S. Supreme Court. Perry. v. Brown, 671 F.3d 1052 (9th Cir. 2012), rehearing en banc denied, 681 F.3d 1065 (9th Cir. 2012), *cert. granted sub nom.* Hollingsworth v. Perry, 2012 WL 3134429 (2012).

32. *Haw. Rev. Stat.* § 572C.

33. The Illinois civil union statute is distinctive in making the status available to both same-sex and opposite-sex couples. California makes its domestic partnership status available to opposite-sex couples if at least one partner is sixty-two years old and eligible for social security benefits.

34. Arising from *Lewis v. Harris*, 908 A.2d 196 (N.J. 2006); *see N.J. Stat.* § 37:1-28.

35. These sorts of unions are also available in many countries. Alternatives to marriage, for same-sex and opposite-sex couples, will be discussed at greater length in chapter 3.

36. The National Conference of State Legislatures has maintained an online list of states with civil unions or domestic partnerships, and the list includes statutory references. *See* http://www.ncsl.org/issues-research/human-services/civil-unions-and-domestic-partnership-statutes.aspx (at the time of writing, updated through November 2012).

some, but far from all, of the state-law rights and obligations of marriage; (4) thirty states have passed state constitutional amendments defining marriage as being between a man and a women; and (5) an additional eleven states have passed state "defense of marriage acts," statutes defining marriage as being between a man and a woman, and refusing, as a matter of public policy, to recognize same-sex marriages from other states.[37]

The level of public support (as expressed in opinion polls) for options—whether called "civil unions," "domestic partnerships," or some other label—that offer the same (state law) rights and obligations as marriage, but under a different label—is consistently significantly higher than the support for same-sex marriage. This difference is initially hard to understand and may seem irrational. The significance seems to be at a symbolic level—a strong feeling for the label that is attached to the social institution, with all the history and religious connections connected with the label "marriage"—even as the legal and social contours of that institution have changed in significant ways.

The fight over the label goes in both directions: both with the large group who would allow same-sex partners the same legal rights and obligations as marriage as long as they did not claim the label, and with the advocates of legal recognition of same-sex unions who are not satisfied with all the legal rights and obligations of marriage if they are denied the label. Where "civil unions" or "domestic partnerships" have been offered to same-sex couples as a compromise, many same-sex couples object that they want "marriage."[38] They object to not having it for reasons connected to

---

37. At the time of writing, updated information on same-sex unions in the states is available at the site for the Human Rights Campaign, http://www.hrc.org.

38. *See In re* Marriage Cases, 43 Cal.4th 757, 183 P.3d 384, 76 Cal. Rptr. 3d 683 (2008) (recognizing state constitutional right for same-sex couples to be included in "marriage," even though they already had access to the same state-law rights and obligations through domestic partnerships). That decision was overturned by state referendum, "Proposition 8," which in turn has been subject to (federal) constitutional challenge in the federal courts, as discussed *supra*, in note 31.

their not being offered it; they understand the exclusion as (at least for some people who have argued for the exclusion) a statement that marriage is something too good or too sacred for same-sex couples to have.

Though this is less discussed, there is another practical disadvantage within many "civil unions" or "domestic partnership" legal options: the authorizing legislation often requires same-sex couples seeking such status to claim that they cohabit, that they commingle their finances, and even that they take care of one another; no such ex ante requirement is ever imposed on opposite-sex couples by marriage laws. Marriage is, in this sense, and at this time, a more flexible institution.[39]

There are two controversial analogies offered by advocates arguing for or against the recognition of same-sex marriages, one on each side of the issue. Those arguing against same-sex marriage claim that if same-sex unions were to be given state recognition, there would be no principled basis for not recognizing polygamous marriages.[40] (Some opponents go further and make a similar, though less persuasive, claim regarding incestuous marriages or bestiality.)

No American state has ever recognized polygamy (plural marriage),[41] there is no indication that recognition via a state legislature or state court is imminent in any state, and there is no evidence of any significant social movement for the legal recognition

39. *See* Mary Anne Case, "Marriage Licenses," *Minnesota Law Review*, vol. 89, pp. 1758–1797 (2005), at pp. 1773–1174.
40. Mary Anne Case has suggested that there is a neutral justification for distinguishing recognizing same-sex marriage from recognizing polygamy: that any two-person union creates administrative efficiencies for various practical purposes, which a multiple-person union does not create. Case, "Marriage Licenses," 1783.
41. The nearest example was the Utah Territory, which briefly recognized plural marriages, but the United States made rejection of plural marriage by the Church of Jesus Christ of Latter-Day Saints (LDS Church), and its prohibition in a state constitution, conditions for recognizing Utah as a state. *See, e.g.*, Nancy F. Cott, *Public Vows* (Cambridge, Mass.: Harvard, 2000), pp. 105–120.

of polygamy in any state.[42] Nonetheless, references to polygamy have become common in debates about same-sex marriages.[43] It is true that a handful of cases challenging restrictions on polygamy, or sanctions grounded on polygamous lifestyles, have been filed, grounded on the Supreme Court decision in *Lawrence v. Texas*.[44] However, no appellate court has upheld claims of this sort, and it is hard to find a legal expert who expects a different outcome in the foreseeable future. Though, of course, to predict that courts would hold that there is no constitutional right to polygamy and that same-sex marriage and polygamy are different for purposes of constitutional law or moral principle, is not the same as saying that either conclusion is correct.[45]

On the other side of the debate, supporters of same-sex marriage argue that refusing to recognize such unions is like the laws that were once present in many states refusing to recognize marriage

---

42. There are American polygamists, numbering in the thousands, mostly heterodox LDS Church members, while the mainstream LDS Church consistently rejects polygamy. And while there is no significant social movement to have polygamy recognized, there have been individual legal challenges, grounding a constitutional claim for recognition on the right to religion. *E.g.*, State v. Holm, 137 P.3d 726 (Utah 2006) (rejecting constitutional freedom of religion challenge to criminal bigamy conviction); Bronson v. Swensen, 500 F.3d 1099 (10th Cir. 2007) (rejecting constitutional freedom of religion challenge to refusal to recognize polygamous marriage).

43. One should note that many countries do recognize plural marriages—especially predominantly Islamic countries, as that religion authorizes a man to have up to four wives. The legality of polygamy in other countries also thus raises issues for polygamous families—legally polygamous in their countries of origin—who want to travel to the United States. *See, e.g.*, Nina Bernstein, "In Secret, Polygamy Follows Africans to N.Y.," *New York Times*, Mar. 23, 2007.

44. 539 U.S. 558 (2003).

45. The polygamy argument has not been the most common or most formidable argument against same-sex marriage. Opponents of same-sex marriage offer arguments based on tradition, historical and religious sources, the best context for raising children, and what is needed to encourage (traditional) marriage, arguments that I do not have time here to summarize or evaluate. For a sample of the arguments against same-sex marriage, see, e.g., Robert P. George & Jean Bethke Elshtain (eds.), *The Meaning of Marriage: Family, State, Market & Morals* (Dallas: Spence Publishing Co., 2006); Lynn D. Wardle, Mark Strasser, William C. Duncan, & David Orgon Coolidge (eds.), *Marriage and Same-Sex Unions: A Debate* (Westport, Conn.: Praeger, 2003).

across racial lines—the anti-miscegenation laws finally invalidated by the Supreme Court decision in *Loving v. Virginia*.[46] Those who proffer the analogy argue that both anti-miscegenation laws and the failure to recognize same-sex unions form an arbitrary exclusion from marriage based on prejudice. Those who resist the analogy argue that there is a difference between excluding a group from marriage based on racism and advocating a significant expansion to what has historically been meant by marriage (by going beyond opposite-sex couples).

✻ F. Heartbalm Actions

Under classical English law, there were a series of common law causes of action meant to protect the interests relating to marriage; they are sometimes collectively called "heartbalm actions." As will be mentioned, these are now mostly matters of history, with only the slightest vestige in modern American (or English) family law, but their past existence—and their present scarcity—may still reveal important aspects of the way we think about marriage.

These causes of action historically included breach of promise to marry,[47] seduction, alienation of affection, and criminal conversation. The meaning of "breach of an agreement to marry" is self-evident; "seduction" traditionally was brought by a father against a man who seduced the petitioner's unmarried daughter (thus significantly reducing her value on the marriage market);[48]

---

46. 388 U.S. 1 (1967).

47. Also sometimes known as "breach of an agreement to marry" or "breach of contract to marry." For a history of this cause of action (focused primarily on English law), see Saskia Lettmaier, *Broken Engagements: The Action for Breach of Promise of Marriage and the Feminine Ideal, 1800–1940* (Oxford: Oxford University Press, 2010).

48. For a modern rethinking and defense of the cause of action of seduction, see Jane Larson, "'Women Understand So Little, They Call My Nature "Deceit"': A Feminist Rethinking of Seduction," *Columbia Law Review*, vol. 93, pp. 374–472 (1993).

"alienation of affection" is traditionally brought by a spouse against a third party who has drawn the other spouse away from his or her marital bond (this is usually brought against a spouse's lover, though there have been cases brought against others,[49] including meddling and hostile in-laws)—there is no need to prove sexual intercourse; "criminal conversation" is adultery, and sexual intercourse must be shown.

Alienation of affection (in its classical form, or slightly different modern variations) is the one heartbalm action that still has some contemporary significance.[50] Seven states still recognize the cause of action (Hawaii, Illinois, Mississippi, New Mexico, North Carolina, South Dakota, and Utah), and plaintiffs have received six-figure sums in a handful of recent cases. Breach of the promise to marry may in principle be recognized in more states (by one count, as many as twenty-two[51]), but significant recent recoveries under that cause of action seem to be rare. Heartbalm actions will also be discussed, briefly, in chapter 9, section B.

---

49. In Heller v. Somdahl, 696 S.E.2d 857 (N.C. App. 2010), the claim was brought against a woman who encouraged the wife's adulterous relationship, and who also prevented communication between wife and husband.

50. Fitch v. Valentine, 959 So.2d 1012 (Miss., 2007) (reaffirming the tort of alienation of affections in Mississippi, affirming $750,000 judgment); Jennifer Fernandez, "The Price of an Affair? $9 Million," *Greensboro News & Record*, Mar. 18, 2010 (reporting jury verdict of $9 million on claims of alienation of affection, criminal conversation, and intentional and reckless infliction of emotional distress).One can even find occasional references to successful suits for breach of contract to marry, e.g., Stephen Gurr, "Jury Awards Jilted Bride $150,000," July 27, 2008, http://www.gainesvilletimes.com/news/article/7296/ (describing Florida case). However, such claims are often brought not under a specific cause of action for "breach of promise to marry" but rather under a general breach of contract action. In South Carolina, the cause of action for breach of promise to marry has not been expressly abolished (though other heartbalm actions, like alienation of affection and criminal conversation have been). Bradley v. Somers, 322 S.E.d2d 665 (S.C. 1984); Campbell v. Robinson, 726 S.E.2d 221 (S.C. App. 2012).

51. *See* Kathryn G. Ross, "Justified Suits or Jilted Brides—An Analysis of the Illinois Breach of Promise Act and the Case of *Buttitta v. Salerno*" (2011), available at http://ssrn.com/abstract=1837620.

✼ G. Formalities

Much of the law of marriage, as such, contains rules for eligibility for marriage—in particular, age of consent—combined with the required formalities required for entry into marriage in the state in question.

All states have a license law (and almost all make obtaining a valid license a prerequisite for a valid marriage[52]).[53] In applying for a license, prospective spouses are asked to give basic information, and that information would include questions that would go to their legal right to marry (e.g., Have the couple ever been married, and, if so, was that marriage dissolved? Are the parties related, and, if so, how closely?). Some states also require a minimal physical examination and a doctor's certification that the patient is free of certain venereal diseases.[54] States also usually require a brief waiting period (a matter of days) between when the marriage license is applied for and when the license is granted or when a valid ceremony can be held. States have varying rules about who is authorized to perform marriages, but this usually includes clergy and judges.

---

52. *See* Hall v. Maal, 32 So.3d 682 (Fla. App. Dist. 2010) (marriage ceremony and couple holding themselves out as married is insufficient for a valid marriage if the couple never obtained a valid marriage license; dissent argued that "substantial compliance" with formalities was sufficient); Betemariam v. Said, 48 So.3d 121 (Fla. App. 2010) (under Virginia law, religious marriage done without license is void *ab initio*); Pinkhasov v. Petocz, 331 S.W.3d 285 (Ky. App. 2011) (refusing to recognize as married a couple who went through religious marriage ceremony but intentionally avoided obtaining civil marriage license). *But see* Rivera v. Rivera, 243 P.3d 1148 (N.M. App. 2010) (holding that license statute is directory only and not mandatory, upholding a marriage where the ceremony was held in New Mexico, but the license was from Texas).

53. For an innovative suggestion for reform of marriage license rules, and an introduction to a symposium about license reform, see Mae Kuykendall & Adam Candeub, "Symposium Overview: Perspectives on Innovative Marriage Procedure," *Michigan State Law Review*, vol. 2011, pp. 1–33.

54. Illinois and Louisiana both briefly required those seeking marriage licenses to take a test for HIV-AIDS. In each case, the requirement was quickly dropped, in part due to the expense of the test and the way that the requirement appeared to be causing a noticeable number of couples either not to marry or to marry in other states.

One state, Montana, does not even require either of the parties to be present to marry—a "double-proxy" marriage is possible—and only recently did the state even impose any form of residency requirement for those taking advantage of the process.[55]

🖋 H. Interjurisdictional Recognition

In general, recognition of a marriage celebrated in another state or country is determined by conflict of laws principles.[56] Established principles state that a marriage valid where celebrated (that is, valid under the laws of the state or country where it was performed) will be recognized as valid in another jurisdiction, unless that marriage is contrary to a strong public policy of the forum state. Until recently, these conflict of laws rules only came up in a relative handful of cases, usually dealing with marriages between first cousins or between an uncle and a niece (that would be invalid in the home state as "incestuous") or, prior to 1967, interracial marriages (that were invalid in many states under anti-miscegenation laws before those laws were invalidated by the U.S. Supreme Court in *Loving v. Virginia*[57]).[58] It is common in those cases to see a forum state (the state where the court is considering the legal effect of the marriage) recognizing marriages even though the rules of the forum state do not allow marriages of that kind, on the basis that many marriages that are not authorized by a state's law may nonetheless not be contrary to the state's "fundamental public policy."[59]

---

55. Dan Barry, "Trading Vows in Montana, No Couple Required," *New York Times*, Mar. 10, 2008. The article explains that recent legislation requires that at least one partner be either a Montana resident or a member of the U.S. Armed Forces. The article further states that all states except Iowa recognize these double-proxy marriages.

56. *See Restatement (Second) of Conflict of Laws* § 283 (2) (1971).

57. 388 U.S. 1 (1967).

58. Andrew Koppelman, *Same Sex, Different States: When Same-Sex Marriages Crosses State Lines* (New Haven: Yale University Press, 2006), pp. 20–50.

59. *E.g.*, Ghassemi v. Ghassemi, 998 So.2d 732 (La. App. 2008) (first-cousin marriage), appeal after remand, ___ So.3d ___, 2012 WL 2060826 (La. App. 2012);

A small number of states have gone further and enacted "marriage evasion laws." These laws state that if citizens of one state go to another state to marry in order to evade marriage laws in the first state, that marriage will not be recognized by the first state (even if valid in the second state where it was celebrated).[60]

The issue of marriage recognition has become particularly significant with the growing availability of same-sex marriages in a number of states (and foreign countries), and the strong opposition in other states to recognizing such unions. It is currently rare for a state that does not itself offer marriage or marriage-like status to its own same-sex couples to recognize such unions from other states (either for the purpose of granting legal benefits, or for making their courts available to dissolve such unions).[61] However, this may be starting to change. At the time of writing, New Mexico and Rhode Island recognize same-sex marriages from other jurisdictions; and New Jersey and New Hampshire recognize such unions as though

---

In re Succession of Hendrix, 990 So.2d 742 (La. Ct. App. 5th Cir. 2008) (common law marriage).

60. *E.g., Ga. Code* § 19-3-43; *Ariz. Rev. Stat.* § 25-112.

61. *In re* Marriage of J.B. and H.B., 326 S.W.3d 654 (Texas Ct. App. 2010) (Texas courts have no subject-matter jurisdiction to dissolve same-sex marriage); Chambers v. Ormiston, 935 A.2d 956 (R.I. 2007) (Rhode Island court lacked subject matter jurisdiction to grant same-sex couple married in Massachusetts a divorce under state statute authorizing divorce); Lane v. Albanese, 2005 WL 896129, 39 Conn. L. Rptr. 3 (Conn. Super. Ct. 2005) (concluding Connecticut courts have no jurisdiction to annul a Massachusetts same-sex marriage); Salucco v. Alldredge, 17 Mass. L. Rptr. 498, 2004 WL 864459 (Mass. Super. Ct. 2004) (Massachusetts divorce statute cannot be applied to Vermont civil union); Procito v. Unemployment Compensation Board of Review, 945 A.2d 261 (Pa. Cmwlth., 2008) (refusing to apply "following the spouse" rule for woman who left job to travel to be with domestic partner; she was thus ineligible for unemployment compensation); Rosengarten v. Downes, 802 A.2d 170 (Conn. App. Ct. 2002) (Connecticut has no jurisdiction to dissolve a same-sex Vermont civil union), opinion later withdrawn. Occasionally, parties get *more* interjurisdictional recognition than they might have wanted. In Elia-Warnken v. Elia, 972 N.E.2d 17 (Mass. 2012), a same-sex marriage partner was refused a divorce, on the basis that the same-sex marriage had been void *ab initio*, because that partner had an undissolved civil union from Vermont, which Massachusetts will treat as a marriage for the purpose of bigamy laws.

they were "civil unions."[62] A New York appellate court has held that its trial courts have, under their general equitable powers, the right to dissolve Vermont civil unions;[63] the Wyoming Supreme Court held that a same-sex marriage from another state or country could be recognized for the limited purpose (only) of granting a divorce.[64] The Maryland Court of Appeals (the highest court in that state), in a decision prior to that state's enactment of a same-sex marriage law, held that same-sex marriages were not contrary to the fundamental public policy of the state, and therefore such marriages from such jurisdictions should be recognized for all legal purposes (including, in that case, granting a divorce).[65]

The question of interjurisdictional recognition of marriage (and marriage-like relationships) goes to the core of the tensions of federalism: the value of having some things (like marital status) be constant throughout the country, in conflict with the desire to let states (or more local government units) make autonomous determinations in line with their citizens' values and preferences. We are an increasingly mobile society, moving from state to state for education, for new jobs or job relocations, for new partners, or just to start over in a place whose opportunities, culture, or climate seem more attractive. There is something jarring about the idea that one might be married in one state but not in the next (or, in the middle of traveling for business or vacation, suddenly being unsure of one's "current" marital status).

Comparable discontinuities happened in the middle decades of the twentieth century, when "migratory divorces" were more common (discussed in chapter 9, section C). People could be married

---

62. New Hampshire and the District of Columbia have legislation on the issue of recognition; New Jersey and New Mexico have attorney general opinions only; Rhode Island has an attorney general's opinion and an executive order by its governor.
63. Dickerson v. Thompson, 928 N.Y.S.2d 97 (A.D. 2011). This decision came down prior to New York's own adoption of same-sex marriage.
64. Christiansen v. Christiansen, 253 P.3d 153 (Wy. 2011).
65. Port v. Cowan, 44 A.3d 970 (Md. 2012).

in one state and divorced in another, or married validly to a second wife or husband in one state and subject to prosecution for bigamy in another.[66] It seems obvious that such uncertainty in a mobile country is not viable for the long term, though how it will be resolved is currently hard to foresee.

The federal Defense of Marriage Act (DOMA)[67] was enacted in 1996, in response to litigation in Hawaii that looked like it might result in legal recognition of same-sex marriages in that state. A number of observers unfamiliar with the Full Faith and Credit Clause of the U.S. Constitution[68] and conflict of laws analysis feared (or hoped) that recognition of same-sex marriages in Hawaii would require the recognition of those marriages in all other states. As will be explained, this view was likely mistaken, but it was widely held.

DOMA had two provisions: one defining marriage for federal law purposes as being (only) between one man and one woman. This provision was significant in that federal law usually simply incorporated each state's decisions regarding who was married and who was not. This part of DOMA has recently been held invalid by two federal appellate courts (and a number of lower federal courts),[69] but those decisions will likely be reviewed by the U.S. Supreme Court.

DOMA's second provision authorizes states not to recognize same-sex marriages that were created in other states. This provision

---

66. *See* Williams v. North Carolina, 317 U.S. 287 (1942) (*Williams I*); Williams v. North Carolina, 325 U.S. 226 (1945) (*Williams II*) (pair of cases involving non-recognition of a Nevada divorce and prosecution of a couple for bigamy). For an overview of the jurisdictional rules for divorce and the possibility of collateral attack on divorce judgments, see Russell J. Weintraub, *Commentary on the Conflict of Laws* (6th ed., New York: Foundation Press, 2010), pp. 345–359, 368–373.

67. Pub. L. No. 104-199, 110 Stat. 2419 (1996), codified at 1 U.S.C. § 7, 28 U.S.C. § 1738C.

68. U.S. Const. art. IV, § 1. On the history and application of that provision, see William J. Reynolds & William M. Richman, *The Full Faith and Credit Clause* (Westport, CT: Praeger, 2005).

69. Massachusetts v. U.S. Dep't of Health & Human Services, 682 F.3d 1 (1st Cir. 2012); Windsor v. United States, 669 F. 3d 169 (2nd Cir. 2012), *cert.* granted, U.S. v. Windsor, 2012 WL 4009654 (2012).

was motivated by two beliefs about the Full Faith and Credit Clause, the first one likely wrong, and the second controversial.

The Full Faith and Credit Clause reads:

> Full faith and credit shall be given in each state to the public acts, records, and judicial proceedings of every other state. And the Congress may by general laws prescribe the manner in which such acts, records, and proceedings shall be proved, and the effect thereof.

Under the view of most experts,[70] DOMA was unnecessary, because marriages are not "public acts, records, [or] judicial proceedings." There are no federal appellate court cases applying the Full Faith and Credit Clause to marriages (though there are cases applying the clause to divorce (judgments), as will be discussed in chapter 9, section C). In any event, as a marriage is just a legal status one has within a given state—my being married in Minnesota is, in some ways, comparable to my license to drive a car in Minnesota or my license to fish (this year) in Minnesota. For another state to give this "full faith and credit" would be simply to recognize (and not deny), for whatever purpose it might be relevant, that I have this status within Minnesota. Iowa has no more constitutional obligation to consider me married in Iowa because I am married in Minnesota than it has to allow me to fish in Iowa because I have a fishing license in Minnesota. As discussed, Iowa *will* recognize my marital status in Iowa, but this will occur under general conflict of laws principles, not under any constitutional compulsion.

DOMA's second provision was controversial because it purports to give states plenary power to avoid recognizing a legal status that the statute assumes that the states must otherwise recognize. The question is whether Congress's power to "prescribe ... the effect" of

---

70. *See, e.g.*, Patrick J. Borchers, "The Essential Irrelevance of the Full Faith and Credit Clause to the Same-Sex Marriage Debate," *Creighton Law Review*, vol. 38, pp. 353–363 (2005).

"acts, records, and proceedings" includes the right to allow them to have no effect at all. As noted, however, this is likely a moot point, as states likely never were under a constitutional obligation to recognize marriages from other states.

Suggested Further Reading

History of Marriage and Marriage Policy

Naomi Cahn & June Carbone, *Red Families v. Blue Families: Legal Polarization and the Creation of Culture* (Oxford: Oxford University Press, 2010).

Stephanie Coontz, *Marriage, a History* (New York: Viking, 2005).

Nancy F. Cott, *Public Vows: A History of Marriage and the Nation* (Cambridge, Mass.: Harvard University Press, 2000).

Robert P. George & Jean Bethke Elshtain (eds.), *The Meaning of Marriage: Family, State, Market & Morals* (Dallas: Spence Publishing Co., 2006).

Robin West, *Marriage, Sexuality, and Gender* (Boulder: Paradigm Publishers, 2007).

John Witte, Jr., *From Sacrament to Contract: Marriage, Religion, and Law in the Western Tradition* (Louisville: Westminster John Knox Press, 1997).

Marital Property

John Tingley & Nicholas Svalina, Updated by Nancy McKenna, *Marital Property Law, rev. 2d* (St. Paul: West, 2011), 3 vols.

Common Law Marriage

Charlotte K. Goldberg, "The Schemes of Adventuresses: The Abolition and Revival of Common-Law Marriage," *William & Mary Journal of Women and the Law*, vol. 13, pp. 483–538 (2007).

Göran Lind, *Common Law Marriage* (Oxford: Oxford University Press, 2008).

Jennifer Thomas, Comment, "Common Law Marriage," *Journal of the American Academy of Matrimonial Lawyers*, vol. 22, pp. 151–167 (2009).

Same-Sex Marriage and Interjurisdictional Recognition

Andrew Koppelman, *Same Sex, Different States: When Same-Sex Marriages Cross State Lines* (New Haven: Yale University Press, 2006).

Nancy D. Polikoff, *Beyond Straight and Gay Marriage: Valuing All Families Under the Law* (Boston: Beacon Press, 2008).

THREE

Alternatives to Marriage

THIS CHAPTER WILL consider legal alternatives and competitors to marriage: long-term cohabitation (by opposite-sex or same-sex partners), domestic partnership, domestic registration, civil unions. Some states and municipalities offer a status that has fewer rights and obligations than marriage and make this status available either only to same-sex couples, or to both same-sex couples and opposite-sex couples. The chapter will consider whether the availability of official alternatives to marriage undermines the promotion of marriage, or whether it is instead a valuable way to allow couples to seek the status that matches their needs. Another basic question facing courts and legislatures is how to respond to couples who have intentionally avoided all forms of legal status (as a mutual choice, or based on the "veto" of one member of the couple): are there circumstances where rights and duties should nonetheless arise from the nature and duration of the relationship? This is also an area that may benefit from comparative scholarship. A number of other countries—in particular, in Europe—have done far more to create legal alternatives for marriage than has the United States.[1]

---

1. Denmark (in 1989) was the first country to recognize legally same-sex partnerships. Among the other countries that offer a relationship *like marriage* (but under another name) for same-sex couples are Andorra, Austria, Brazil, Croatia, Czech Republic, Finland, France, Germany, Hungary, Ireland, Israel, Luxembourg, Mexico (some states only), New Zealand, Slovenia, Switzerland, United Kingdom, and Uruguay. In many of these jurisdictions, there remain important differences between these unions and marriage, often relating to parentage rights (e.g., the right to adopt or to use certain forms of new reproductive technologies). A small number of these jurisdictions open these marriage-like (or "marriage-lite") relationships to opposite-sex couples as well.

The question about allowing forms of legal recognition that differ from or fall short of marriage[2] turns on the benefits of marriage on one hand versus the value of responding to individual interests on the other. The question about allowing legal recourse to couples outside of marriage often turns on the "ex ante vs. ex post" decision making discussed in chapter 1. On one side is the argument that the state should be encouraging couples to marry—for the sake of society, for the sake of children who might be born to the couple, or perhaps for the sake of the couple themselves. And, the argument goes, when the state makes some of the advantages of marriage available to nonmarried couples (like the ability to demand equitable division of property or other equitable claims on a partner after the union has ended), that decreases the relative attractiveness of marriage, and fewer couples will take up marriage. The contrary argument focuses on fairness to the individuals concerned: that it would be unfair to not allow them some recourse if they have made sacrifices for the household, even if they were not married.

It is probably helpful to begin the analysis with some notion of why couples in long-term cohabitation relationships do not marry.[3] Sometimes the decision not to marry is mutual, sometimes it is unilateral, but at least one partner must have a motivation for avoiding marriage. Motivations can vary from principled objections to civil marriage (perhaps based on a belief that civil marriage is an essentially hierarchical and patriarchal institution), to a desire to keep earnings from being subject to being given to the other spouse as part of property division or alimony at divorce, to a fear of commitment, to a desire to maintain the current level of public benefit (if it would be reduced by marriage).

---

2. Premarital agreements (discussed in chapter 8) raise identical concerns, as they effectively allow couples to create for themselves a form of marriage with altered—or, some might argue, "diluted"—terms (e.g., where one party might have decreased obligations to the other upon divorce).

3. Of course, cohabiting same-sex partners may fail to marry because the state in which they live does not make same-sex marriage available.
Many cohabiting couples eventually marry, and at that point they are able to take advantage of state laws dividing property and granting alimony at the dissolution of the marriage.

🎗 A. Long-Term Cohabitation

Cohabitation outside of marriage is now both common and commonly accepted. Even though there are a handful of states where criminal prohibitions on extramarital cohabitation are still on the books,[4] these laws are almost never enforced (and the validity of such enforcement under the U.S. Constitution after *Lawrence v. Texas*[5] is, in any case, in doubt).

There is a common "folk belief" that a sufficient period of cohabitation creates a "common law marriage."[6] This misunderstands the concept: as discussed in chapter 2, section D, "common law marriage" simply reflects a way of entering marriage by private agreement rather than by public ceremony in those states in which it is allowed. In principle, no period of cohabitation is required; the references to periods of cohabitation come as *evidence* (sometimes required as a matter of statutory or decisional law) that the couple had a private agreement to marry. No marital status arises from the cohabitation alone.

One state, Washington, creates a (nonmarital) legal status grounded on long-term cohabitation, which it calls a "committed intimate relationship."[7] Under this status, each partner gains an equitable claim in property owned by the other partner; but the status does not affect intestacy laws, nor does it create marital status

---

4. According to one news report, Florida, Michigan, Mississippi, North Carolina, Virginia, and West Virginia have such laws. "N.D. Anti-Cohabitation Law Repealed," Associated Press, Mar. 2, 2007. North Dakota repealed its law in 2007.

5. 539 U.S. 558 (2003) (criminal law prohibiting sodomy held to be unconstitutional).

6. One can find a similar phenomenon in Britain, where there is no such legal category. Rebecca Probert, "Why Couples Still Believe in Common-Law Marriage," *Family Law*, vol. 37, pp. 403–406 (2007).

7. The status was originally labeled, "meretricious relationship," the term used in other jurisdictions to refer to the types of nonmarital connections or contracts (exchange of sex for money) that are usually not given legal recognition. In 2007, the courts changed the label to "committed intimate relationship." Olver v. Fowler, 168 P.3d 348, 350 n.1 (Wash. 2007).

for the purpose of state or federal statutes.[8] This status has been extended to cover same-sex cohabitants.[9]

A number of states have recognized contractual claims arising out of long-term cohabitation (sometimes called "palimony"), where one partner alleges that the other promised "to take care" of him or her, as part of an inducement for companionship, homemaker services, and the like.[10] These sorts of claims, when recognized,[11] are usually analyzed in terms of express contracts and implied-in-fact contracts[12] or related claims of restitution or promissory estoppel. Even where successful, the cohabitant is likely to receive only a fraction of what he or she would have received had the claim been one of property division and alimony relating to a divorce.

---

8. In Scotland, when a long-term cohabitation ends other than by death of one of the partners, the court has discretion to order a financial payment from one partner to the other, where this is justified based on financial advantages suffered by one partner or financial advantages gained by the other partner, during the cohabitation. *See* Family Law (Scotland) Act 2006, section 28; Gow v. Grant, [2012] UKSC 29.

9. Connell v. Francisco, 127 Wash.2d 339, 898 P.2d 831 (1995). Vasquez v. Hawthorne, 33 P.3d 735, 737 (Wash. 2001); Gormley v. Robertson, 120 Wash. App. 31, 83 P.3d 1042 (2004).
New Zealand offers long-term nonmarried cohabitants comparable protections.

10. The first important case was *Marvin v. Marvin*, 557 P.2d 106 (Cal. 1976). The plaintiff in that case, Michele Triola Marvin, ended up recovering nothing in her suit against Lee Marvin. Marvin v. Marvin, 122 Cal.App.3d 871, 176 Cal. Rptr. 555 (1981). In an apparent "victory of hope over experience," she then cohabited outside of marriage with another star, Dick Van Dyke. However, this cohabitation lasted thirty years, until Ms. Marvin's death in October 2009, at age seventy-six.

11. By one count, twenty-six states and the District of Columbia have recognized such claims, five have expressly rejected such claims, and many states have yet to decide the issue. Marsha Garrison, "Nonmarital Cohabitation: Social Revolution and Legal Regulation," *Family Law Quarterly*, vol. 42, pp. 309–331 (2008), at 315–322.

12. Courts in New York, New Hampshire, New Mexico, and Massachusetts have indicated that they would recognize express agreements (including express *oral* agreements), but not implied-in-fact agreements. Morone v. Morone, 50 N.Y.2d 481, 413 N.E.2d 1154 (1980); Tapley v. Tapley, 449 A.2d 1218 (N.H. 1982); Merrill v. Davis, 673 P.2d 1285 (N.M. 1983); Wilcox v. Trautz, 693 N.E.2d 141 (Mass. 1998).

Additionally, a number of states have rejected these claims entirely,[13] arguing that recognizing such claims undermines marriage, or placed significant procedural hurdles in their way (e.g., requiring the agreements to be in writing), worried in part about the possibility of fraudulent claims.[14]

Unsurprisingly, few claimants have been successful under this legal standard.[15] Couples are unlikely to have entered express agreements prior to, or during, long-term cohabitation. And reference to unjust enrichment seems inapplicable in all but the most extreme and idiosyncratic cases. Beyond that, both parties simply expect to offer and receive benefits in a roughly mutual way, and likely expect (optimistically) that the harmonious partnership will never end. For most people, there is no expectation—and almost certainly no agreement—about what would happen after a breakup.

B. Marriage-like Status

A growing number of states—and foreign countries—have a legal status that is less than marriage in terms of rights and obligations. Many of these legal status options were created in large part to offer some official recognition for same-sex couples, though they are usually characterized in neutral terms such that they are open to opposite-sex couples as well. In France, it is the Civil Solidarity

---

13. Three states have expressly refused recovery in these cases: Illinois, Georgia, and Louisiana. Hewitt v. Hewitt, 394 N.E.2d 1204 (Ill. 1979); Rehak v. Mathis, 238 S.E.2d 81 (Ga. 1977); Schwegman v. Schwegman, 441 So.2d 316 (La. App. 1983).

14. *See, e.g., Minn. Stat.* § 513.075 (writing requirement); *Tex. Fam. Code* § 1.108 (same). *See also* the New Jersey statute described in the next note.

15. There is one state that had been relatively receptive to palimony claims, New Jersey. *See, e.g., In re* Estate of Quarg, 938 A.2d 193 (N.J. Super. A.D. 2008); Connell v. Diehl, 938 A.2d 143 (N.J. Super. A.D. 2008). However, that state changed its laws in 2010 to limit palimony claims. Under *N.J. Stat.* § 25:1-5(h), agreements between cohabitants for support "or other consideration" will be enforceable only when they are in writing and with both parties having been advised by independent counsel.

Pact (*Pacte Civil de Solidarité*, or PACS), which has been used by half a million people in its first ten years (it was introduced in 1999); in 2008, for every two marriages in France, there was one PACS union, and the vast majority of the couples using the PACS are now opposite-sex couples.[16]

In the United States, the marriage-like options are quite diverse. Hawaii makes available to those legally prohibited from marrying (most obviously, same-sex couples, but also close relatives) the ability to register as "reciprocal beneficiaries" and to gain some (but far from all) of the benefits of marriage.[17] Vermont provides the status of "reciprocal beneficiaries" for couples who are prevented from marrying or forming a civil union because they are related.[18] In Maine, registered domestic partners (either same-sex or opposite-sex) are granted spousal rights on inheritance and are given certain rights (generally similar to, but less substantial than those of spouses) regarding a deceased partner and that partner's estate.[19] As already discussed, Washington State has a status for long-term cohabitants that requires no formal ceremony or registration; Oregon has a comparable status, whereby those in a "domestic partnership" (a long-term cohabitation in which resources were pooled) gain the right to an equitable division of property at the end of the relationship.[20]

Colorado has established "designated beneficiary agreements," by which any two people (same-sex or opposite-sex), not already married or in a designated beneficiary agreement with other people, can establish certain marriage-like legal protections: for example,

---

16. Edward Cody, "Straight Couples in France Are Choosing Civil Unions Meant for Gays," *Washington Post*, Feb. 14, 2009; *see also* Joëlle Godard, "Pacs Seven Years On: Is It Moving Towards Marriage?," *International Journal of Law, Policy, and the Family*, vol. 21, pp 310–321 (2007).

17. *Haw. Rev. Stat.* § 572C.

18. *Vt. Stat.* tit. 15, § 1303(3).

19. 2004 *Legis. Serv.* 672; *Me. Rev. Stat. Ann.* tit. 18-A, §§ 2-102, 5-309; *id.*, tit. 22, §§ 2710, 2846.

20. *See* Beal v. Beal, 577 P.2d 507 (Or. 1978); *In re* Greulich, 243 P.3d 110 (Or. App. 2010).

joint ownership of property, hospital visitation rights, medical decision making, and the ability to sue for wrongful death.[21]

While a handful of "marriage lite" forms of legal status are thus available, sparsely scattered across different American jurisdictions, the availability (and use) of such forms of status (recognized by the state, but without the name "marriage" and with fewer rights and obligations) are far more numerous—and far more accepted and used—in various European countries.

To recount, there are justice-based arguments in favor of status and contract-based claims for long-term cohabitants, as parties are made vulnerable by sacrifices made during the years of the cohabitation. The primary argument against such claims is that marriage is beneficial to both individuals and society, and the more marriage-like benefits are available to unmarried couples, the lower the incentive to marry.

Suggested Further Reading

Cohabitation

Cynthia Grant Bowman, "Social Science and Legal Policy: The Case of Heterosexual Cohabitation," *Journal of Law & Family Studies*, vol. 9, pp. 1–52 (2007).

Palimony

Symposium, "Unmarried Partners and the Legacy of *Marvin v. Marvin*," *Notre Dame Law Review*, vol. 76, pp. 1261–1490 (2001).

---

21. *Colo. Rev. Stat.* §§ 15-22-101 to 15-22-112.

✐ PART THREE

Parenthood

FOR A LONG time, parental rights and obligations were in a sense secondary, deriving from marital status (this is not a claim of the relative importance of parenthood, only a claim about how legal rights and obligations in this area worked). Married parents had significant rights and obligations regarding their children; unmarried parents had neither.

More recently, parental rights and obligations were presumptively correlated with genetic connections: the biological mother would have rights and obligations regarding her child regardless of her marital status, and the biological father would as well under most circumstances.[1] Under current social practices and medical technology, there is now a third level of complexity: situations where (through artificial insemination, in vitro fertilization (IVF), and/or surrogacy) the intended parents of a child may not be the genetic parents. The factors of marital status, genetic connection, and "intended parent" may now point in different directions, leaving the law in these areas highly unsettled.

---

1. As will be discussed, there were (and are) two important exceptions. First, if an unmarried father had not created a significant relationship with the child (or when dealing with a newborn, with the child's mother), states are constitutionally free to disregard his interests in the child, and some will do so (e.g., in allowing the child to be adopted without notifying the child's father). *See* Lehr v. Robertson, 463 U.S. 248 (1983). Second, where the mother is married, but the father is not the mother's husband, states are constitutionally free to create a conclusive presumption that the mother's husband is the legal father. *See* Michael H. v. Gerald D., 491 U.S. 110 (1989).

Additionally, when talking about parenthood, one must keep in mind adoption: a court judgment that creates a legal parent-child relationship where there had not been one before. The practice and principles of adoption will be discussed in chapter 5.

FOUR

Parental Authority
General Rights and Obligations

IN THE PAST, a parent's (in particular, a father's) relationship to children was analogized either to an owner's relationship to property or to a monarch's relationship to the monarch's subjects. Additionally, there were aspects of both political and religious thought in the Western tradition that would give parents almost absolute powers over their children.[2]

As already mentioned, a parent's obligations to a child (and a child's rights against a parent) depended significantly on marital status, with an illegitimate child treated by the law "as the child of no one." Both of these aspects of parenting law have changed drastically in recent decades: with parents (fathers and mothers equally) being seen as caretakers, there to promote the best interests of their children; and parental rights and duties being separated almost entirely from marital status.

This chapter will also consider some issues that connect to Part II: for example, how should the state deal with parental rights arising from unconventional family formations (ranging from step-parents, to "kinship" caregivers, to co-parenting by same-sex partners, and parents in polyamorous relationships)? Here we see the courts and

---

2. The early modern political theorists Jean Bodin (1529/30–1596) wrote: "It is needful in a well-ordered commonweal to restore unto parents the power of life and death over their children, because domestical justice and power of fathers [are] the most sure foundations of laws, virtue, piety, wherewith a commonwealth ought to flourish." Jean Bodin, *The Six Books of a Commonwealth* (Kenneth Douglas McRae ed., Cambridge, Mass.: Harvard University Press, 1962) [1606], pp. 22–23.

legislatures trying to resolve colliding themes of encouraging marriage, protecting the prerogatives of parents, defining parenthood in "functional" rather than bright-line or legal terms, and protecting the best interests of children.

The current legal view of parents is as guardians[3] of their minor children: having significant rights and powers regarding those children, but tied to an underlying duty to act in the best interests of the children. As will be discussed in greater detail in chapter 7, if parents fall below a certain minimal level of care in protecting the children's interests, the state has the right (and perhaps the duty) to remove the children from that household and also, in extreme cases, to terminate the parents' legal connection with the children.

Legal parents have significant rights and obligations relating to their children. They have the right and duty to make all significant decisions, including where their children live, where they go to school, provision of their food and clothing, and what medical care they receive, all of these within quite broad discretion (again, subject to falling below a minimum that would constitute "abuse" or "neglect"—the topic of chapter 7). There is a strong legal presumption that the decisions parents make on behalf of their children are in the best interests of those children.

Consistent with traditional views, the law states that a child can have no more than two legal parents. The problems of that restriction, including the legal consequences for "step-parents," will be considered later in this chapter.

A. Nonmarital Children

The treatment of nonmarital (illegitimate) children is one of the areas of American family law which has changed most radically.

---

3. There is a specific legal status of guardianship, often used to refer to the selected legal representative for a legally incompetent adult. I am using the term here in a related way, but meant to be broader or more metaphorical.

And this has reflected a change in social practices and social norms: we have moved from a time when children born out of wedlock were a matter of shame (and it was considered reasonable to punish those children, as a way of encouraging (other) parents to marry) to a time when nearly 40 percent of births are to unmarried mothers, and individual births out of wedlock are (in most places) hardly worthy of comment, let alone public shaming.[4]

In ancient Roman law, fathers had no obligation to support children not born within "legitimate marriage or of the recognized Roman form of concubinage."[5] The common law similarly recognized no right of nonmarital children to inherit from their parents (or to make any other claim of support), but some commentators have argued that in England this principle merely reflected that such questions were left to the ecclesiastical courts, where parents *were* held to have obligations to support even nonmarital children.[6] In England, the Elizabethan Poor Law of 1576 gave local justices of the peace the power to impose duties of support for nonmarital children on their parents, eventually displacing the church court remedies.[7]

---

4. Stephanie J. Ventura, "Changing Patterns of Nonmarital Childbearing in the United States" (Center for Disease Control and Prevention, National Center for Health Statistics, May 2009), available at http://www.cdc.gov/nchs/data/databriefs/db18.pdf. This is not a uniquely American phenomenon; the same report noted that a number of European countries have nonmarital birth figures comparable to, or higher than, those in the United States.
5. R. H. Helmholz, "Support Orders, Church Courts, and the Rule of *Filius Nullius*: A Reassessment of the Common Law," *Virginia Law Review*, vol. 63, pp. 431–448 (1977), at pp. 433–434. Under Roman law, illegitimate children might ask the praetor for rights under the estate of their mothers but not under the estate of their fathers. Bruce W. Frier & Thomas A. J. McGinn, *A Casebook on Roman Family Law* (Oxford: Oxford University Press, 2004), p. 334.
6. *See* Helmholz, "Support Orders, Church Courts, and the Rule of *Filius Nullius*"; cf. Charles J. Reid, Jr., "The Rights of Children in Medieval Canon Law," in Patrick Brennan (ed.), *The Vocation of the Child* (Grand Rapids, Mich.: William B. Eerdmans, 2008), pp. 243–265, also available at http://papers.ssrn.com/abstract=1015403 (arguing that medieval canon lawyers repudiated Roman law, and argued that even illegitimate children had rights of paternal support).
7. *See* Helmholz, "Support Orders, Church Courts, and the Rule of *Filius Nullius*," 446–447.

The American treatment of nonmarital children initially gave such children no rights against their parents. By the late twentieth century, this had changed, and the U.S. Supreme Court announced that it was unconstitutional to treat nonmarital children differently from marital children.[8] This position was later codified and strengthened by the Uniform Parentage Act and related state legislation.

While not all states have enacted the Uniform Parentage Act, the current state of American law is fairly uniform: (1) nonmarital children are treated the same as marital children for nearly all legal purposes; and (2) for almost all legal purposes, it is a person's parental status (parent or nonparent) relative to a child that determines his or her rights and obligations toward that child, while marital status plays little to no role. A few courts have recently used the Uniform Parentage Act as grounds for treating a biological mother's same-sex partner as a legal parent, if that partner has "held out" the child the couple was raising as her own—thus meeting a criterion the Uniform Parentage Act had established for determining when to treat a man as a child's father.[9]

A different aspect of the legal approach of nonmarital children can be seen in the traditional common law presumption of legitimacy. This is the topic for the next section.

✼ B. Presumptions of Paternity

As the prior section indicated, family law (and social norms) once created significant disabilities on children born outside of marriage. (The value of encouraging marriage was once considered sufficiently important as to justify the imposition of significant social and legal burdens on nonmarital children.[10] It is rare to find that

---

8. Gomez v. Perez, 409 U.S. 535 (1973).

9. *See, e.g.,* Chatterjee v. King, 280 P.3d 283 (N.M. 2012).

10. James Fitzjames Stephen, the prominent nineteenth-century British legal commentator, wrote:

    Take the case of illegitimate children. A bastard is *filius nullius*—he inherits nothing, he has no claim on his putative father. What is all this except

cost-benefit analysis defended today.[11]) The law related to marriage and legitimacy historically included the marital presumption.[12]

Under the traditional form of that presumption, if a child is born to a married woman, the child would be conclusively presumed[13] to be the legitimate child of both husband and wife, unless the husband could be proven to have been sterile or impotent, or not to have had access to the wife during the prior year or nine months. Many states continue to maintain some (nonconclusive) version of the presumption.[14] However, other states now allow a biological father to claim legal parentage, even if the mother was married to someone else at the time of birth.

This is an area where there are tensions between, on one hand, the emphasis on genetics in parental rights, the de-emphasis of marital status, and the greater social and legal toleration of children born outside of wedlock, and, on the other hand, continuing concerns about shoring up marital households where one can. It might seem that a household in which one spouse had a child through an

---

the expression of the strongest possible determination on the part of the Legislature to recognize, maintain, and favour marriage in every possible manner as the foundation of civilized society? ... It is a case in which a good object is promoted by an efficient and adequate means.

James Fitzjames Stephen, *Liberty, Equality, Fraternity and Three Brief Essays* (Chicago: University of Chicago Press, 1991) (1873), p. 156.

11. *Cf. In re* Baby M, 537 A.2d 1227, 1257 (N.J. 1988) (rejecting argument that custody of child should be given to surrogate mother, even if against child's best interests, as a way of deterring surrogate agreements).

12. In the context of immigration, the children of unmarried U.S. citizens are still treated differently from the treatment of married U.S. citizens, and the children of unmarried U.S.-citizen fathers differently from the children of U.S.-citizen mothers. *See, e.g.*, Nguyen v. I.N.S., 533 U.S. 53 (2001).

13. This is much stronger than conventional presumptions, which simply create tie-breaking rules, or rules for establishing who has the burden of proof. For those, the presumption can be overcome if enough evidence is brought forward for a contrary conclusion. A conclusive presumption, however, cannot be overcome, whatever the quantity or strength of the evidence for a different conclusion.

14. On the presumption and whether it should be reformed or removed, see Susan Frelich Appleton, "Presuming Women: Revisiting the Presumption of Legitimacy in the Same-Sex Couples Era," *Boston University Law Review*, vol. 86, pp. 227–294 (2006).

adulterous relationship would not be a marriage with much commitment left to shore up, but there have been marriages where the married couple reconciles after such an event, and the presumption of legitimacy allows the couple to effectively exclude third parties who might otherwise disrupt marital stability by claims to spend time with the child.[15]

A growing number of states have made the marital presumption of paternity less absolute and, in some jurisdictions, more of a case-by-case matter.[16] This move is frequently justified by the lower stigma of illegitimacy.[17]

Today the courts often combine the marital presumption with the tool of equitable estoppel. Estoppel can be used in two different sorts of contexts: (1) to prevent a man who has held himself out as a child's father, and allowed that child to bond with him, from later trying to rid himself of legal paternal status; and (2) to prevent a mother who has told a man that he is the biological father (when he in fact is not) or who has encouraged such a man to take up the role of father, from later excluding him from paternal status when it no longer suits her purposes.[18] Equitable parental status is considered further in section D, below.

---

15. This appears to have been the fact situation of the *Michael H.* Supreme Court case, cited earlier. Michael H. v. Gerald D., 491 U.S. 110 (1989).
16. This discussion derives in part from June Carbone & Naomi Cahn, "Which Ties Bind? Redefining the Parent-Child Relationship in an Age of Genetic Certainty," *William & Mary Bill of Rights Journal*, vol. 11, pp. 1011–1070 (2003).
17. *See, e.g.,* J.A.S. v. Bushelman, 342 S.W.3d 850 (Ky. 2011) (change from irrebuttable marital presumption to rebuttable presumption, justified in part on the lower burden on nonmarital children).
18. *See, e.g.,* K.E.M. v. P.C.S., 38 A.3d 798 (Pa. 2012) (after reviewing policy and commentary regarding parenthood by estoppel, concluding that whether the doctrine should be applied to a man who was not a biological father, and knew he was not, but who held himself out as the child's father, turns on the best interests of the child); *see also* Wanda M. v. Lawrence T., 80 A.D.3d 765, 915 N.Y.S.2d 610 (2011) (equitable estoppel used to reject putative father's denial of paternity and to refuse ordering of genetic test, where the putative father had held himself out as the child's father, and the child would be hurt if he were to be declared no longer the child's father). These issues are obviously related

✇ C. Step-Parents

When a legal parent to a child marries someone other than the child's other parent, that spouse is a step-parent to the child. Under most state laws, step-parents have limited rights and obligations regarding such children, and most of these rights and obligations end when the marriage to the legal parent ends.[19] For custody purposes in many states, step-parents are considered "nonparents," and so would be at a significant legal disadvantage in most states in any later custody fight (against either their former spouse, or against the child's other legal parent), even if the step-parent had played a very significant role in the child's care.[20]

There is a legal process of step-parent adoption, by which step-parents can become the legal parents of their spouses' children. However, such adoptions will usually not be granted unless the children's other legal parent (generally the other biological parent of the child) either consents, or the consent is considered unnecessary because that other parent has had little contact with the children and adoption by the step-parent is found to be in the children's best interests.[21]

---

to the somewhat different question of when, if at all, men who were misled regarding their parental status should be able to sue for "paternity fraud." On that topic, see Melanie B. Jacobs, "When Daddy Doesn't Want to Be Daddy Anymore: An Argument Against Paternity Fraud Claims," *Yale Journal of Law and Feminism*, vol. 16, pp. 193–240 (2004).

19. However, "when a stepfather actively interferes with the child's support from the natural father, he may be equitably estopped from disclaiming that obligation in the future, even after the marriage to the biological mother has ended." Laura W. Morgan, "Child Support Fifty Years Later," *Family Law Quarterly*, vol. 42, pp. 365–380 (2008), at p. 379 (footnote omitted).

20. Some states, by statute or case law, expressly give step-parents standing to seek visitation or custody. *See, e.g.,* 750 ILCS 5/607(b)(1.5) (Illinois' step-parent visitation provision).

21. Consent would also be unnecessary if the other legal parent had been shown to be an unfit parent in some other way—for example, through past abuse or neglect.

✻ D. Equitable Parents

As already discussed, American law (and the law of many other countries) has developed to the point where one's rights and duties regarding one's biological children no longer depend on one's marital status. Unmarried biological mothers and fathers have the same, or almost the same, set of rights and obligations regarding their children as married parents do. The prior section discussed step-parents, and step-parenthood might be thought of as a special subcategory within a more general one: persons who function as parents to children without having any biological ties to them or the formal status of parenthood granted by legal adoption.

Courts in some jurisdictions have recognized doctrines of "de facto parenthood," "psychological parent," or "parenthood by estoppel" as a way of granting parental rights and obligations to parties who would otherwise not meet the (biological or statutory) criteria for legal parenthood.[22] These "functional" approaches to parental status have also been encouraged by the American Law Institute.[23]

One set of situations where this status is especially important is with same-sex couples raising children, at least for those couples who do not have access to the legal formalization of same-sex marriage, civil unions, domestic partnership, or second-parent adoption.[24] A handful of jurisdictions have recognized "de facto

---

22. The doctrine is occasionally the product of legislation. *See, e.g., Del. Code* tit. 13, § 8-201; *see also* Smith v. Guest, 16 A.3d 920 (Del. 2011) (upholding against constitutional challenge the legislative directive that the de facto parenthood status have retroactive effect and not be precluded by *res judicata*).

23. American Law Institute, *Principles of the Law of Family Dissolution: Analysis and Recommendations* (Newark: LexisNexis, 2002), § 2.03(1).

24. In a small number of states, no judicially created or equitable doctrine is required: members of a same-sex couple raising a child together can both be named legal parents of the child. *E.g.,* Elisa B. v. Superior Court, 37 Cal.4th 108, 117 P.3d 660 (2005) (under California's version of Uniform Parentage Act, child may have two female parents, and partner who contributed significantly to the process of having and raising the child can be the presumed parent under the statute); Charisma R. v. Kristina S., 44 Cal. Rptr. 3d 332 (Cal. App. 2006)

parenthood," "psychological parent," or "parenthood by estoppel" status for partners in same-sex couples raising children; a number of relevant court cases are listed in the footnote below.[25] On the other hand, a few jurisdictions have expressly refused to recognize any quasi-parental status, on the basis that it was contrary to their public policy regarding parental rights and responsibilities.[26]

Even in those states where some form of quasi-parental status is recognized, there is no guarantee that both members of a couple raising a child together will be granted parental status. For the partner who is not the biological or adoptive parent of the child, it is usually a fact-sensitive, all-things-considered judgment, which is often far from predictable. Some recent cases, showing a range of outcomes, are presented in the footnote below.[27] One particularly tricky area involves step-parents who are generally deeply involved

---

(applies *Elisa B.* to hold that former same-sex partner has standing to seek parental rights to child born to partner during their relationship; clarifies that nothing turns on whether ex-partner supports action or not).

25. Psychological Parent: *In re* E.L.M.C., 100 P.3d 546 (Colo. App. 2004); Kinnard v. Kinnard, 43 P.3d 150 (Alaska 2002); V.C. v. M.J.B., 748 A.2d 539 (N.J. 2000); *In re* Clifford K.*, 619 S.E.2d 138 (W. Va. 2005); A.C. v. C.B., 829 P.2d 660 (N.M. App. 1992).

  In loco parentis: Spells v. Spells, 378 A.2d 879 (P. Super. Ct. 1977); Robinson v. Ford-Robinson, 196 S.W.3d 503 (Ark. App. 2004), *aff'd*, 208 S.W.3d 140 (Ark. 2005); Logan v. Logan, 730 So.2d 1124 (Miss. 1998); Russell v. Bridgens, 647 N.W.2d 56 (Neb. 2002); T.B. v. L.R.M., 786 A.2d 913 (Pa. 2001).

  De facto parenthood: *In re* H.S.H.-K.: Holtzman v. Knott, 193 Wis.2d 649, 533 N.W.2d 419 (1995); C.E.W. v. D.E.W., 845 A.2d 1146 (Me. 2004); Soohoo v. Johnson, 731 N.W.2d 815 (Minn. 2007); Mason v. Dwinnell, 660 S.E.2d 58 (N.C App. 2008); E.N.O. v. L.M.M., 711 N.E.2d 886 (Mass. 1999).

26. *E.g.*, Heatzig v. MacLean, 664 S.E.2d 347 (N.C. Ct. App. 2008) (rejecting "parenthood by estoppel"); Jones v. Barlow, 154 P.3d 808 (Utah 2007) (declining to adopt *de facto* parent or psychological parent doctrine to allow standing to seek visitation by former partner, and civil union partner, who had been involved in the process of having and raising a child for two years).

27. A.H. v. M.P., 857 N.E.2d 1061 (Mass. 2006) (mother's same-sex partner denied de facto parent status, despite her significant role in the IVF process and her financial support for the child; court emphasized her failure to follow through on adoption of the child, and her actions, especially during litigation, that "demonstrated an inability to place the child's need above her own"); Jones v. Jones, 884 A.2d 915 (Pa. Super. 2005), appeal denied, 912 A.2d 838 (Pa. 2006) (mother's former same-sex partner had *in loco parentis* status and met clear

in the raising of children, but whose legal rights and duties involving those children are often significantly diminished (as discussed in the previous section); it is rare for step-parents to succeed in obtaining "*de facto* parent" (or similar) status.[28]

E. Co-Parenting Agreements

Unmarried partners sometimes enter agreements to parent a child together (the agreement often includes, centrally, a promise not to contest the other partner's parental rights in court). This occurs with some frequency among same-sex couples who live in states in which same-sex marriage or an alternative status ("civil union" or "domestic partnership") is not available.[29] Additionally,

---

and convincing evidence standard to be granted custody in contest with legal mother); K.M. v. E.G., 37 Cal. 4th 130, 117 P.3d 673 (2005) (woman who donated eggs to partner to have child and joined her in a registered domestic partnership is a parent to the resulting children, despite language of sperm donor statute); King v. S.B., 837 N.E.2d 965 (Ind. 2005) (in the context of former lesbian partner's claim for parental rights, holding that, in general, people other than natural parents can be awarded such rights where it is in the child's best interests to do so); C.E.W. v. D.E.W., 845 A.2d 1146 (Me. 2004) (recognizing de facto parent status for former lesbian partner of biological mother for child they had raised together); T.B. v. L.R.M., 786 A.2d 913 (Pa. 2001) (former lesbian partner *in loco parentis* for child the couple raised together, can seek partial custody and visitation); Santos v. Banister, No. 1566 (Md. Ct. Spec. App., August 14, 2007) (mother's former lesbian partner *de facto* parent of only one of two children born during their relationship); Wakeman v. Dixon, 921 So.2d 669 (Fla. App. 2006) (refusal to grant lesbian ex-partner parental rights despite a co-parenting agreement); *In re* Parentage of L.B., 122 P.3d 161 (Wash. 2005) (finding *de facto* parentage available in principle for long-term lesbian partner).

28. *See, e.g., In re* Parentage of M.F., 228 P.3d 1270 (Wash. 2010) (de facto parental status denied to step-parent, because of adequacy of statutory protections for step-parents, including right to seek custody); *In re* Parentage of J.M.W., 158 Wash. App. 1017, 2010 WL 4159385 (Wash. App. 2010) (de facto parental status denied to step-parent, despite involvement in child's life and a co-parenting agreement with the legal parent).

29. Discussion of co-parenting agreements aimed at same-sex couples and a sample agreement can be found on the Human Rights Campaign site, http://www.hrc.org/resources/entry/co-parenting-agreement. *Cf. In re* Wells, 373 S.W.3d

fertility clinics will sometimes accept unmarried couples (same-sex or opposite-sex) as patients only if they agree to sign a document of this sort; or the agreement may, in some other way, be part of a gamete donor arrangement.[30]

Courts have to date generally been reluctant to enforce co-parenting agreements.[31] One case where a co-parenting agreement was not directly enforced, but where it did play a role in the court's decision recognizing parental rights, is *Mason v. Dwinnell.*[32] In that case, a co-parenting agreement was one piece of evidence among others that the biological parent had chosen to share parental decision making with her partner, and for that reason could not later claim a constitutional right to exclude the partner from contact with the child.[33]

It seems clear that this remains an area where courts (and legislatures) are reluctant to encourage private ordering. One justification and explanation is the courts' role as guardians of the best interests of children, combined with the view that this can be vouchsafed only when traditional institutions or state-created processes relating to parental status are followed. Of course, it is

---

174 (Tex. App. 2012) (without same-sex marriage or co-parenting agreement, same-sex partner who helped to raise the couple's child from its birth is considered only a "non-parent," who lacked standing to seek visitation with the child).

30. *See* Wakeman v. Dixon, 921 So.2d 669, 670 (Fla. App. 2006) (provision in sperm donor agreement); *In re* Sullivan, 157 S.W.3d 911 (Tex. App. 2005) (sperm donor who entered co-parenting agreement with intended mother has standing to maintain a proceeding to adjudicate parentage).

31. *See, e.g.,* Alison D. v. Virginia M., 572 N.E.2d 27 (N.Y. 1991); Sporleder v. Hermes (*In re* Interest of Z.J.H.), 471 N.W.2d 202 (Wis. 1991); Wakeman v. Dixon.

32. 660 S.E.2d 58 (N.C. Ct. App. 2008). There are other cases where the agreement is noted but plays no role in granting access rights to the party seeking those rights. *E.g.,* J.A.L. v. E.P.H., 682 A.2d 1314, 1321 (Pa. Super. Ct. 1996). In *Holtzman v. Knott* (*In re* H.S.H.-K.), 533 N.W.2d 419, 434–435 (Wis. 1995), the court allowed visitation based on the party's past parental function, though dicta indicates that the decision might also have been grounded on the co-parenting agreement.

33. *Mason,* 660 S.E.2d at 66–71.

probable that another part of the explanation is that the states (or, more precisely, the judges and lawmakers) that view same-sex unions as immoral and their recognition as contrary to strong public policy[34] are unlikely to be quick to recognize a contract process that would allow same-sex couples to circumvent state policy and opt into state recognition of their status as "co-parents."

There are hints in recent cases that some jurisdictions might be reversing the current conventional approach to co-parenting agreements. For courts in these states, instead of seeing agreements as having no independent significance, and only relevant as evidence of factual and functional co-parenting (which in turn grounds some form of equitable parenting status, or some waiver of the constitutional prerogatives of the biological and legal parent), the new emphasis is on the need for an actual agreement (in which the legal parent waived his or her constitutional parental rights), and look at practical and functional co-parenting as, at most, evidence of an implied agreement to waive.[35]

Even those sympathetic to the private ordering in co-parenting agreements might not want to grant full enforcement based on the agreement alone.[36] Such agreements are usually executed, and later litigated, in cases where partners share in the conceiving and raising of a child. If one of the parties to such an agreement rarely or never partook of the financial or caregiving obligations as regards a child, courts might reasonably be reluctant to ascribe parental rights to that party (courts and legislatures take a similar attitude toward unmarried biological fathers who have not taken on the obligations of parenthood[37]).

---

34. By one recent count, as of June 2010, roughly forty states "expressly refuse to recognize same-sex marriage of other jurisdictions, and some of those more broadly refer to other same-sex relationships." Matthew J. Eickman, "Same-Sex Marriage: DOMA and the States' Approaches," BNA *Fam. L. Rep.*, pp. 1383, 1385 (June 22, 2010).

35. *See In re* Mullen, 953 N.E.2d 302 (Ohio 2011).

36. I am grateful to Courtney Joslin for reminding me of this point.

37. *See* Lehr v. Robertson, 463 U.S. 248 (1983).

❦ F. Sharp Distinctions and the Rule of Two

Under U.S. law, when a child is born, it almost always has two legal parents, no more and no less. Through the process of adoption (including step-parent adoption), who the legal parents are can change, but the number usually does not. One can lose a legal parent through that parent's death, but the legal system generally does not allow one to gain a legal parent if one already has two, unless and until another legal parent loses his or her parental rights (through surrender or termination).

From one perspective, one might argue that the legal treatment of parental status at times can be unwisely rigid, even in the face of social norms that are far more nuanced and flexible. There are occasions—rare and sporadic—when family law does show some signs of flexibility and pragmatism toward parental status. In 2007, at roughly the same time, an American (Pennsylvania) court and a Canadian (Ontario) court both came down with decisions recognizing three legal parents for a child. In the Pennsylvania case, a state Superior Court dealt with a lesbian couple who had been raising a child, with ongoing parental contributions from the sperm donor they had used, a sperm donor who was also a friend of the couple.[38] When the lesbian couple broke up, one question that was raised in the litigation over custody and support was whether all three had child support obligations. The court held that all three were parents, and all had support obligations.

The structure of the case and the outcome were similar in a Canadian decision, where the Court of Appeal for Ontario again dealt with a lesbian couple and the sperm donor they had used.[39] The couple had wanted the sperm donor in the child's life, and he was already recognized as the legal father; and the birth mother was the legal mother. The action before the Ontario court was

---

38. Jacob v. Shultz-Jacob, 923 A.2d 473 (Pa. Super. 2007).
39. A.A. v. B.B., 83 O.R.3d 561 (2007) (Court of Appeal of Ontario).

the lesbian partner's effort to also be named as a legal parent, and the appellate court used its *parens patriae* jurisdiction to grant the parental right to the partner.[40] This sort of ruling in either the United States or Canada is unusual, to say the least, in large part because the statutes and case law all assume or assert that children have two, and no more than two, (legal) parents.[41]

Some of the commentators responded sharply to these two cases. In discussing the three-parent cases just mentioned, the conservative commentator Elizabeth Marquardt wrote:

> Astonishingly, few legal experts, politicians or social commentators have considered the enormous risks these rulings and proposals pose for children.[42]

The alarm was sounded from other culturally traditional commentators as well.[43] Stanley Kurtz offered as his first objection to multiple parenthood that "[o]nce parental responsibilities are parceled out to more than two people ... it becomes easier for any one parent to shirk his or her responsibilities." This seems, paradoxically, a good argument for only having one parent (likely not Mr. Kurtz's intentions)—a single parent who would then have no opportunity to

---

40. In July 2010, the Attorney General for British Columbia published a white paper, which recommended rules for parental rights that (the paper recognizes) would lead to some children having three parents. Ministry of Attorney General, "White Paper on *Family Relations Act*: Reform Proposals for a New Family Law Act" (July 2010), available at http://www.ag.gov.bc.ca/legislation/index.htm.

41. Even states like California "progressive" enough to have the two legal parents of a child be of the same gender balk at declaring a child to have three legal parents. *See In re* M.C., 195 Cal.App.4th 197, 123 Cal. Rptr. 3d 856 (Cal. App. 2011) (trial court in dependency case correctly determined that subject child had three presumed parents but conflicting presumptions must be resolved to leave only two legal parents).

42. Elizabeth Marquardt, "When Three Really Is a Crowd," *New York Times*, July 16, 2007.

43. *E.g.*, Stanley Kurtz, "Heather Has 3 Parents," *National Review Online*, Mar. 12, 2003, http://www.nationalreview.com, responding to an earlier stage of the Ontario case.

shirk. It works less well as an argument for removing legal responsibilities from an adult ("the third parent") who has a caretaking role in the child's life, just because two other adults equally qualify.

In the commentators' responses, the bogeyman of "three parents" quickly leads back to that other bogeyman: polygamy. Marquardt wrote: "If more children are granted three legal parents, what is our rationale for denying these families the rights and protections of marriage? America, get ready for the group-marriage debate."[44] Stanley Kurtz offered the same specter: "[J]ust as gay adoption has set a legal precedent for group parenthood, so will group parenthood pave the way to group marriage."[45]

However, things look far less drastic if matters are put into context. The three-parent cases (or potential three-parent cases) that get the most attention are those involving same-sex couples and a third-party gamete donor,[46] but there are numerous other contexts in which parental roles are split more than two ways, and in which there is either social acceptance of such splits, or even limited legal recognition.

And we do not need to even speak about the sort of cases that make conservative and traditional commentators most antsy— same-sex couples, or children born from gamete donors or with the help of surrogates. In a world where divorce is relatively common and accepted, and remarriage of one or both parents far from rare, children frequently grow up with three or four (or, with multiple divorces and remarriages, potentially more) parental figures. As discussed in section C, above, step-parents in a number of states have

---

44. Marquardt, "When Three Really Is a Crowd."
45. Kurtz, "Heather Has 3 Parents." And beyond that, for Kurtz, the abyss: "Once we cross the border into legalized multiple parenthood, we have virtually arrived at the abolition of marriage and the family." *Id.*
46. Such cases are discussed in greater detail in chapter 6. Scientists in 2008 reported success in creating human embryos from three genetic parents— with one female contributing mitochrondial DNA and a male and a female contributing nuclear DNA. Ben Hirschler, "Scientists Create Three-Parent Embryos," *Reuters*, Feb. 5, 2008. However, no cases have been reported to date of children being created from this three-genetic-parent process.

a level of legal recognition of rights and responsibilities for the children they help raise (one might believe, far fewer rights and responsibilities than they should have, but that is a different debate). And the law here clearly lags behind the social reality of step-parents being real social parents, most of the time, for the children they raise. Original legal parents, plus step-parents, equals three, frequently four, sometimes more, parents. Also, in many communities, a significant amount of parenting occurs by "kinship caregivers," who also do not fit into the simple "rule of two."[47]

A second increasingly common scenario involves children being placed for adoption, but with an express or informal agreement for the child to maintain some contact with one or both birth parents: a so-called open adoption (discussed in chapter 5, section C). Adoptive parents, plus continued connection with birth parent(s), equals three (and perhaps four) parents.

There are other more or less conventional situations: for example, with extended kinship care networks or grandparents helping out with parenting. There are also legal contexts where a man who has chosen to hold himself out as the legal father even though he has no genetic ties to a child is given some or all parental rights; or similar legal rights are recognized for a man who has been misled into believing that he is the genetic father of a child when in fact he is not (topics discussed earlier in this chapter). In such circumstances, if the real genetic father also has legal status or social authority in relation to the child, then there will be more than two parents.

One can even find reported cases—not many of them, to be sure, but from perfectly respectable courts (and in fairly conservative, traditional jurisdictions)[48]—where the judge finds three parents:

47. Sacha M. Coupet, "'Ain't I a Parent?': The Exclusion of Kinship Caregivers from the Debate Over Expansions of Parenthood," *New York University Review of Law & Social Change*, vol. 34, pp. 595–656 (2010).

48. *See* Smith v. Cole, 553 So. 2d 847 (La. 1989); Nebraska v. Mendoza, 481 N.W.2d 165 (Neb. 1992); Green v. Green, 666 So. 2d 1192 (La. Ct. App. 1995); Sinicropi v. Mazurek, 760 N.W.2d 520 (Mich. App. 2008).

two legal fathers to go along with one mother.[49] In these cases, there is a biological father and a putative or presumed father, or a father who accepted paternity in a legal action. There is no evidence that these rulings were considered earth-shattering by commentators (conservative or otherwise). Perhaps we are just accustomed to the state chasing after all possible male child support obligors, or perhaps children born of adulterous unions are not as scandalous as they once were.

On the whole, neither traditionalists nor their critics are against multiple caregivers: some may have moral or policy qualms about nannies or about day care, and others may raise objections to alternative family formation, but it would be hard to find anyone objecting to extended family being involved in child care, or the occasional use of babysitters. The objection to grandparents comes only when courts give them parental rights, or the equivalent, over the objections of conventional parents.[50]

To be fair, the conservative commentators have not missed that children often have multiple parental figures. For example, after noting the multiple parents involved in step-parent situations and some adoptions, Elizabeth Marquardt added (with some exasperation):

> Those who have noticed tend to say they are nothing new, because many children already grow up with several parent figures. But this fails to recognize that stepchildren and adopted children still have only two legal parents.[51]

This is true, of course, but merely restates the legal status quo, without explaining why it is better than the alternatives.

---

49. *Cf.* Smith v. Cole, 553 So.2d 847 (La. 1989) (recognizing three legal parents—mother, mother's husband, and biological father—in order both to maintain legitimacy of child and to impose support obligations on the biological father).
50. Troxel v. Granville, 530 U.S. 57 (2000).
51. Marquardt, "When Three Really Is a Crowd."

It is hard not to suspect that much of the shocked reaction to the three-parent cases is grounded in the visceral response to both same-sex couples on one hand, and new reproductive technologies (in vitro fertilization gamete donation, and surrogacy in particular) on the other.[52]

As Susan Appleton has pointed out,[53] there are also likely gender aspects to some of the decisions in multiple-parenting cases, and to some of the objections. Both the Pennsylvania and Ontario cases involved a male parental figure supplementing an otherwise dual-female parenting structure. Given the traditionalist objection to same-sex parenting, that it is important for children to have role models of both sexes, perhaps multiple parenting orders will always be easier when "the missing gender" is involved, rather than, say, seeking a third mother for a child who still has no legal father.

As in most debates about marriage and parenting in family law (and probably everything else), the debates often come down to claims about the consequences for children. Traditionalists argue that only conventional parenting—by two parents of opposite sexes in a marital relationship—is good for children, while nontraditionalists disagree.

In her commentary against recognizing three parents, Elizabeth Marquardt noted that three-parent litigation often involves same-sex parents and a gamete donor—almost inevitably parties who live in two (or more) different households. And, she continued, research shows that children of divorce who shuttle between households—especially households where the adults are not on the best of terms—often have bad long-term outcomes. This may not

---

52. Nancy Polikoff reports that courts in a number of states have authorized what is in effect "third-party adoptions": adding a legal parent (the partner of an existing legal parent), while both legal parents retain parental rights (a variation of the step-parent and second-parent adoptions discussed in chapter 5, section D). Nancy Polikoff, "Where Can a Child Have Three Parents?," *Beyond (Straight and Gay) Marriage* (Blog), July 14, 2012, available at http://beyond-straightandgaymarriage.blogspot.com/2012/07/where-can-child-have-three-parents.html.

53. Susan Frelich Appleton, "Parentage by the Numbers: Should Only Two Always Do?," *Hofstra Law Review*, vol. 37, pp. 11–69 (2008).

be the strongest argument against multiple parenting, but it points to the type of argument most likely to hold up under scrutiny: that allowing certain sorts of legal claims would result, in the short term or the long term, in harm to children.

We may be beginning to know something about the long-term effects of divorce and single parenthood on children, though even here the data is difficult to gather and too easy to over-read. As for the effects of multiple parenting, there is unsurprisingly, very little data: only armchair speculation and attempts to extrapolate from the data already in hand on other nontraditional family forms. The problem is that there is little data about unconventional, multiple-parenting families, and what data there is, would, in any event, be confounded by the effects of the social marginalization of these families.[54]

Even if one accepts, for the purpose of the current discussion, that multiple parenting is less good for children in comparison with traditional family structures, it is not clear where that gets us as a policy matter. The question is, when starting from an unconventional family structure, is it better for all the adults with a social, genetic, or caretaker role in the child's life to have their relationship formalized in law with all the attendant legal rights and obligations, or is it better for the number of legal parents to be limited in some way?

On one hand, there is an argument that with divorces and step-parents, we already have the *social* recognition of more than two parents, even if not always the *legal* recognition. Additionally, the move toward more legal recognition of *functionally* defined parents seems to be leading to a *legal* recognition of more than two parents. On the other hand, there is still something like the objection Mary Anne Case offered[55] for the legal recognition of polygamy: there is simply greater administrative convenience when dealing with one or two legal parents that is substantially lost when we move to three or more legal parents.

---

54. Another point made in Appleton, "Parentage by the Numbers."
55. Mary Anne Case, "Marriage Licenses," *Minnesota Law Review*, vol. 89, pp. 1758–1797 (2005).

In 2012, the California legislature passed a bill that would have given judges authority to recognize more than two legal parents, but the bill was vetoed by the governor.[56]

Suggested Further Reading

Evaluating Parental Claims

June Carbone & Naomi Cahn, "Marriage, Parentage, and Child Support," *Family Law Quarterly*, vol. 45, pp. 219–240 (2011).

Marital Presumption and Parenthood by Estoppel

June Carbone, "The Legal Definition of Parenthood: Uncertainty at the Core of Family Identity," *Louisiana Law Review*, vol. 65, pp. 1295–1344 (2005).

June Carbone & Naomi Cahn, "Marriage, Parentage, and Child Support," *Family Law Quarterly*, vol. 45, pp. 219–240 (2011).

Step-Parents

Margaret M. Mahoney, "Stepparents as Third Parties in Relation to Their Stepchildren," *Family Law Quarterly*, vol. 40, pp. 81–108 (2006).

Nonmarital Children

Susan Frelich Appleton, "Illegitimacy and Sex, Old and New," *American University Journal of Gender, Social Policy, and Law*, vol. 20, pp. 347–384 (2012).

Carlos Ball, "Rendering Children Illegitimate in Former Partner Parenting Cases: Hiding Behind the Façade of Certainty," *American University Journal of Gender, Social Policy & the Law*, vol. 20, pp. 623–668 (2012).

R. H. Helmholz, "Support Orders, Church Courts, and the Rule of *Filius Nullius*: A Reassessment of the Common Law," *Virginia Law Review*, vol. 63, pp. 431–448 (1977).

John Witte, Jr., *The Sins of the Fathers: The Law and Theology of Illegitimacy Reconsidered* (Cambridge: Cambridge University Press, 2009).

Multiple Parents

Susan Frelich Appleton, "Parentage by the Numbers: Should Only Two Always Do?," *Hofstra Law Review*, vol. 37, pp. 11–69 (2008).

---

56. *See* Jim Sanders, "Jerry Brown Vetoes Bill Allowing More Than Two Parents," *Sacramento Bee*, Sept. 30, 2012; for critical reaction to the original proposal, see John Culhane & Elizabeth Marquardt, "California Should Not Pass 'Multiple Parents' Bill," *Huffington Post*, Aug. 17, 2012, http://www.huffingtonpost.com.

FIVE

Adoption

% A. History and General Rules

Adoption is the creation of a legal parent-child relationship through the action of a court rather than through birth. Currently, about 130,000 to 140,000 children are adopted each year, though only 15–20 percent of these "conform to the traditional model of a healthy ... infant placed voluntarily by an unwed mother with an infertile ... couple."[1]

While there have been forms of adoption in Western societies for millennia,[2] adoption as we know it—the adoption primarily of

---

1. Joan Heifetz Hollinger & Naomi Cahn, "Forming Families by Law: Adoption in America Today," *Human Rights*, pp. 16–19 (Summer 2009), at p. 17. The remainder of the adoptions include step-parent adoptions, the adoptions of older children out of foster care, and the adoptions of children by extended family members.
2. For example, the Roman emperors frequently "adopted" an adult they wanted to succeed them. (On adoption in Roman law, see generally Paul du Plessis, *Borkowski's Textbook on Roman Law* (4th ed., Oxford: Oxford University Press, 2010), pp. 132–135.) In Japan, adult adoption (which is the vast majority of adoptions in that country) is used for a comparable reason: creating a worthy successor in a "family" company. Vikas Mehrotra et al., "Adoptive Expectations: Rising Sons in Japanese Family Firms" (unpublished manuscript, 2010), linked at http://www.freakonomics.com/2011/08/09/the-church-of-scionology-why-adult-adoption-is-key-to-the-success-of-japanese-family-firms/.

   The early church developed forms of adoption to find new homes for unwanted children, a process that the medieval canon lawyers developed into somewhat more formal arrangements. *See* Charles J. Reid, Jr., "The Rights of Children in Medieval Canon Law," in Patrick Brennan (ed.), *The Vocation of the Child* (Grand Rapids, Mich.: William B. Eerdmans, 2008), pp. 243–265, also available at http://papers.ssrn.com/abstract=1015403.

young children, accomplished through legal decree, which terminates all (or nearly all[3]) legal ties to the former parent(s)—is surprisingly recent, coming into existence in the mid-nineteenth century.[4] The principles and rules of adoption exemplify interesting aspects of the role of money, genetics, and consent in family law matters. Developing rules on "open adoptions," like some of the developments relating to new reproductive technologies (see chapter 6) test the willingness of courts and legislatures to consider the legal recognition of (and legal protection for) unconventional family forms.

Every stage of the adoption process has raised its own distinct set of issues: the consent by the original parent(s) to give up a child for adoption, the determination of the fitness of the adopting parents, whether there is recourse for the adopting parents for fraud in the process, and what rights adopted children have regarding inheritance and learning about their background.

The basic rule—and the basic objective—of American adoption law is to create a legal parent-child relationship equivalent to that created when a child is born. However, finding procedures and standards that can adequately protect the interests of all the relevant parties (not least the best interests of the child to be adopted) as well as the public interest has proven both difficult and controversial.[5]

---

3. Under some state adoption laws, the adopted child retains its rights to inherit from its original parents, even after the adoption has been finalized and the original parental rights terminated.

4. Most commentators point to an 1851 Massachusetts law, An Act to Provide for the Adoption of Children, 1851 Laws Mass. ch. 324, though comparable practices were authorized prior to that date through individual legislative acts. *See, e.g.*, Lawrence M. Friedman, "Rites of Passage: Divorce Law in Historical Perspective," *Oregon Law Review*, vol. 63, pp. 649–669 (1984), at p. 656. For an interesting article tying the change in adoption law to the change in thinking about child custody, see Jamil S. Zainaldin, "The Emergence of a Modern American Family Law: Child Custody, Adoption, and the Courts, 1796–1851," *Northwestern University Law Review*, vol. 73, pp. 1038–1089 (1979). The 1851 Act is reproduced in Naomi Cahn & Joan Heifetz Hollinger (eds.), *Families by Law: An Adoption Reader* (New York: New York University Press, 2004), pp. 9–10.

5. The Uniform Law Commission promulgated a Uniform Adoption Act in 1994—the full text can be found at http://www.law.upenn.edu/bll/archives/ulc/fnact99/1990s/uaa94.htm. To date, the Act has been adopted in only one state, Vermont.

In recent decades, a significant portion of adoptions in the United States were of children from other nations. Between 1999 and 2011, there were 233,934 international adoptions.[6] However, other countries have imposed restrictions in recent years that have decreased the total number of these international adoptions (from 22,991 in 2004 to 9,319 in 2011).[7]

⁂ B. Nonmarital Fathers

As noted, in Anglo-American law, parental rights were once tied closely to marital status. Married parents had significant rights and duties regarding a child, but when a child was born outside of marriage, fathers in particular had few rights or obligations, and mothers' rights and obligations were also often limited. In the United States (and many other countries) today, unmarried parents retain many of the rights and obligations of married parents, but there are some differences, and these differences are sharpest with unmarried fathers.

While mothers (married or unmarried) have constitutionally protected rights relating to their children from their children's birth, the U.S. Supreme Court has held that unmarried fathers have constitutionally protected rights only if they have maintained a certain level of contact with the child in question.[8] According to the Court, the genetic tie the father has with a child (where the father is not married to the mother) gives that father a "unique opportunity" to create a (constitutionally protected) tie with the child, but nothing more.[9]

---

6. U.S. Department of States statistics, available at http://adoption.state.gov/about_us/statistics.php.

7. *See id.*

8. Lehr v. Robertson, 463 U.S. 248 (1983).

9. A postscript to *Lehr*: the birth father in that case, Jonathan Mathias Lehr, continued to try to have contact with the daughter ("Jessica Martz") who was adopted in that case. In 2005, he posted information on the Internet site, adoption.com, searching for her, http://registry.adoption.com/records/452561.html. There is no indication that his daughter ever contacted him.

This creates complications where the parents are not married, and either the mother does not allow the father to have contact with her or the child (or perhaps does not even inform him that she is pregnant or (later) that he is the father of a child that was born), or the mother seeks to place the child for adoption soon after birth. Under such situations, the father can hardly be said to be at fault for not creating a relationship with his biological child. In some cases of this type, a court has focused on whether the father tried to support the mother-to-be through her pregnancy (though there will remain problems where the father's failure to support the mother-to-be was due to her efforts to avoid continued contact with him).

A persistent problem with the adoption of newborns is balancing, on one hand, the protection of a father's rights—in particular, his right to be heard prior to the another couple's adoption of the father's biological child (an action that will terminate the biological father's parental rights)—and, on the other hand, the value of finality in the adoption process (because allowing the intervention by a biological father might delay or unsettle an adoption). This question also comes up with recent state initiatives to provide places where women can anonymously, and without legal liability, drop off newborn babies whom the mothers wish to abandon ("infant safe haven" laws).[10]

On one hand, there are highly publicized cases where a father has been allowed, somewhat late in the process, to upset an adoption process, where the child had already become settled in the new family setting.[11] In many of these cases, the biological father did not know that he had a child or that the child had been put up for adoption. And sometimes the long bonding process between the children and the couples who want to adopt them comes from their (understandable) determination to fight the issue in court even after being

---

10. *See* Jeffrey A. Parness, "Lost Paternity in the Culture of Motherhood: A Different View of Safe Haven Laws," *Valparaiso Law Review*, vol. 42, pp. 81–98 (2007).
11. In the Interest of *B.G.C.*, 496 N.W.2d 239 (Iowa 1992) ("Baby Jessica" case); *In re* Kirchner, 649 N.E.2d 324 (Ill. 1995) ("Baby Richard" case); Adoptive Couple v. Baby Girl, 731 S.E.2d 550 (S.C. 2012), cert. granted, 2013 WL 49813, 81 USLW 3198 (2013).

informed that the child's father has not consented to the adoption. Sometimes the father does not find out about the child until the adoption has been finalized and can no longer be challenged. In *Wyatt v. McDermott*, a father claimed that the mother (to whom he was not married) had promised him that they would raise the child together; he claimed that instead she hid the child from him and eventually arranged for its adoption by a Utah couple. Under a question certified to the Virginia Supreme Court by a federal court hearing the dispute, the Virginia court concluded that the state did recognize a common law tort for interference with parental rights.[12] The Virginia court reported that a comparable claim had been recognized under the English common law as early as 1607 and that the "overwhelming majority" of other (American) jurisdictions had recognized the cause of action. The biological father thus had potential grounds for seeking damages against the biological mother (if his allegations were found to be true), though likely this would be small consolation for being denied contact with and legal rights regarding his biological child.

There are no easy solutions to the tension between a father's interests and rights on one side and the interest in speed and finality in the adoption process on the other side. In one notoriously bad effort to resolve the tension, Florida in 2001 passed a law requiring a birth mother to publish

a physical description, including, but not limited to, age, race, hair and eye color, and approximate height and weight of the minor's mother and of any person the mother reasonably believes may be the father; the minor's date of birth, and any date and city, including the county and state in which the city is located, in which conception may have occurred.[13]

However, a court struck down this statute as unconstitutional in 2003.[14]

---

12. Wyatt v. McDermott, 725 S.E.2d 555 (Va. 2012).
13. G.P. v. State, 842 So. 2d 1059, 1062 (Fla. App. 2003).
14. *See* G.P. v. State.

✍ C. Open Adoption and Open Records

Open adoption involves ongoing contact between the adopted child and its birth mother (or, more rarely, both birth parents).[15] In the early and middle decades of the twentieth century, it was customary for the adopting parents and the birth parents not to know one another's identity. The consensus view of government officials, social services officials, social scientists, and the general public was that this secrecy and anonymity was best for all concerned. Frequently the mother giving up the child for adoption had become pregnant outside of marriage, and nonmarital births were then generally treated as shameful. It was also sometimes thought embarrassing, from the perspective of the adopting parents, not to be able to have one's own biological children. So the anonymous and secret passing of the child from the pregnant mother to the state (or state-sanctioned) agency to the adoptive parents allowed all concerned to pretend to norms and a normality that was not in fact present. It was also considered best for adopted children not to know that they had been adopted—another reason for secrecy.[16] Also, birth mothers were promised that they would be protected from the prospect of their secret children, born out of wedlock, later reappearing in their lives, potentially undermining the conventional life that they had (it was hoped) acquired by then.

---

15. *See* Kirsten Widner, "Continuing the Evolution: Why California Should Amend Family Code Section 8616.5 to Allow Visitation in All Postadoption Contact Agreements," *San Diego Law Review*, vol. 44, pp. 355–386 (2007), at pp. 357–361 (2007); *see also* U.S. Department of Health and Human Services, *Postadoption Contact Agreements Between Birth and Adoptive Families* (2011), available at http://www.childwelfare.gov/systemwide/laws_policies/statutes/cooperative.cfm [hereinafter, *Postadoption Contact Agreements*]. California has recently begun to recognize "tribal customary adoption," under which an adoption follows the rules and traditions of a child's tribe, and need not involve termination of parental rights. *California Welfare and Institutions Code* § 366.24.

16. The idea that being adopted is something to be ashamed of, or a second-class status, has not entirely disappeared in contemporary American, but it is far less prevalent than it once was.

The social context in which adoption occurs has changed radically in recent decades. On the one hand, having children outside of marriage is far more acceptable than it once was, as is obtaining children through adoption. Also, many psychologists and social scientists consider it beneficial for adopted children to have some contact with their birth parents at some point. While open adoption agreements in earlier times were not encouraged by adoption agencies for the reasons summarized above, and were generally treated as unenforceable by courts (because they were contrary to the "public policy" of anonymity in adoption, or because they altered the terms of a state-created status[17]), such agreements are now far more common and more commonly legally recognized and enforced. One commentator has reported that "[o]pen adoption has now become the norm for all types of adoption,"[18] though perhaps this only indicates the greater frequency of adoptive parents knowing the identity of birth parents rather than any predominance of actual contact agreements among adoptive families.

In any event, there is a growing use of open adoption agreements, which has been justified and explained in part by a growing view that it is beneficial for an adopted child to know of and have contact with its birth parents. A quite different part of the explanation is the reality that far more parents are seeking to adopt than there are healthy babies and infants available for adoption,[19] creating a

---

17. *E.g., In re* Adoption of Hammer, 487 P.2d 417 (Ariz. App. 1971). It would be more precise to say that the parties were thought not to have the power to create *enforceable* alterations of the state-created status. Nothing prevents adopting parents from allowing or encouraging ongoing contact between the child and its birth parents, if the identity of the birth parents is known to the adopting parents.

18. Annette Ruth Appell, "Reflections on the Movement Toward a More Child-Centered Adoption," *Western New England Law Review*, vol. 31, pp. 1–32 (2010), at p. 4 (footnote omitted). One assumes that the quotation was directed only to domestic adoptions; it seems unlikely that open adoptions are common in international adoptions.

19. The "supply" to "demand" ratio is much higher when speaking about the adoption of older children, children who have been in foster care for long periods, and children with disabilities.

situation where (1) a parent considering putting his or her child up for adoption is in a position to set terms (e.g., of ongoing contact) that the adopting parents might not otherwise prefer; and (2) there is an interest in creating options (like enforceable open adoption) that "free up" more children for adoption.[20]

One should note that these agreements are not universally recognized. By statute and case law, open adoption agreements are valid and enforceable in twenty-six states and the District of Columbia,[21] and even in those states, such agreements are often treated with suspicion or hostility by some judges. Under the Minnesota statute, for example, an open adoption agreement must be approved by the court and is then subject to modification by the court (if "exceptional circumstances" have arisen that make modification necessary for the best interests of the adopted child).[22]

A separate significant change to confidentiality in adoptions has occurred largely through legislative changes, pressed by adoptees after they have reached adulthood: open access to birth records. Until relatively recently, parents giving up children for adoption were promised confidentiality, and the identity of those birth parents was generally only given to adopted children upon a court order, an order that in turn was usually only given upon a very strong showing (e.g., for medical

---

20. *See generally* Annette Ruth Appell, "The Move Toward Legally Sanctioned Cooperative Adoption: Can It Survive the Uniform Adoption Act?," *Family Law Quarterly*, vol. 30, pp. 483–518 (1996). Open adoptions are increasingly being offered as a "choice" to a parent, when a social services agency is threatening to terminate that person's parental rights (due to allegations of abuse or neglect). *See* Carol Sanger, "Acquiring Children Contractually: Relational Contracts at Work at Home," in Jean Braucher, John Kidwell, & William Whitford (eds.), *Revisiting the Contracts Scholarship of Stewart Macaulay: On the Empirical and the Lyrical* (Hart Publishing, 2013). As Sanger concludes, in such circumstances, open adoption agreements are less like commercial or premarital agreements, and more like criminal law plea bargains.

21. *Postadoption Contact Agreements*, at 2.

22. *Minn. Stat.* § 259.58. The Minnesota Supreme Court has not yet answered the question of whether "modification" of the agreement would include the power to invalidate it in total. C.O. v. Doe, 757 N.W.2d 343, 352 n.10 (Minn. 2008). Other states, e.g., Oregon and Washington, have comparable legislation. *Wash. Stat. Ann.* § 26.33.295; *Or. Rev. Stat. Ann.* § 109.305.

reasons). Many states have maintained registries that allow adopted children to find the biological parents who gave them up for adoption—but only if those birth parents consented to be found. However a few states now go further in allowing adopted children information about their birth parents.[23] Maine, for example, recently became the eighth state to allow adult adoptees full access to their birth certificates and, thus, the identity of one, and perhaps both, birth parents.[24]

✺ D. Step-Parent and Second-Parent Adoption

Under the normal adoption process, when a child is adopted, all legal ties with its former parents are cut off (subject to the exceptions discussed in the previous section on open adoption). However, all states, by statute or court decision, now have an option by which the spouse of a legal parent can adopt a child without terminating the parental rights of that parent: so-called "step-parent adoption."[25]

"Second-parent adoption" is the name given to same-sex partners[26] trying to use step-parent adoption, or a close analogy, to allow a same-sex partner to adopt his or her partner's child.[27] In many states, appellate courts have read their adoption statutes broadly

---

23. *See, e.g.*, Doe v. Sundquist, 2 S.W.3d 919 (Tenn. 1999) (upholding against state constitutional challenge of Tennessee law which allowed disclosure of sealed adoption records to adopted persons at the age of 21).

24. Wendy Koch, "Many States Usher in New Laws with the New Year," *USA Today*, Dec. 29, 2008.

25. The one state that created step-parent adoption through court decision rather than legislation was California. *See* Marshall v. Marshall, 239 P. 36 (Cal. 1925) (reading a step-parent adoption provision into the general California adoption statute).

26. In principle, opposite-sex unmarried couples could, and occasionally do, also seek a second-parent adoption. *See In re* Adoption of Shelby L.B., No. M2010-00879-COA-R9-PT, 2011 WL 1225567 (Tenn. App. 2011) (refusing second-parent adoption in case brought by opposite-sex couple).

27. There has been at least one case where the "second parent" was not a same-sex partner but rather a grandfather to the child. *See In re* Adoption of A.M., 930 N.E.2d 613 (Ind. App. 2010) (approving "second-parent" adoption by grandfather, terminating the rights of the child's father but not that of the mother). In states where same-sex marriages are recognized, same-sex married couples should be able to use step-parent adoption.

to allow such adoptions;[28] in other states, the appellate courts have argued that adoption, as a statutory product, needs to be read narrowly, and second-parent adoptions cannot be done until there is express legislative authorization. In a third group of states, the appellate courts have not spoken on the issue one way or the other, and in those states some trial court judges are performing second-parent adoptions even though they do not have clear authorization either from the legislature or from an appellate court.[29]

✻ E. Race and Religion

In *Palmore v. Sidoti*,[30] the U.S. Supreme Court declared that it was unconstitutional for a court to base a custody determination on direct or indirect racial discrimination, including in that case the effort to protect a child from the bad effects of other people's racial prejudices. While some commentators had read that case as requiring that race play no role in child placement decisions, it has been a common practice for state and private adoption agencies to try to place children with parents of the same race.

In part, race-matching was a reaction to prior practices, in which the placement of minority children with white families had become common. In response to such placements, in 1972 the National Association of Black Social Workers promulgated a "Position Statement on Transracial Adoption," stating that a "white

---

28. *See, e.g., In re* Jacob, 660 N.E.2d 397 (N.Y. 1995) (allowing second-parent adoption); Sharon S. v. Superior Court, 73 P.3d 554 (Cal. 2003) (same).

29. This has obvious risks. In North Carolina, the second-parent adoptions "granted" by trial courts were later held to be void when the state supreme court finally considered the issue and determined that second-parent adoptions were not authorized by the state adoption statute. Boseman v. Jarrell, 704 S.E.2d 494 (N.C. 2010); *cf.* Bates v. Bates, 730 S.E.2d 482 (Ga. App. 2012) (suggesting that it is "doubtful" that Georgia law permits second-parent adoption, but not deciding the issue; challenge to particular second-parent adoption rejected on *res judicata* grounds).

30. 466 U.S. 429 (1984).

home is not a suitable placement for black children."[31] (The National Association of Black Social Workers continues to stand by its 1972 statement.[32]) There was a sense that "race-matching" in adoption would benefit the children being adopted, as parents would be in a better position to teach children about their racial, ethnic, or cultural identity, and would be better positioned to prepare them for the challenges they would meet.[33]

On the other hand, there was a growing concern that the effort to "match" children racially too often resulted in children of color being left in foster care or orphanages when loving adoptive homes (of potential parents of another race) were available. In response to such concerns, Congress passed the Multiethnic Placement Act in 1994.[34] This Act, strengthened by subsequent congressional action two years later, made federal funding of adoption agencies dependent on those agencies *not* delaying or denying a child's placement based on race.[35] These actions do not forbid race-matching (only delays in placement based *solely* on race-matching); additionally, there are indications that many agencies may still be acting contrary to both the spirit and letter of those rules.[36]

As regards religion in adoption, many state-sanctioned adoption agencies are run by religious organizations, and this contributes to

31. National Association of Black Social Workers, "Position Statement on Transracial Adoption" (September 1972), reprinted in The Adoption History Project, http://www.uoregon.edu/~adoption/archive/NabswTRA.htm.

32. *See* National Association of Black Social Workers, "Preserving Families of African Ancestry" (January 2003), http://www.nabsw.org/mserver/Preserving Families.aspx?menuContext=757.

33. *See* Ruth-Arlene W. Howe, "Race Matters in Adoption," *Family Law Quarterly*, vol. 42, pp. 465–479 (2008).

34. Pub. L. No. 103-382, 108 Stat. 4056 (codified as amended at 42 U.S.C. § 622).

35. Removal of Barriers to Interethnic Adoption Act of 1996, Pub. L. No. 104-188, 110 Stat. 1904, codified at 42 U.S.C. § 622.

36. *See* Ralph Richard Banks, "The Multiethnic Placement Act and the Troubling Persistence of Race Matching," *Capital University Law Review*, vol. 38, pp. 271–290 (2009). For a fairly positive assessment of the federal enforcement of the Multiethnic Placement Act, see U.S. Commission on Civil Rights, *The Multiethnic Placement Act: Minorities in Foster Care and Adoption* (July 2010), available at http://www.usccr.gov/pubs/MEPABriefingFinal_07-01-10.pdf.

an unofficial practice of choosing adoptive parents of the same religion as the birth parent(s), or at least the same religion as the organization supervising the adoption process. This practice is arguably as prevalent as racial matching but has been less controversial and has received far less public and government attention.

✹ F. Indian Child Welfare Act

The Indian Child Welfare Act (ICWA)[37] was enacted in 1978 in response to concerns about improper governmental practices, by which a high rate of Indian children were being separated from their families and their tribes, and adopted by non-Indian families.[38]

The ICWA affects both the forum for adoptions and the criteria for determining placement. As regards forum, tribal courts are to have exclusive jurisdiction over actions regarding the placement of children who reside on or are domiciled within tribal reservations.[39] For other Indian children, tribal courts have concurrent jurisdiction (with state courts), and this jurisdiction is "presumptive."[40]

On the substantive side, regardless of which court hears a case, preference should be given in the placement of Indian children (absent "good cause") to (1) members of the child's extended family; (2) other members of the same tribe; and (3) other Indian families (in that order).[41] The ICWA also contains a provision allowing a birth parent to retract consent to adoption up until the date that

---

37. 92 Stat. 3069, 25 U.S.C. §§ 1901–1963.

38. The background of the legislation is summarized in *Mississippi Band of Choctow Indians v. Holyfield*, 490 U.S. 30 (1989). Some states have their own versions of the ICWA, which supplement the federal law for child placements within that state. *See, e.g., Iowa Code* § 232B.9(6).

39. 25 U.S.C. at § 1911(a).

40. *Id.* at § 1911(b). "Presumptive" here means that a parent or a tribe has the right to transfer a proceeding from state court to tribal court, upon request, and absent "good cause," objection of the other parent, or the tribal court's declining jurisdiction. *Id.*

41. *Id.* at § 1915.

the adoption is judicially finalized,[42] which is contrary to the growing trend elsewhere (e.g., in the Uniform Parentage Act[43]), which makes consents irrevocable far sooner.[44]

There is an obvious tension between the federal policy of the ICWA and the policy on the treatment of race in placement decisions. As discussed in the previous section, case law and legislative action have generally moved in the direction of forbidding use of race by government or private social service agencies in placing children, and particularly discouraging "race-matching," while the ICWA requires matching of tribal identity (to the extent possible) between children to be adopted and adopted parents.[45]

In *Pierce v. Society of Sisters*, the U.S. Supreme Court stated that "[t]he child is not the mere creature of the State."[46] With the ICWA, however, we can see the implied claim that while children may not belong to the state, they do, at least in some circumstances, belong to their (tribal) communities. A similar sentiment underlies *Wisconsin v. Yoder*,[47] where the argument against enforcing the mandatory school attendance policy against the Wisconsin Old Order Amish turned largely on the argument (based on expert testimony, and accepted by the Court) that enforcement would endanger the continued existence of that religious community.[48]

---

42. 25 U.S.C. § 1913(c).

43. *See* Uniform Parentage Act §§ 2-404, 2-409 (consent irrevocable eight days after birth, unless consent is given before a judge, in which case it is immediately irrevocable).

44. For an example of a recent case where an attempted adoption by a non-Indian couple of a child with an Indian father was denied because of the requirements of the ICWA, see *Adoptive Couple v. Baby Girl*, 731 S.E.2d 550 (S.C. 2012), cert. granted, 2013 WL 49813, 81 USLW 3198 (2013).

45. The line-drawing based on tribal membership is treated as connected with political association rather than race (thus avoiding strict scrutiny under the Equal Protection Clause of the Fourteenth Amendment). *See* Barbara Ann Atwood, *Children, Tribes, and States: Adoption and Custody Conflicts over American Indian Children* (Durham, N.C.: Carolina Academic Press, 2010).

46. Pierce v. Society of Sisters, 268 U.S. 510, 535 (1925).

47. 406 U.S. 205 (1972).

48. *See, e.g., Yoder*, 406 U.S. at 209.

G. Sexual Orientation

A small number of states expressly restrict the ability of homosexuals to adopt. Florida had a statutory ban on homosexuals adopting in that state that went back to 1977, but a court invalidated that ban in 2010 under the equal protection provision of the Florida state constitution.[49] There are restrictions still in place on adoption by same-sex couples in Mississippi, Alabama, and Oklahoma.[50] According to the American Academy of Adoption Attorneys, quoted in a 2011 article, in thirty-four states only married couples and single men and women can adopt (thereby excluding both same-sex and opposite-sex unmarried couples).[51]

In November 2008, Arkansas passed a referendum prohibiting unmarried "sexual partners" from adopting children or from serving as foster parents. By its terms, the initiative expressly applied to both opposite-sex and same-sex couples, but the proposal was widely understood to be aimed primarily at gays (and the sponsor described the initiative as being aimed at the "gay agenda").[52] It was struck down by a court under state constitutional privacy grounds.[53]

It is hard to find a way to interpret or defend these restrictions charitably. It is not sufficient to claim that married, opposite-sex parents are always, or nearly always, better for the objective best

---

49. Florida Dept. of Children and Families v. Adoption of X.X.G., 45 So.3d 79 (Fla. App. 2010). The ban had earlier been upheld under a challenge based on the federal constitution. Lofton v. Department of Children and Family Services, 358 F.3d 804 (11th Cir. 2004).
50. *Miss. Code* § 93-17-3(2); *Ala. Code* § 26-10A-5 (excluding any unmarried couple); *Okla. Stat. Ann.* § 10-7503.1.1 (same).
51. Anita Kumar, "Kaine: Gay Couples Should be Allowed to Adopt," *Washington Post*, May 18, 2011; *see, e.g., Utah Code* § 78B-6-117 (3): "A child may not be adopted by a person who is cohabiting in a relationship that is not a legally valid and binding marriage under the laws of this state."
52. Jon Gambrell, "Ark. Voters OK Unmarried Foster, Adoption Bans," Associated Press, Nov. 5, 2008.
53. Arkansas Department of Human Services v. Cole, 2011 Ark. 145, ___ S.W.3d ___, 2011 WL 1319217 (Ark. 2011).

interests of the children in their care. For this would justify, at most, a presumption in favor of that category of parents, not an absolute ban.[54] There is also the issue that a legislatively imposed presumption or ban indicates a lack of trust in the agency or judicial personnel who would otherwise make the adoption decisions. Additionally, a ban often does not change who cares for the child, but merely means that a long-term foster parent or a partner of a legal parent has no opportunity to gain formal legal protections for their existing connections with the children for whom they are caring.

Suggested Further Reading

Overview

Naomi R. Cahn & Joan Heifetz Hollinger (eds.), *Families by Law: An Adoption Reader* (New York: New York University Press, 2004).

National Council for Adoption, *Adoption Factbook V* (Alexandria, Va.: National Council for Adoption, 2011).

History

Naomi Cahn, "Perfect Substitutes or the Real Thing?," *Duke Law Journal*, vol. 52, pp. 1077–1166 (2003).

Stephen B. Presser, "The Historical Background of the American Law of Adoption," *Journal of Family Law*, vol. 11, pp. 443–516 (1971).

Race and Religion

Ralph Richard Banks, "The Multiethnic Placement Act and the Troubling Persistence of Race Matching," *Capital University Law Review*, vol. 38, pp. 271–290 (2009).

Elizabeth Bartholet, "Where Do Black Children Belong? The Politics of Race Matching in Adoption," *University of Pennsylvania Law Review*, vol. 139, pp. 1163–1256 (1991).

Donald L. Beschle, "God Bless the Child? The Use of Religion as a Factor in Child Custody and Adoption Proceedings," *Fordham Law Review*, vol. 58, pp. 383–426 (1989).

---

54. Arizona has a presumption of this sort: *Ariz. Stat.* § 8-103(C): "If all relevant factors are equal and the choice is between a married man and woman certified to adopt and a single adult certified to adopt, placement preference shall be with a married man and woman."

Ruth-Arlene W. Howe, "Race Matters in Adoption," *Family Law Quarterly*, vol. 42, pp. 465–479 (2008).

Nonmarital Fathers

Laura Oren, "Thwarted Fathers or Pop-Up Pops?: How to Determine When Putative Fathers Can Block the Adoption of Their Newborn Children," *Family Law Quarterly*, vol. 40, pp. 153–190 (2006).

SIX

New Reproductive Technologies

MEDICAL TECHNOLOGY (not all of it particularly "high tech") regarding egg donation, sperm donation, surrogacy, and related matters has undermined traditional understandings of parenthood, especially in the way that it has allowed a weakening in the connection between legal parents, genetic parents, and gestational mothers.

The essential scientific and medical breakthrough was the ability to fertilize a human embryo outside a woman's body (hence the early term, "test tube babies") before implanting the fertilized embryo in a woman to be carried to term. Fertilization outside the body is known as in vitro fertilization (IVF). The first successful IVF pregnancy resulted in the birth of Louise Brown in Cambridge, United Kingdom, on July 25, 1978.

Around 3 percent of all births now occur with the help of some form of reproductive technology.[1] Worldwide, it is estimated that approximately 250,000 babies are born each year through assisted reproduction.[2] Another source estimates that four million children have been born using IVF, 59,000 in the United States in 2010 alone.[3]

---

1. *See* Judith F. Daar, "Accessing Reproductive Technologies: Invisible Barriers, Indelible Harms," *Berkeley Journal of Gender Law & Justice*, vol. 23, pp. 18–82 (2008), at p. 29, citing data from U.S. Department of Health and Human Services Centers for Disease Control and Prevention, *2005 Assisted Reproductive Technology Success Rates* (2007), report available at http://www.cdc.gov/art/PDF/508PDF/2005ART508.pdf.
2. William Saletan, "You: The Updated Owner's Manual," *New York Times Book Review*, Aug. 2, 2009, p. 23.
3. Denise Grady, "Lesley Brown, Mother of First 'Test Tube Baby,' Dies at 64," *New York Times*, June 23, 2012.

This chapter will consider how the new reproductive technologies have forced American lawmakers and judges to rethink legal parenthood and will explore the repercussions the laws in this area have had for other areas of family law. American family law is based on the principles, rules, and doctrines that developed during the centuries during which there was never any doubt that the birth mother was the legal and genetic mother, and married fathers sometimes feared that their wives' children might not be their own blood (genetic) children, but there was not, until relatively recently, any way for the husbands to gain certainty on that matter.

Family law in this area (like many other areas) tends to vary significantly from state to state, and one has a clear sense of law trying desperately—though not always successfully—to catch up with both changing technology and changing social practices and norms.

✻ A. Egg and Sperm Donation

According to one recent estimate, between 30,000 and 60,000 children are born every year as a result of sperm donation, and 6,000 as a result of egg donation; the same estimate suggests at least one million American adults are the biological children of sperm donors.[4]

Sperm donation has a long history going back (in both the United States and France) at least to 1884; egg donation is significantly more recent, dating back only to 1985.[5] In the earliest cases

---

4. Ross Douthat, "The Birds and the Bees (via the Fertility Clinic)," *New York Times*, May 30, 2010. I follow conventional usage in using the term sperm and egg "donor," even though in a large percentage of the cases, the party providing the egg or sperm have been paid to do so.

5. Institute for American Values, *My Daddy's Name Is Donor: A New Study of Young Adults Conceived Through Sperm Donation* (Institute for American Values, 2010), available at http://familyscholars.org/my-daddys-name-is-donor-2/, pp. 5, 18. Some sources place the practice of sperm donation further back, to 1790 in England, and 1866 in the United States. Jeffrey M. Shaman, "Legal Aspects of Artificial Insemination," 18 *Journal of Family Law* 331, 331 & n.1 (1979–1980).

on the issue, it seemed like the courts did not know what to make of sperm donation. In one case arising from a custody dispute after a divorce, an Illinois court held a child born by sperm donor (where the father was not the donor) was illegitimate and the husband had no rights to the child.[6]

These are the sort of novel fact situations that make law in general, and legal reasoning (especially the sort of analogical reasoning that is distinctive to common law judging) in particular, look bad. The courts try to find an existing legal or factual category in which to slot the new practice, that the law of the existing category might be applied to the new dispute. And gamete donation and surrogacy services just are too different from the analogies and categories the courts have brought to bear (e.g., adultery, adoption, baby-selling).

Eventually, courts came around to the conclusion that, at least where the sperm donation involves a married couple and the husband had fully consented, the husband was to be treated as the legal father of the resulting child.[7] Over time, many states adopted sperm donation statutes (in many cases, as part of the Uniform Parentage Act). Statutes (or case law) covering egg donation are far less common.[8]

The donor statutes (and cases) tend to set the default rule under which the intended parents are the legal parents, and the gamete donor has neither the rights nor the duties of a legal parent. Some states limit the application of this statute to intended parents who

---

For an interesting history of how the early medical practice of artificial insemination for human beings was transformed by legal factors and social concerns, see Kara W. Swanson, "Adultery by Doctor: Artificial Insemination, 1890–1945," *Chicago-Kent Law Review*, vol. 87, pp. 591–633 (2012).

6. Doornbos v. Doornbos, 23 U.S.L.W. 2308 (Cook County, Illinois, Sup. Ct., Dec. 13, 1954), appeal dismissed on procedural grounds, 139 N.E. 2d 844 (Ill. 1956); *see also* Gursky v. Gursky, 242 N.Y.S.2d 406 (Sup. Ct. 1963) (child of sperm donation is illegitimate).

7. *E.g., In re* Adoption of Anonymous, 345 N.Y.S.2d 430 (Surr. Ct. 1973); People v. Sorensen, 68 Cal. 2d 280, 437 P.2d 495 (1968).

8. *E.g.*, in Minnesota, there is a statute covering sperm donation, *Minn. Stat.* § 257.56, but no statute for egg donation.

are married, and some statutes only apply if a physician is involved in the process.[9]

Increasingly, sperm donation is being used by unmarried couples (both same-sex and opposite sex) and also by individuals who intend to be single parents.[10] Additionally, the donated sperm is frequently being obtained from friends or acquaintances rather than from an anonymous donor from a sperm bank. Sometimes the parties want the donor to have a role in the life of the resulting child, sometimes they do not, and sometimes the parties have (or claim to have) different views of what the "shared understanding" is or was. Sometimes the parties put their understandings into writing, though more often they do not. And sometimes the parties' subsequent behavior is contrary to their original understanding. Some of the sperm donation statutes state that if (and only if) the parties enter an express written agreement, the donor can have parental rights.[11] In some states where no comparable provision is in the statute, courts have indicated that an exception for agreements on paternity may need to be read into the statute to make it constitutional.[12] It is frequently left to courts, years later, to create legal structure out of a factual mess. Consider two examples.

---

9. Both the married parents restriction and the licensed physician restriction were present in the sperm donor provisions (Section 5) of the original 1973 version of the Uniform Parentage Act, available at http://www.law.upenn.edu/bll/archives/ulc/fnact99/1990s/upa7390.htm. In *Jhordan C. v. Mary K.*, 179 Cal. App. 3d 386, 224 Cal. Rptr. 530 (1986), the court refused the request to reject the donor's claim to paternity on the basis that the statutory requirement of a licensed physician had not been met.

   Both the married and licensed physician limitations are absent from the relevant part (Section 7) of the 2002 revised version of the Uniform Parentage Act. Http://www.law.upenn.edu/bll/archives/ulc/upa/final2002.htm.

10. C.M. v. C.C., 377 A.2d 821 (N.J. Cumberland Cty. Ct. 1977), was apparently the first court to deal with a known donor and an unmarried carrier and intended mother. Holding that there was a public policy in favor of children having both mothers and fathers, the court concluded that the donor had the legal rights and duties of a natural father.

11. *E.g., Kan. Stat.* § 38-1114(f); *Ark. Code Ann.* § 9-10-201; *Fla. Stat.* § 742.14; *N.H. Rev. Stat. Ann.* § 168-B:3(I)(e); *N.J. Stat. Ann.* § 9:17-44(b).

12. McIntyre v. Crouch, 98 Or. App. 462, 472, 780 P.2d 239 (1989); C.O. v. W.S., 64 Ohio Misc.2d 9, 12, 639 N.E.2d 523 (1994).

In *In re* Thomas S. v. Robin Y.,[13] a lesbian couple had an informal relationship with a sperm donor—all three were lawyers, but (surprisingly) they wrote no formal document. The evidence was that the donor had agreed at the beginning not to assert parental rights, but after the child was born he continued to have regular contact with the two parents and the child. When the child was nine years old, a dispute arose that led to the litigation. The court held that the baseline was the donor's parental rights, and whether the parties had complied with New York's statutory requirements for relinquishing paternity. The oral agreement, especially in light of post-birth behavior, was held to be insufficient to divest the donor of his parental rights.

In *Ferguson v. McKiernan*,[14] a man agreed with his former lover to donate sperm for IVF, on the condition that he not seek visitation and that he not be liable for support for any resulting child. This agreement was held to be enforceable, where neither party later acted inconsistently with the agreement. The donor had not been involved with the intended mother's prenatal medical care nor paid any prenatal expenses (he did attend the delivery, but only when asked to do so as a friend); and he had no contact with the twins that were subsequently born or with their mother, until the mother sought child support from the donor when the children were five years old. The court held that there was a public policy reason to enforce the agreement, in order to allow women to secure known donors rather than use anonymous donors.[15]

The problem in this area is that there is a public interest both in creating a mechanism for donors *not* to have parental rights (if that is what the relevant parties prefer) and in allowing them *to* have

---

13. 618 N.Y.S.2d 356 (N.Y. App. Div. 1994).

14. 940 A.2d 1236 (Pa. 2007).

15. *See also* Brown v. Gadson, 654 S.E.2d 179 (Ga. App. 2007) (enforcing Florida agreement for man to donate sperm in return for being relieved of any parental responsibility); *In re* K.M.H., 169 P.3d 1025 (Kan. 2007) (upholding against constitutional challenge a state rule creating a presumption against paternal rights for sperm donors unless there is a written agreement to the contrary).

parental rights (if *that* is what the relevant parties prefer). Within that tension, one needs clear default rules, and one begins to understand the value of a writing requirement to channel the parties toward clarifying their own views, and creating clear documentation of those views in case of a later challenge.[16] Especially where such written forms are not made (though not only then), chaotic outcomes that seem unfair to some of the parties are inevitable.

With informal sperm donation, it is more and more common for children to know their donor parent and for that person to have a role in the child's life. There is an ongoing debate about whether non-anonymity for donors should be not only possible but required. Since 2005, Britain has required that sperm donors be identified once a child turns eighteen.

✇ B. Surrogacy

Surrogacy involves a woman carrying a child for another person or couple, usually in exchange for a significant payment; the carrier is not an intended parent. Surrogacy arrangements are often divided along various lines: commercial versus "altruistic" surrogacy, depending on whether the surrogate is being paid (beyond her expenses) for carrying the child (altruistic carriers are often relatives or close friends of the intended parent(s)); and gestational versus "traditional" surrogates, where a traditional surrogate also provides the egg, and thus is genetically related to the child, while a gestational surrogate is not genetically related to the child (and the egg comes either from the intended mother or from an egg donor).

The first major litigated surrogacy case was the highly publicized *Baby M* case.[17] *Baby M* involved an agreement to hire a commercial,

---

16. *See* Lon L. Fuller, "Consideration and Form," *Columbia Law Review*, vol. 41, pp. 799–824 (1941), at pp. 800-801 (on the evidentiary, cautionary, and channeling functions of form).

17. *In re* Baby M, 537 A.2d 1227 (N.J. 1988).

traditional surrogate and a child born from that arrangement. While the trial court enforced the agreement, the New Jersey Supreme Court ultimately held the agreement unenforceable, because contrary to public policy. The court had numerous objections to the standard surrogacy agreement: that it involved turning over the surrogate's parental rights before the baby was born (and before the usual "cooling off period" used in adoption to allow parental change of mind); the assignment of parental rights to a new parent without any legal determination of the fitness of the new parent or the best interests of the child (as is required with conventional custody determinations and adoptions); and that the surrogate's consent to surrendering parental rights was held to have been tainted by the substantial payment promised.

The court thus concluded that the surrogacy agreement was unenforceable, and this left the genetic parents (the surrogate and the intended father) as the legal parents. A custody determination was then made, not grounded on the surrogacy agreement but on the best interests of the child: custody was eventually given to the intended father and his wife, with substantial visitation to the surrogate.

Over time, traditional surrogacy (where the woman carrying the child is also genetically related to the child) has become rarer,[18] and gestational surrogacy (where the intended parents use the intended mother's egg, or use a donor egg, and the woman carrying the child is thus not genetically related to the child) has become the norm.[19] Legislative and judicial responses to gestational surrogacy have often differed from the response to traditional surrogacy.

In 1993, the California Supreme Court held in a case of gestational surrogacy that the intended parents were the legal parents

18. Though one still sees occasional cases involving traditional surrogacy. *See, e.g., In re* the Paternity of F.T.R., No. 2011AP2166, 2012 WL 3205579 (Wis. App. 2012).

19. Another trend is the increasing use of (less expensive) surrogates from other countries, including India. *See, e.g.,* Nilanjana S. Roy, "Protecting the Rights of Surrogate Mothers in India," *New York Times,* Oct. 4, 2011. In the United States, apparently a large number of surrogates are military wives. Lorraine Ali & Raina Kelley, "The Curious Lives of Surrogates," *Newsweek,* Apr. 7, 2008.

and the woman who carried the child had no legal rights.[20] In passing, that court also rejected the *Baby M* court's argument that surrogacy agreements were contrary to public policy. Illinois currently has a statute that legalizes, recognizes, and regulates gestational surrogacy, its Gestational Surrogacy Act.[21] It sets requirements that must be met by the surrogate, the intended parents, and the contract between them (allowing payment above the surrogate's expenses), but if these requirements are met, then the intended parents are the legal parents from birth, and a legal parent-child relationship can be established even prior to birth.[22]

California and Illinois, however, are exceptional. Most states are far less friendly to surrogacy arrangements: most states will not directly enforce surrogacy agreements, and will treat the surrogate as the legal mother of the child born to her (and the intended mother must then, with the cooperation of the surrogate, legally adopt the child). A small number of states make surrogacy (or *commercial* surrogacy) illegal.[23]

C. Division of Embryos

The IVF process often involves the creation of more embryos than the couple uses. If the couple using the process breaks up before all

---

20. Johnson v. Calvert, 5 Cal. 4th 84, 851 P.2d 776 (1993); *see also* Buzzanca v. Buzzanca, 72 Cal. Rptr. 2d 280 (1998) (intended father is legal parent even when not genetically related to child); *cf.* J.F. v. D.B., 879 N.E.2d 740 (Ohio 2007) (in the context of a breach of contract action, court holds that gestational surrogacy agreement is not unenforceable because contrary to public policy, even when agreement contains provision requiring the surrogate not to claim parental rights).

21. 750 ILCS 47.

22. Outside Illinois it is rare (but not unheard of) for prebirth parentage orders to be granted in cases involving surrogates. *See Cal. Fam. Code* § 7633 (authorizing prebirth orders); *see generally* Steven H. Snyder & Mary Patricia Byrn, "The Use of Pre-Birth Parentage Orders in Surrogacy Proceedings," *Family Law Quarterly*, vol. 39, pp. 633–662 (2005).

23. For a summary of the current law (as of 2011) on surrogacy, see Diane S. Hinson & Maureen McBrien, "Surrogacy Across America," *Family Advocate*, vol. 34(2), pp. 32–36 (Fall 2011).

the embryos are used, and the parties disagree about the disposition of the embryos, courts must resolve the disagreement. In some early divorce cases in which the issue came up, the courts tried to figure out whether the division of embryos better fit the category of "custody" or "property division."[24]

Partly in response to such litigation, IVF centers have become better at requiring couples to jointly fill out and sign prior designations as to what should be done with any frozen embryos in case of divorce or the death of either party.

In the absence of an agreement as to the disposition of embryos, the question in cases of party disagreement[25] is whether the desire to parent (or to donate the embryos to another couple who will use them to parent) should prevail over the desire not to be a (genetic) parent. Almost every state court that has considered the question (and every foreign supreme court, bar one[26]) has come to the conclusion that the right *not* to parent should prevail over the right to parent. The one exception involved a case where the woman was likely made sterile by cancer treatments and use of the embryos would likely be her only chance to have a (genetic) child.[27]

Where there has been an agreement, the question is whether these agreements should always be enforced (in circumstances

24. Davis v. Davis, 842 S.W.2d 588 (Tenn. 1992) (enforcing ex-husband's desire that embryos not be used; in dicta: rule is to enforce prior agreements and, in the absence of prior agreement, to weigh the parties' interests, with the understanding that a desire not to parent will usually prevail over a desire to parent).

25. There are commentators who view the embryos as having the moral status of human beings and therefore would reject the destruction of the embryos even where both parties favor it. The American legal system, however, does not treat the embryos in this way, and the parties' agreement to dispose of them is dispositve.

26. The exception was the Israeli Supreme Court decision in A.H. 2401/95, *Nachmani v. Nachmani*, 50(4) P.D. 661 (Israel 1997), enforcing a woman's right to parent over her partner's objection. For an argument in favor of a woman's right to parent in such circumstances, see Anne Morris & Sue Nott, "Rights and Responsibilities: Contested Parenthood," *The Journal of Social Welfare & Family Law*, vol. 31, pp. 3–16 (2009).

27. Reber v. Reiss, 42 A.3d 1131 (Pa. Super. 2012).

where one of the parties now challenges the agreement he or she once signed). Many courts will enforce all such agreements (subject to the usual contract law defenses, like duress and undue influence), while other courts have given priority to the parties' *current* wishes, holding that even those who have signed such an agreement have a right to change their mind, and that the use of embryos will only rarely be authorized against subsequent objection by either party.[28]

There have also been statutes in a handful of states touching on the issue of division of embryos. The Florida statute requires the couple to enter an agreement, but then provides what will occur without an agreement:

A commissioning couple and the treating physician shall enter into a written agreement that provides for the disposition of the commissioning couple's eggs, sperm, and preembryos in the event of a divorce, the death of a spouse, or any other unforeseen circumstance. [] Absent a written agreement, any remaining eggs or sperm shall remain under the control of the party that provides the eggs or sperm. [] Absent a written agreement, decisionmaking authority regarding the disposition of preembryos shall reside jointly with the commissioning couple. [] Absent a written agreement, in the case of the

28. *See* Kass v. Kass, 696 N.E.2d 174 (N.Y. 1998) (enforcing contract); J.B. v. M.B., 783 A.2d 707 (N.J. 2001) (no clear agreement in the case, but indicating that such an agreement would be enforceable, though each party could change his or her mind up to point of use or destruction; in case of dispute, the right not to procreate will usually prevail); Roman v. Roman, 193 S.W.3d 40 (Texas Ct. App. 2006), review denied (Aug. 24, 2007) (agreement that frozen pre-embryos were to be discarded upon divorce was enforceable); *In re* Marriage of Witten, 672 N.W.2d 768 (Iowa, 2003) (prior agreement not enforced if one party has changed his or her mind; no use or destruction of embryos without agreement of both parties).The British courts, affirmed by the Grand Chamber of the European Court of Human Rights, reached a similar conclusion, upholding British law that required the continuing consent of the woman's partner for her to use frozen embryos. Natallie Evans v. Amicus Healthcare Ltd. and Others (Secretary of State for Health intervening), [2004] EWCA (Civ.) 727, [2004] FLR 766; Evans v. United Kingdom, Application No. 6330/05, Judgement of 10 April 2007 (Grand Chamber).

death of one member of the commissioning couple, any eggs, sperm, or preembryos shall remain under the control of the surviving member of the commissioning couple ...[29]

By contrast, the Texas statute focuses on the ability of parties to withdraw their consent to use of an embryo: "The consent of a former spouse to assisted reproduction may be withdrawn by that individual in a record kept by a licensed physician at any time before the placement of eggs, sperm, or embryos."[30]

D. Posthumous Reproduction

The same IVF technology that allows the fertilization of embryos outside the body and the storage of eggs, sperm, and embryos, has created a different legal and social issue: what to do about children born from embryos created and implanted long after the biological father has died, or implanted in another woman after the biological mother's death.

Many of the legal questions to date have gone to the relatively mundane issue of benefit payments. In *Astrue v. Capato*,[31] the U.S. Supreme Court upheld the Social Security Administration's interpretation of the Social Security Act, holding that posthumously conceived children are entitled to dependents' benefits under the Act only if they would qualify for inheritance from their biological father under state intestacy law. There are comparable interpretive issues relating not only to state benefit laws but also to intestacy laws and to the interpretation of will provisions.

Of course, there are also more general moral and policy questions regarding the "harvesting" of sperm from a seriously ill patient, a patient who is comatose, or one who recently died (is the patient's

---

29. *Fla. Stat. Ann.* § 742.17.
30. *Tex. Fam. Code Ann.* § 160.706(b).
31. 132 S. Ct. 2021 (2012).

prior consent sufficient?), and regarding whether posthumous use of the sperm should be allowed and, if allowed, whether it should only be allowed for a spouse, partner, or someone designated by the sperm "donor."

Suggested Further Reading

New Reproductive Technology Generally

American Bar Association, "Model Act Governing Assisted Reproductive Technology February 2008," *Family Law Quarterly*, vol. 42, pp. 171–202 (2008).

Susan Frelich Appleton & D. Kelly Weisberg, *Adoption and Assisted Reproduction: Families Under Construction* (New York: Aspen Publishers, 2009).

Naomi R. Cahn, *Test Tube Families: Why the Fertility Market Needs Legal Regulation* (New York: New York University Press, 2009).

Naomi Cahn & the Evan B. Donaldson Adoption Institute, "Old Lessons for a New World: Applying Adoption Research and Experience to ART," *Journal of the American Academy of Matrimonial Law*, vol. 24, pp. 1–32 (2011).

J. Herbie DiFonzo & Ruth C. Stern, "The Children of Baby M.," *Capital University Law Review*, vol. 39, pp. 345–411 (2011).

Marsha Garrison, "Law Making for Baby Making: An Interpretive Approach to the Determination of Legal Parentage," *Harvard Law Review*, vol. 113, pp. 835–923 (2000).

Charles P. Kindregan, Jr., & Steven H. Snyder, "Clarifying the Law of ART: The New American Bar Association Model Act Governing Assisted Reproductive Technology," *Family Law Quarterly*, vol. 42, pp. 203–229 (2008).

Elizabeth Marquardt, Norval D. Glenn, & Karen Clark, *My Daddy's Name Is Donor* (New York: Institute for American Values, 2010), available at http://familyscholars.org/my-daddys-name-is-donor-2/.

Division of Embryos

I. Glenn Cohen, "The Right Not to Be a Genetic Parent?," *Southern California Law Review*, vol. 81, pp. 1115–1196 (2008).

Theresa M. Erickson & Megan T. Erickson, "What Happens to Embryos When a Marriage Dissolves? Embryo Disposition and Divorce," *William Mitchell Law Review*, vol. 35, pp. 469–488 (2009).

Mark P. Strasser, "You Take the Embryos but I Get the House (and the Business): Recent Trends in Awards Involving Embryos upon Divorce," *Buffalo Law Review*, vol. 57, pp. 1159–1225 (2009).

Surrogacy

Elizabeth S. Scott, "Surrogacy and the Politics of Commodification," *Law and Contemporary Problems*, vol. 72, pp. 109–146 (2009).

Posthumous Reproduction

Benjamin C. Carpenter, "A Chip Off the Old Iceblock: How Cryopreservation has Changed Estate Law, Why Attempts to Address the Issue Have Fallen Short, and How to Fix It," *Cornell Journal of Law and Public Policy*, vol. 21, pp. 347–430 (2011).

Charles P. Kindregan, Jr., & Maureen McBrien, "Posthumous Reproduction," *Family Law Quarterly*, vol. 39, pp. 579–597 (2005).

SEVEN

Abuse and Neglect

THERE ARE LIMITS to parental rights and limits to state deference to parental choices. These are expressed in doctrines of abuse and neglect—which are both categories of criminal liability and civil liability terms for when children can be taken from their parents. Sometimes the override of parental prerogative is for a limited time and a limited purpose (regarding parental decision making in (e.g.) medical, educational, and religious matters), where particular decisions are thought to be extremely harmful to the child, but that the caregiving competence of the parent(s) is not otherwise questioned.[1]

There was a time, and not that long ago, when what happened within a family (especially if it occurred in the privacy of the home, but even to some extent if it spilled out into public places) was considered "not anyone else's business," and certainly not the government's business—with few limits this side of murder. This is no longer the case:[2] abuse of children, like the domestic abuse of adult partners, is considered a crime and, in the case of children,

---

1. For example, this might come about in relation to a parent's religiously based refusal of medical care for a child. That issue is considered, briefly, in section C, *infra*, and again in chapter 16, section E.
2. The interaction of social norms and government action in that process is well documented in Barbara Nelson, *Making an Issue of Child Abuse* (Chicago: University of Chicago Press, 1984). Nelson is particularly good in showing how various pressures led to a construction of the problem in terms of (medical) deviance, discounting structural or systemic explanations, and possible connections with poverty.

appropriate grounds for removing children, and, in more serious cases, the termination of parental rights.

According to a recent report of the U.S. Department of Health and Human Services,[3] 772,000 children were maltreated in the United States in 2008, slightly more than 1 percent of all children.[4] Of those, 71 percent suffered neglect, 16 percent were physically abused, 9 percent were sexually abused, and 7 percent suffered psychological maltreatment.[5]

While much of the law of child abuse is relatively uncontroversial—few would argue that those who severely beat their children or molest them sexually should not be subject to punishment—there are some areas where the borders of appropriate behavior are more controversial: for example, regarding which forms of corporal punishment are acceptable (this example is revisited in section B, below). Also, as already noted, the finding of abuse can be separated from the question of when children should be separated—temporarily or permanently—from their parents.

Children can also be taken from their parents' home on the grounds of "neglect." Neglect is a failure of a parent to give his or her children a sufficient amount of food, clothing, shelter, or medical care to reach minimal standards of child care, or a general failure to supervise the child.[6]

One should note that both law and social practice seem to move, pendulum-like, between a focus on protecting children (even if that

---

3. U.S. Department of Health and Human Services, *Child Maltreatment 2008* (2010), available at http://www.acf.hhs.gov/programs/cb/pubs/cm08.

4. According to the same study, this was a significant decrease from a total of 903,000 in 2006.

5. "New Federal Report Shows Drop in Child Abuse Rates," Associated Press, Apr. 1, 2010.

6. Some medical and legal authorities also refer to emotional neglect, where it is claimed that a child can suffer greatly in a household where the child is not shown even minimal levels of loving support, and can suffer severe and long-term harm from the deprivation, even in cases where the child otherwise receives adequate food, shelter, clothing, and medical care and is not the subject of physical or sexual abuse.

means breaking up families) and a focus on maintaining families (even if that means keeping some children in situations where their well-being is clearly at risk).

✄ A. Standards for Abuse and Neglect

The standards of abuse and neglect vary from state to state; they are usually set by statute, though often in terminology too vague to give much guidance either to parents or to courts.[7] Of the two, abuse tends to be the more clearly defined; however, even with abuse laws, there are many areas of controversy and uncertainty. One such area is corporal punishment: at what point—with what means of punishment, or level of injury caused—does discipline become abuse (or battery)? Both the social services agencies and the courts vary greatly in their response to such questions.[8]

There are policy questions about possible secondary legal effects of a finding of abuse. For example, if a parent abuses one child in that parent's care, should that be a sufficient ground for removing (temporarily or permanently) other children from that parent's care, even if there is no evidence of that parent having harmed those other children? If a parent knows of but does not stop the abuse

---

7. However, most claims that such statutes are so vague as to be unconstitutional have been rejected. *See, e.g.*, State v. Watkins, 659 N.W.2d 526 (Iowa 2003). Such claims do occasionally succeed, though often there are additional factors, e.g., suspicion that the statute is being applied in an egregiously racist way. *See, e.g.*, Roe v. Conn, 417 F. Supp. 769 (M.D. Ala. 1976).

8. *See, e.g.*, Willis v. State, 888 N.E.2d 177 (Ind. 2008) (mother's punishment of "five to seven swats on [an eleven-year-old son's] buttocks, arm, and thigh" was within her parental privilege, and thus a full defense to a charge of battery on a child); DYFS v. K.A., 996 A.2d 1040 (N.J. App. Div. 2010) (mother's striking of child several times did not constitute child abuse); Dep't of Children v. C.H., 5 A.3d 163 (N.J. App. Div. 2010) (mother's striking of child several times did constitute child abuse; *K.A.* distinguished on the basis that it was a single isolated incident, while *C.H.* involved a pattern of excessive corporal punishment and inflicting injuries in vulnerable areas); Simons v. State, 803 N.W.2d 587 (N.D. 2011) (father's twenty-four swats over two hours with wooden back-scratcher on two-year-old because child would not say "sir" constituted abuse).

of that parent's child by someone else in the house (whether the other legal parent, a step-parent, a temporary partner, or someone else), is that sufficient grounds for taking the child away from that parent (perhaps on the basis that the failure to protect is a kind of "neglect")?[9] Answers to these questions tend to vary greatly.

By its nature, child abuse is a harm that often occurs without witnesses (other than the child, who may be too young or too scared to offer helpful testimony). Often the evidence of abuse is circumstantial—the injuries suffered by the child. While abusers often explain such injuries away as the result of unfortunate accidents, doctors have developed criteria for determining what sorts of injuries are almost certainly caused by abuse, not accident—"battered child syndrome."[10]

Regarding neglect law, there are two significant issues: when parental poverty should be a "defense" to charges of neglect; and what to do in cases where refusal of medical treatment is grounded on sincere religious belief. As already noted, "neglect" is usually defined in terms of a failure to provide children with a minimal level of food, clothing, shelter, medical care, and so forth. This is usually understood as some fault on the parent's side. However, as there are now limits and conditions on the grant of state support for the poor,[11] there is a real possibility that a parent's failure to provide minimum levels may be based on short-term financial limits rather than any unwillingness or incompetence on the parent's part.[12]

---

9. *E.g.*, State v. Williquette, 385 N.W.2d 145 (Wis. 1986).

10. C. Henry Kempe et al., "The Battered Child Syndrome," *Journal of the American Medical Association (JAMA)*, vol. 181, pp. 17–24 (July 7, 1962).

11. Under what had been known as welfare reform—the new official title is "Temporary Assistance for Needy Families" (TANF).

12. *See, e.g.*, Erica Turcios, "Remaining versus Removal: Preventing Premature Removal When Poverty Is Confused with Neglect," *Michigan Child Welfare Law Journal*, vol. 12(4), pp. 20–28 (Summer 2009). As others have pointed out, there often appears, in practice, to be two different family law systems: one for the relatively rich (deferential and nonintrusive) and one for the poor (intrusive, demanding, and leading to a much higher frequency of parental rights suspensions and terminations). *See* Jacobus tenBroek, "California's Dual System of Family Law: Its Origin, Development, and Present Status" (Parts I, II, & III),

※ B. Cultural and Religious Defenses

A different sort of question comes when the parental misbehavior is grounded on sincere religious belief. This comes up regularly for parents who refuse to give their children conventional medical care because of the parents' beliefs (for example, Jehovah's Witnesses or Christian Science). A number of states have express legislative exceptions holding that when refusal of medical treatment is religiously based, it will not count as "neglect."[13] (Courts in some of these same states have held that this protection is limited to neglect actions and does not extend to prosecutions which involve charging a parent with causing a child's death through a failure to intervene medically.[14])

※ C. Procedural Protections

Where the state is attempting to terminate a parent's rights based on an accusation of abuse or neglect, proof must meet the heightened "clear and convincing" standard (rather than the usual standard of proof for civil cases, "preponderance of the evidence").[15] At the same time, there is no federal constitutional requirement that legal counsel be provided to parties who are facing termination of their parental rights.[16]

Stanford Law Review, vol. 16, pp. 257–317, 900–981 (1964), vol. 17, pp. 614–682 (1965); *see also* Marsha Garrison, "Why Terminate Parental Rights?," *Stanford Law Review*, vol. 35, pp. 423–496 (1983), at p. 432 ("[t]he foster care system's lack of concern for natural parents reflects centuries of a dual family law—one for the rich and one for the poor.").

13. A related question comes when a parent applies what local social and legal norms consider to be excessive corporal punishment, but justifies the action, in the face of an abuse charge, by stating that this level of punishment is required by sincere religious belief or by the foreign culture in which the parents were raised.

14. *E.g.*, Hall v. State, 493 N.E.2d 433 (Ind. 1986); Walker v. Superior Court, 763 P.2d 852 (Cal. 1988); Commonwealth v. Twitchell, 617 N.E.2d 609 (Mass. 1993).

15. Santosky v. Kramer, 455 U.S. 745 (1982).

16. Lassiter v. Department of Social Services of Durham County, N.C., 452 U.S. 18 (1981).

✺ D. Foster Care

Within family law and practice, foster care is the in-between place. Foster caregivers are nominally employees of the state, hired to care for children temporarily, subject to termination at the will (and sometimes at the whim) of the state agency in charge. Though long-term foster caregivers frequently build strong bonds with the children in their care, the caregivers generally have no legal right to continued contact with those children, unless such a right is expressly given by the state.[17] Children are sent to foster care when there are doubts about their parents' ability to care for them, but the objections are not (or not yet) strong enough to justify termination of parental rights. (Foster care is also used as a temporary home for children whose parents *have* had their rights terminated, but the hope is that foster care placement in that case will be short-term, while a permanent, adoptive placement is arranged.)

According to recent data,[18] a little over 400,000 children are in foster care at any given date, and about 646,000 are in foster care at some point during the year. Of that number, about 104,000 are officially "waiting to be adopted," and about 51,000 were in fact adopted during the course of the year. "In most states, a third or more of the children placed from foster care are being adopted by the individuals or couples who had served as their foster parents."[19] Federal law has attempted to speed the movement of children from

---

17. In *Smith v. Organization of Foster Families For Equality and Reform*, 431 U.S. 816 (1977), the question was officially left open, but the Supreme Court strongly hinted that foster caregivers had no constitutional liberty interests in continued contact with the children in their care. More recent federal appellate courts have come to the same conclusion.

18. U.S. Department of Health and Human Services, Administration for Children & Families, Children's Bureau, Trends in Foster Care and Adoption, FY 2002–FY 2011 (2012), available at http://archive.acf.hhs.gov/programs/cb/stats_research/afcars/trends_july2012.pdf.

19. Joan Heifetz Hollinger & Naomi Cahn, "Forming Families by Law," *Human Rights*, pp. 16–19 (Summer 2009), at p. 18.

foster care to permanent adoption placements,[20] but there clearly remains much work to be done.[21]

Suggested Further Reading

Elizabeth Bartholet, *Nobody's Children: Abuse and Neglect, Foster Drift, and the Adoption Alternative* (Boston: Beacon Press, 2000).

Sarah H. Ramsey & Douglas E. Abrams, "A Primer on Child Abuse and Neglect Law," *Juvenile and Family Court Journal*, vol. 61, pp. 1–31 (2010).

U.S. Department of Health and Human Services, Child Welfare Information Gateway, *Acts of Omission: An Overview of Child Neglect* (2001), available at http://www.childwelfare.gov/pubs/focus/acts/.

---

20. Under the Adoption and Safe Families Act of 1997, 42 U.S.C. §§ 671(a)(15)(D), 675(5)(e), states receiving federal funds must, under most circumstances, seek the termination of parents' rights when a child has been in nonkinship foster care for fifteen of the previous twenty-four months.

21. For a critique of the child welfare system and recent moves to speed adoption, arguing that both work against the interest of families and children who are poor or racial minorities, see Dorothy E. Roberts, "Poverty, Race, and New Directions in Child Welfare Policies," *Washington University Journal of Law & Policy*, vol. 1, pp. 63–76 (1999).

EIGHT

Children's Rights

⁂ A. Children's Rights

In recent decades, discussion of parents' rights over, or in relation to, their children has evoked a response in terms of "children's rights." This way of speaking has also been asserted in terms of (children's') rights against the state, potentially unrelated to the claims or preferences of parents (e.g., in the context of schools or the criminal justice system[1]).

There are a number of conceptual and practical complexities relating to the issue of children's rights. First, one should note that enlarging the rights of children necessarily limits the rights or prerogatives of adults, including parents and teachers. Second, the mere assertion of "children's rights" often hides an important underlying question: who is most likely to know what is best for children—their parents, the state, the children themselves, or lawyers appointed to act on the children's behalf? Third, even the strongest advocate for children's rights would admit that very young children are not capable of acting in their own best interests; there thus remains the difficult question regarding when older children should have partial or complete rights to make choices on their own behalf.[2]

---

1. Some see the children's rights movement as beginning with the Supreme Court decision of *In re* Gault, 387 U.S. 1 (1967), which established the constitutional due process rights of juveniles facing criminal charges.

2. I am putting aside the abstract, conceptual questions of whether children (or any other person or entity unable to make legally competent choices on its own) is the type of subject to whom rights can sensibly be ascribed. Under

Additionally, it is hard to take a general view on children's rights, as the questions raised differ substantially as one moves from educational decisions to health-care decisions (including examples as disparate as abortion, forced sterilization of the permanently incompetent, altruistic organ donation, and "voluntary" institutionalization) to the right of participation in foster care, adoption, visitation, and custody decisions.

Consider some of the variations on the theme:

1. When the question involves the right of minors to have an abortion, it often entails a right to have a medical procedure without the consent of the child's parents, and usually without the parents having been informed.[3]

2. The right of children against the state (e.g., First Amendment claims not to be forced to affirm certain ideas) may in fact be claims made on behalf of the child by a parent, with or without the child's actual agreement.[4]

A partly substantive, partly procedural question is at what age rights ascribed to children by the legal system should reflect the children's own choices rather than (or in supplement to) some third party's guess as to what would be objectively best for that child. In some jurisdictions, it is common to appoint a "guardian ad litem" to represent the interests of a child in a custody case, and, if the child

---

some "will theories" of rights, only entities capable of making choices exercising or waiving claims can be said to have rights, or to have rights "in their fullest sense."

3. *See* Carol Sanger, "Regulating Teenage Abortion in the United States: Politics and Policy," *International Journal of Law, Policy and the Family*, vol. 18, pp. 305–318 (2004).

4. Famously, in the Pledge of Allegiance case, the claim was being brought on behalf of a minor by her noncustodial father, when the custodial mother disagreed with his position (and the child's position was not made clear); the Supreme Court ultimately held that the noncustodial parent did not have standing to bring the case on behalf of his daughter. Elk Grove Unified School Dist. v. Newdow, 542 U.S. 1 (2004).

is old enough, either to order that representative to advocate for the outcome the child chooses, or to have a second advocate appointed to represent the child's expressed wishes.

※ B. Children's Duties

In discussions of the legal status of children, children's rights properly have received most of the attention. However, a word should be added about children's duties—more precisely, the duties grown (adult) children owe to their parents. At one point or another, nearly every state has had a statute using either civil liability or the criminal law to impose a duty on adult children to support parents incapable of self-support.[5] However, many of those states subsequently repealed those laws, and, of the twenty-eight states that still have such laws, eleven states have never enforced them, and only a few enforce them actively.[6] It is clear that these statutes are more of a public declaration of a moral position rather than an effort by the state to actually impose or enforce that moral view.

Suggested Further Reading

David William Archard, "Children's Rights," *Stanford Encyclopedia of Philosophy* (2010), http://plato.stanford.edu/entries/rights-children/.

Stephen G. Gilles, "On Educating Children: A Parentalist Manifesto," *University of Chicago Law Review*, vol. 63, pp. 937–1034 (1996).

Martin Guggenheim, *What's Wrong with Children's Rights* (Cambridge, Mass.: Harvard University Press, 2005).

Barbara Bennett Woodhouse, "Hatching the Egg: A Child-Centered Perspective on Parent's Rights," *Cardozo Law Review*, vol. 14, pp. 1746–1865 (1993).

---

5. Allison E. Ross, "Taking Care of Our Caretakers: Using Filial Responsibility Laws to Support the Elderly Beyond the Government's Assistance," *Elder Law Journal*, vol. 16, pp. 167–209 (2008), at p. 173.

6. *Id.* at 173–174.

PART FOUR

Divorce

ONE ASPECT OF family law that puzzles law students when they first study it is the predominance of rules relating to divorce. The rules of marriage themselves seem to be slight—and frequently unenforced, except as they relate to grounds for and financial consequences of divorce. This emphasis on postdissolution regulation reflects not just a desire to avoid interference with ongoing relationships (an idea sometimes called "family privacy"[1]) but also the fact that the financial rules of divorce can both express symbolically our ideas about marriage and can have significant effects on marital behavior; the relative burdens and benefits the rules of divorce create play a part in whether married couples stay married.

One additional basic point is that both the rules relating to divorce and its social perception have changed radically—whether one thinks in terms of centuries or in terms of decades—and those transformations have also contributed significantly to changes in the institution of marriage.

---

1. *See* McGuire v. McGuire, 59 N.W.2d 336 (Neb. 1953). The family law notion of "family privacy," discussed in chapter 1, is not to be confused with the constitutional protections that go under the rubric of privacy.

NINE

Divorce
Grounds and Jurisdiction

THIS CHAPTER WILL give an overview of the history of divorce: including a time when divorce was not allowed (or only rarely); fault approaches to divorce; no-fault divorce; and current movements to try to again make divorce more difficult (e.g., "covenant marriage," mentioned in chapter 2 and discussed in section B of this chapter). The chapter will also discuss the conflicting social science data regarding the effects of divorce rules.

❦ A. History of Divorce Grounds

As in most areas of American law, the origins of American divorce law are in English law. England had divorce in only exceptional circumstances, and through the difficult (and expensive) process of legislative enactment, until well into the nineteenth century.[2] Among the American colonies, there was a split: with the New England colonies always more receptive to divorce than the Southern colonies (the

---

2. The first UK parliamentary divorce was given to Lord Roos in 1670. The National Archives, "Divorce Records Before 1858," http://www.nationalarchives.gov.uk/records/research-guides/divorce-before-1858.htm.

    Some countries did not make divorce available until recently. Ireland did not legalize divorce until a constitutional amendment was approved by referendum in 1995 and signed into law in 1996. Malta changed its constitution to allow divorce only in 2011. Now only the Philippines and the Vatican remain as places where divorce is not legally available.

Plymouth Colony granted a divorce as early as 1639[3]), and this difference continued long after Independence.[4] Northern states were quicker to allow divorce and to move divorce from legislatures to courtrooms.[5]

However, one should not assume that a society without divorce was a world where everyone lived together happily ever after. For unhappily married people, there were other forms of recourse. Hendrik Hartog has shown that in England and colonial America, and well into the nineteenth century, desertion and bigamy were common responses to marital unhappiness.[6] And in England prior to the establishment of judicial divorce, there were even documented cases of wife selling (apparently as often initiated by the wife as by the husband).[7] Some of these involved prearranged bidding on market day, where the wife, her property, and responsibility for her transferred from one husband to another.[8]

---

3. Glenda Riley recounts:

   In December 1639, James Luxford's wife asked for a divorce because Luxford already had a wife. An unidentified magistrate granted a divorce and took this hapless woman and her children under the court's protective wing by seizing Luxford's property and transferring it to her. Next, the court turned its wrath on the deceitful Luxford. Not content with levying a fine of £100 on the bigamist, it sentenced him to 'be set in the stock an hour upon the market day after the lecture,' and to be banished to England 'by the first opportunity.'"

   Glenda Riley, *Divorce: An American Tradition* (New York: Oxford University Press, 1991), p. 12.

4. Lawrence M. Friedman, *A History of American Law* (3rd ed., New York: Simon and Schuster, 2005), pp. 142–144. *See also* Joel A. Nichols, "Multi-Tiered Marriage: Ideas and Influences from New York and Louisiana to the International Community," *Vanderbilt Journal of Transnational Law*, vol. 40, pp. 135–196 (2007), at pp. 142–147.

5. In a number of southern states, even while judicial divorces were allowed, legislative divorces remained an option, sometimes until the middle of the nineteenth century. Glenda Riley, *Divorce: An American Tradition* (New York: Oxford University Press, 1991), pp. 35–36.

6. Hendrik Hartog, *Man and Wife in America: A History* (Cambridge, Mass.: Harvard University Press), pp. 36, 63, 84.

7. Peter T. Leeson, Peter J. Boettke, & Jayme S. Lemke, "Wife Sales," unpublished manuscript (2011), available at http://www.peterleeson.com; John deP. Wright, "Wife Sale," *Green Bag 2d*, vol. 7 (2004), pp. 169–173.

8. The National Archives, "Divorce Records Before 1858," http://www.national-archives.gov.uk/records/research-guides/divorce-before-1858.htm.

Eventually, all American states allowed divorce,[9] but in the battle over allowing divorce, the compromise almost all states settled on was to allow divorce, but only to a wronged and innocent spouse. This was the fault divorce system that dominated American family law until the last decades of the twentieth century.

Different states offered a range of available grounds for divorce: almost all had adultery, abandonment, and extreme cruelty, and many had impotence, imprisonment, and insanity. As divorce was like a tort law action, where one had to show the other spouse's faulty behavior and one's own relative innocence, it is not surprising that the fault law regime also contained "defenses" that the other spouse could raise to defeat the petition for divorce. These included collusion, provocation (that one's faulty behavior was in response to the petitioning spouse's faulty behavior—e.g., that one's abandonment was in response to physical abuse); connivance (the petitioning spouse in some way participated in or looked the other way—usually with adultery); condonation (that the faulty behavior was forgiven; under case law, sexual intercourse after learning of the faulty behavior was sometimes considered conclusive evidence of forgiveness); and recrimination (the defendant spouse may be bad but the petitioning spouse was even worse). This last defense, recrimination, in some ways sums up the fault system and why it seems so strange to contemporary readers. In one case involving recrimination (two faulty spouses), the court opined:

> The fact that married people do not get along well together does not justify a divorce.... Testimony which proves merely an unhappy union, the parties being high-strung temperamentally and unsuited to each other … is insufficient to sustain a decree [of divorce].[10]

---

9. While South Carolina had allowed divorce during a ten-year period in the late nineteenth century, it then changed its mind and prohibited divorce, removing that prohibition only in 1949. Riley, *Divorce: An American Tradition*, 156–157.

10. Rankin v. Rankin, 124 A.2d 639, 644 (Pa. 1956).

Under the fault regime, the punishment for being a bad spouse was usually that the other (more virtuous spouse) was allowed to divorce you; the punishment for both spouses being bad, apparently, was that they were stuck with one another—divorce as reward, marriage as penalty.[11]

A marriage can also be dissolved by annulment (an alternative still favored by those who have religious objections to divorce). An annulment is a legal conclusion that the marriage, in effect, never existed, due to fraud or duress in entering the marriage, some legal incapacity at the time of marriage, or the existence of a prior undisclosed marriage. Not just any intentional misrepresentation (fraud) will suffice, as it is generally understood that courtship commonly involves people presenting themselves as better than they actually are. To ground an annulment, the intentional misrepresentation must usually go to "the essence" of the marriage,[12] which under case law included lies about whether one was pregnant, and whether one was able to have children or was willing to have children.[13] Some jurisdictions have been willing to stretch the idea of "essentials" in a more subjective direction, as when an Orthodox Jewish woman had made it clear that she could only marry someone who shared her level of piety, a man's lie about his orthodoxy was adjudged sufficient grounds for an annulment.[14]

---

11. *Cf.* Melissa Murray, "Marriage as Punishment," *Columbia Law Review*, vol. 112, pp. 1–65 (2012).

12. *But see* Desta v. Anyaoha, 371 S.W.3d 596 (Tex. App. 2012) (in granting annulment where the woman had lied to the man to marry him for a "green card," court concluded that Texas annulment statute required only showing of fraud, not fraud going to "the essentials of the marriage relationship"); *cf. In re* Marriage of Joel, ___ P.3d ___, 2012 WL 3127305 (Colo. App. 2012) (concluding that immigration-based fraud similar to *Desta* did go "to the essence of the marriage").

13. One leading case in this areas is Reynolds v. Reynolds, 85 Mass. 605 (1862) (annulment granted where woman claimed to be "chaste and virtuous" but was in fact pregnant by another man); *cf.* Johnston v. Johnston, 18 Cal. App.4th 499, 22 Cal. Rptr. 2d 253 (1993) (lies about drinking problem insufficient to ground annulment).

14. Bilowit v. Dolitsky, 304 A.2d 774 (N.J. Super. 1973); *cf. In re* Marriage of Farr, 228 P.3d 267 (Colo. App. 2010) (annulment granted for man's lies that he was suffering from a terminal disease; woman claimed she married him only because she did not want him to die alone).

In most jurisdictions, the remedies available after an annulment are the same as those available after a divorce, including division of property, alimony, and child custody and support orders.[15]

𝒲 B. No Fault and Beyond

Most commentators on the history of divorce in the United States focus on the adoption of no-fault divorce by the state of California in 1970, and there is no doubting the influence of that event. However, at least four states had some no-fault ground for divorce earlier than that, including New Mexico's adoption of the ground of "incompatibility" as far back as 1933, and Maine and Connecticut's short-lived experiment with no-fault-like grounds in the middle of the nineteenth century.[16]

The California reform was preceded by a report by the Governor's Commission on the Family.[17] Along with rehearsing the many problems with fault divorce, the report offered a picture of a future family court that would be focused on bringing resources to help keep couples together.

One argument for those seeking reform had been that the traditional fault "grounds" for divorce were more symptoms of the underlying problems of the marriage, and that was where the proper focus should be. Adultery could be a response to the other spouse's emotional cruelty or emotional withdrawal; why focus only on the adultery? A marriage that was irretrievably broken should

---

15. *E.g., Minn. Stat.* § 518.03.
16. *See* Lawrence M. Friedman, "Rights of Passage: Divorce Law in Historical Perspective," *Oregon Law Review*, vol. 63, pp. 649–669 (1984), at p. 654.
17. In Britain, a committee appointed by the Archbishop of Canterbury published his report, "Putting Asunder: A Divorce Law for Contemporary Society," at roughly the same time (January 1964), making comparable recommendations (that "marital breakdown" should be the sole ground for divorce). The resulting British law allowed no-fault divorce only after a lengthy separation: two years where both parties agree, five years where only one party sought the divorce.

be dissolved; one that could be saved, however, should be, even if wrongful actions had occurred.

Additionally, there was concern that fault divorce, as practiced, was tarnishing the reputation of the legal system. Where couples had agreed to divorce—either because both wanted out of the marriage, or because one had offered the other economic incentives to buy that spouse's consent—it became a matter of fabricating the ground for divorce, and perhaps even the "evidence" for that ground. In New York, in particular (where adultery was effectively the only available ground for obtaining a divorce), some women made considerable sums pretending to be "the other woman" in divorce actions.[18]

However, when no-fault divorce was enacted, the pictured ideal was not realized: resources were not provided, and the result was primarily one of a quicker and easier divorce, with no need for a public declaration (or public admission) of blame. Additionally, instead of the courts making searching inquiries as to whether the marriages before them could be saved, both in general perception and common practice, "no fault divorce" is "divorce on demand" ("unilateral divorce"), with divorce being granted (following whatever required waiting period the jurisdiction has—usually six months or a year) on the unilateral demand of one spouse, even if the other spouse objects. By the recent count of one commentator, perhaps only two states vary from that approach: Mississippi and Tennessee both seem to require mutual consent, for the parties to have entered a written separation agreement and to have lived separate and apart for a stated period of time.[19] (One still occasionally

---

18. Dorothy Jarvis let herself be named (and photographed) as part of many divorce actions, and was the subject of a 1934 *New York Sunday Mirror* magazine section article titled "I Was the Unknown Blonde in 100 New York Divorces." Lawrence M. Friedman, "A Dead Language: Divorce Law and Practice Before No-Fault," *Virginia Law Review*, vol. 86, pp. 1497–1536 (2000), at p. 1512.

19. Ira Mark Ellman & Sharon Lohr, "Marriage as Contract, Opportunistic Violence, and Other Bad Arguments for Fault Divorce," *University of Illinois Law Review*, vol. 1997, pp. 719-772, at p. 723 n.8. Ellman & Lohr in fact list three states, but the third, New York, changed to unilateral no-fault in 2010, as discussed in the text.

comes across cases where a court concludes that there are not suf-ficient objective indications of that the marriage has "irretrievably broken down," and therefore no divorce decree will be granted,[20] but these are extremely rare.)

Some form of no-fault divorce—either a pure no-fault system, where fault grounds (and defenses) were abolished, or the addition of no-fault grounds as an alternative to fault-based divorce—was soon adopted in nearly every state. New York State had been (for many years) one of the last holdouts against "unilateral" no-fault, but it passed no-fault legislation in August 2010.[21]

There was much talk in the early days of "no-fault" divorce of an ideal of creating a "clean break" between the parties, and one can still see references to such a purported ideal (often in the course of a court's rejection of permanent alimony). Whether this was ever a realistic, or even attractive, ideal for couples without minor children, it has never been realistic for couples with minor children. Finances can be disentangled and divided; alimony can either be denied or made temporary (a topic covered in chapter 12), but child support and issues of joint parenting are (or should be) a continuing matter, at least until the children reach the age of majority (topics discussed in chapters 13 and 14).

No-fault divorce remains controversial, as commentators have raised questions about the long-term effects of easier and more fre-quent divorce on women and children.[22] Partly in response to those

---

20. *See, e.g.,* Vandervort v. Vandervort, 134 P.3d 892 (Okl. Ct. Civ. App. 2005) (spouses colluded to obtain divorce, to use division of assets to make wife eligible for state payment for nursing home care; decree of divorce based on "incompat-ibility" vacated on appeal).

21. Under its prior law, couples could seek divorce on a "no-fault" ground of hav-ing lived separately and apart for one year after the granting of a legal separa-tion or the signing of a written separation agreement. This, however, required the cooperation of the other spouse; if the other spouse refused to agree to a legal separation or a separation agreement, a fault ground had to be proven before the divorce could be granted.

22. *See* Judith S. Wallerstein, Julia Lewis, & Sandra Blakeslee, *The Unexpected Legacy of Divorce: A 25 Year Landmark Study* (New York: Hyperion, 2000); Lenore J. Weitzman, "The Economics of Divorce: Social and Economic Consequences of Property, Alimony and Child Support," *UCLA Law Review*, vol.

arguments, many states have considered, and three states have passed, a compromise between those who support no-fault divorce and those who think that it makes divorce too easy. Covenant marriage (discussed briefly in chapter 2) is a means for a couple about to marry, and also for couples already married, to opt into something like the old fault system, where divorce is allowed only after counseling and only on fault grounds or an extended period of separation (usually two years rather than, say, six months).[23] Additionally those choosing covenant marriage agree to premarriage counseling and predivorce counseling. Beyond the three states that passed covenant marriage shortly after it was introduced (Louisiana in 1997, Arizona in 1998, and Arkansas in 2001[24]), no states have passed it in the dozen years since the last enactment, and the take-up percentage for covenant marriage in the three states that have it has been in the low single digits.[25]

Louisiana, which was the first state to offer the option of covenant marriage, more recently introduced a two-track system of no-fault divorce (for those who are not in a covenant marriage): couples with minor children will have to live apart for a year before

---

28, pp. 1181–1268 (1981). While social scientists have questioned the extent of the postdivorce financial loss women suffer, they have generally agreed that there is an effect. *See* Ira Mark Ellman, Paul M. Kurtz, Lois A. Weithorn, Brian H. Bix, Karen Czapanskiy, & Maxine Eichner, *Family Law: Cases, Text, Problems* (5th ed., LexisNexis, 2010), pp. 424–429 (while Weitzman claimed a 73 percent loss, later theorists, using Weitzman's own data found a loss closer to 30 percent).

23. Of the three states, only Arizona's covenant marriage law allows no-fault divorce upon the agreement of both parties. *Ariz. Rev. Stat.* § 25-903(8).

24. *La. Rev. Stat.* §§ 9: 272-279, 307–309; *Ariz. Rev. Stat.* §§ 25-901 to 25-906; *Ark. Code Ann.* §§ 9-11-801 to 9-11-808.

25. For a good overview of the background and implications of Louisiana's covenant marriage law, see Joel A. Nichols, "Louisiana's Covenant Marriage Law: A First Step toward a More Robust Pluralism in Marriage and Divorce Law?," *Emory Law Journal*, vol. 47, pp. 929–1001 (1998). For some conflict of laws complications, see Peter Hay, "The American 'Covenant Marriage' in the Conflict of Laws," in John Witte, Jr. & Eliza Ellison (eds.), *Covenant Marriage in Comparative Perspective* (Grand Rapids, Mich.: William B. Eerdmans Publishing Co., 2005), pp. 294–316.

divorcing; couples without minor children can divorce after living apart for six months.[26]

The need, or at least the strong desire, in the context of a marital breakup, to blame and to seek public vindication, is powerful, and with the move to no-fault divorce, that impulse sometimes gets pushed to other arenas. As discussed earlier (chapter 2, section F), in a small number of states, a heartbalm action like "alienation of affection" is available, to gain civil remedies against someone who has broken up one's marriage. Additionally, in the context of a divorce, and often as part of the same proceeding, one spouse may accuse the other of a tort arising from behavior during the marriage. Like the heartbalm actions, claims that one's (former) spouse was guilty of "intentional infliction of emotional distress," or the like, seems to approximate fault-based divorce, and therefore such actions tend to be limited by the courts on public policy grounds.[27] Both of these options are only infrequently available and successful; somewhat more common are state laws that allow consideration of marital fault as a factor in determining the division of property and award of alimony upon divorce. These topics are considered in chapters 11 and 12.

✇ C. Jurisdiction

Jurisdiction is the power of a court to hear a case. To hear a case, a court must have the power to deal with disputes of the kind before it ("subject matter jurisdiction"), and it must have the power to rule over the parties in the dispute ("personal jurisdiction").

---

26. Louisiana Act 743; *La. Civil Code* art. 103.1. The act went into effect Jan. 1, 2007, and would not affect situations where there has been physical or sexual abuse of a spouse or child, where a protective order has been issued, or where the divorce is grounded on adultery or a spouse's imprisonment, *id.*; *La. Civil Code* arts. 102, 103, 103.1(b), (c).

27. *See, e.g.*, Harry D. Krause, "On the Danger of Allowing Marital Fault to Re-Emerge in the Guise of Torts," *Notre Dame Law Review*, vol. 73, pp. 1355–1367 (1998).

The jurisdictional rules of marriage dissolution are intricate and not always easy to follow.

First and foremost, jurisdiction to grant a divorce (or a legal separation or civil annulment) has different rules—different grounds—than jurisdiction to make financial and child custody rules incident to the dissolution of the marriage. It is common for a court to have the power to resolve all the issues together, but there are also cases where courts can deal with some issues but not others. Where a court has the power to end the marriage but not to resolve other related issues, this is sometimes called "divisible divorce."

To have the power to end a marriage, the *res* ("thing") of the marriage must be before the court; that is, the marriage must be "in the jurisdiction." Where does a marriage "live" for the purposes of American family law? The answer is: in the domiciles[28] of the two spouses. Thus, the marriage can exist in two states, if the spouses are currently domiciliaries of different states, and the state courts in either of those states would have the power to dissolve the marriage.

How do these rules of divorce jurisdiction reflect the basic themes of American family law? On the whole, they do not. The jurisdictional rules derive from the archaic (one might be tempted to say "scholastic" or "medieval"—and, historically speaking, one would not be far wrong) rules of Anglo-American legal procedure. However, even if the jurisdictional rules are neither distinctive to family law nor reflective of modern interests (relating to family law policy or otherwise), those jurisdictional rules create unintended consequences that do get played out in ways that reflect the themes we have been discussing throughout this book.

---

28. A person's domicile is the most recent state in which that person has lived with the intention of remaining in that state indefinitely. Thus, current residence is neither sufficient nor necessary for domiciliary status. One can fail to be a domicile in a place one is living, and even where one has lived in a state for some years (e.g., a university student who intends to leave a state after her studies is not a domiciliary of the university's state). On domicile, see Russell J. Weintraub, *Commentary on the Conflict of Laws* (6th ed., New York: Foundation Press, 2010), pp. 16–54.

For example, the rules of divorce jurisdiction mean that the court that hears a divorce case may be in a state that has little connection with the married life of the spouses (if one of the spouses moved from the state where he or she had lived for most of the marriage). When this is combined with the fact that courts hearing divorce cases tend to apply their own law to divorce disputes rather than the law of the jurisdiction where the parties married or lived their married life, a tension in federalism comes to the surface: how do we effectively delegate policy-making power to the states in a context where individuals frequently move from one state to another?

This also means that there are significant limits on the ability of any state to create effective marriage policy. A state could best control choices couples made about marriage if it set the terms for the couple's marriage and subsequent divorce (if any). However, we have already seen that one can circumvent a state's marriage law by simply marrying in another state; the marriage will be recognized in one's home state, as long as it is not contrary to the home state's significant public policy. And one can evade a home state's divorce policies by moving to another state, becoming a domiciliary of that state, and filing for divorce in that second state. The accumulative effect of the state-law governance over family law and significant party autonomy regarding in which state marriage and divorce take place is substantial constraints on the ability of state governments to regulate marriage.

Suggested Further Reading

History

Norma Basch, *Framing American Divorce: From the Revolutionary Generation to the Victorians* (Berkeley: University of California Press, 1999).

Lawrence M. Friedman, "A Dead Language: Divorce Law and Practice Before No-Fault," *Virginia Law Review*, vol. 86, pp. 1497–1536 (2000).

Hendrik Hartog, *Man and Wife in America: A History* (Cambridge, Mass.: Harvard University Press, 2000).

Covenant Marriage

Steven L. Nock, Laura Ann Sanchez, & James D. Wright, *Covenant Marriage: The Movement to Reclaim Tradition in America* (New Brunswick: Rutgers University Press, 2008).

John Witte, Jr. & Eliza Ellison (eds.), *Covenant Marriage in Comparative Perspective* (Grand Rapids, Mich.: William B. Eerdmans Publishing Co., 2005).

Jurisdiction

Courtney G. Joslin, "Modernizing Divorce Jurisdiction: Same-Sex Couples and Minimum Contacts," *Boston University Law Review*, vol. 91, pp. 1669–1722 (2011).

TEN

Agreements

AS SUBSEQUENT CHAPTERS will discuss, divorce litigation entails determination of the financial and child-centered details arising from the breakup of a shared life. In approximately 90 percent of American divorces, these details are worked out in a negotiated agreement between the parties, a separation agreement.[1] Additionally, parties sometimes try to set some of the terms of divorce either prior to the beginning of the marriage (a premarital or "antenuptial" or "prenuptial" agreement) or during the marriage (a marital or "reconciliation" agreement). However, it must be remembered that there are many aspects of divorce and the financial and child-related consequences of divorce that couples are not able to control, or are only able to alter at the margins. It is for the courts, in the end, to grant decrees of divorce—the couple cannot end their marriage by simple agreement (and state statutes usually set requirements for mandatory waiting periods)—and courts have significant responsibilities relating to the best interests of children, as will be discussed later in this chapter.

How much deference courts give agreements depends on the timing and circumstances of the agreements, and states vary significantly

---

1. A rate of 90 percent settlement is a figure commonly thrown out both for civil lawsuits generally and for divorce litigation in particular. As regards civil lawsuits generally, recent empirical work has shown a wide range of settlement rates across types of cases, with some categories closer to 50 percent than 90 percent. Theodore Eisenberg & Charlotte Lanvers, "What Is the Settlement Rate and Why Should We Care?," *Journal of Empirical Legal Studies*, vol. 6, pp. 111–146 (2009), also available at http://ssrn.com/abstract=1276383.

in how they treat agreements. The issues lead to useful discussions of the way in which modern marriage is moving from a purely "status" arrangement (where the state sets all the terms) to more of a "contract" relationship (where the parties control many terms, subject to some level of state protection of vulnerable parties).[2]

A. Premarital Agreements

1. History

Until the 1970s, nearly every jurisdiction refused to enforce agreements entered prior to marriage that purported to affect the financial terms of divorce. The legal terrain then changed radically in a relatively short period of time. Currently, no jurisdictions refuse enforcement of all premarital agreements, though quite a few direct the courts to enforce only those that meet significant tests of procedural or substantive fairness. According to one survey, currently 3 percent of those who are married or engaged to be married have a premarital agreement.[3]

Premarital agreements are entered when marriage is imminent, to settle or modify certain rights between the parties during their marriage, upon the death of one of the spouses, or upon divorce. Most of the litigation and academic commentary has focused on the agreements, and provisions within agreements, that purport to modify the rights of the (former) spouses upon divorce.

Forty years ago, state courts generally refused to enforce premarital agreements that altered the parties' right at divorce, on the

---

2. The reference here is to Sir Henry Maine's famous (if now somewhat clichéd) quotation: "[W]e may say that *the movement of progressive societies* has hitherto been a movement from Status to Contract." Henry Sumner Maine, *Ancient Law* (J. Murray ed., 10th ed., 1920), p. 141 (end of chapter 5) (emphasis in original).

3. Laura Petrecca, "Prenuptial Agreements: Unromantic, but Important," *USA Today*, Mar. 8, 2010.

basis that such agreements were attempts to alter the terms of a status (marriage), or because they had the effect of encouraging divorce (at least for the party who would have to pay less in alimony or give up less in the division of property). Over the course of the 1970s and 1980s, nearly every state changed its law, and currently every state allows at least some divorce-focused premarital agreements to be enforced, though the standards for regulating those agreements vary greatly from state to state.[4] (The law relating to premarital agreements affecting the parties' rights at the death of a spouse had historically been less hostile than the treatment of such agreements affecting the rights of the parties at divorce.[5])

The move toward greater enforceability of premarital agreements was strengthened by the 1983 promulgation of the Uniform Premarital Agreement Act (UPAA),[6] a strongly pro-enforcement law that was subsequently adopted by twenty-six jurisdictions.[7] For example, the UPAA notoriously held that a premarital agreement would be enforceable even if it were found to be unconscionable (sufficient grounds for refusing enforcement for conventional, commercial agreements), as long as there had been adequate financial disclosure.[8] It should be noted that roughly half of those jurisdictions have made significant amendments to the UPAA and that most of these changes involve adding greater protection for vulnerable parties.[9]

---

4. The history of the enforceability of divorce-focused premarital agreements is summarized in Brian Bix, "Bargaining in the Shadow of Love: The Enforcement of Premarital Agreements and How We Think About Marriage," *William & Mary Law Review*, vol. 40, pp. 145–207 (1998), at pp. 148–158.

5. The ability of a wife to waive her dower rights goes back to the sixteenth-century Statute of Uses. 227 Hen. VIII, c. IO, § 6 (1535).

6. The text of the UPAA can be found at http://www.law.upenn.edu/bll/archives/ulc/fnact99/1980s/upaa83.htm.

7. By way of full disclosure, I should note that I was the Reporter for the Uniform Law Commission's "Uniform Premarital and Marital Agreements Act," promulgated in 2012, which was intended to supersede the UPAA (and also intended to bring greater uniformity to the legal treatment of marital agreements).

8. UPAA § 6(a)(2).

9. *See* Amberlynn Curry, Comment, "The Uniform Premarital Agreement Act and Its Variations throughout the States," *Journal of the American Academy of Matrimonial Lawyers*, vol. 23, pp. 355–383 (2010). For examples of jurisdictions

While there is no reliable data regarding premarital agreements—how many are entered into each year, who uses them, the motivations behind them, what percentage are contested, what percentage of contested agreements are upheld, and so forth—there is certainly a standard view of such agreements, reflected in media and academic discussions. The standard story is that most premarital agreements are initiated by wealthy partners who are unwilling to share their wealth should their marriages fail. The standard view sometimes notes that a minority of such agreements are entered for the seemingly more laudable purpose of protecting the interests of children born of a prior marriage.

The current law on premarital agreements is not easy to summarize without distortion, in large part because the rules vary from state to state, and even when courts (whether in the same state or in different states) are applying the same law, they will often do so in ways which differ significantly.[10]

There is a consensus across jurisdictions that premarital agreements must be in writing.[11] There is similar unanimity on the requirement that there have been substantial financial disclosure of assets by the party seeking enforcement of an agreement.[12] While

---

altering the UPAA significantly, see, e.g., *Cal. Fam. Code* §§ 1612, 1615 (limiting right to waive alimony and making access to independent legal counsel central to determining voluntariness of agreement); *Conn. Gen. Stat.* § 46b-36g(2) (unconscionability to be tested not just at time of execution but also at time of enforcement).

10. *See, e.g.,* Judith T. Younger, "Lovers' Contracts in the Courts: Forsaking the Minimal Decencies," *William & Mary Journal of Women and the Law,* vol. 13, pp. 349–428 (2007), at pp. 359–400 (summarizing the divergent interpretations between states and within individual states in applying UPAA standards).

11. However, even here, the same sorts of exceptions to the Statute of Frauds in other contexts may be allowed for premarital agreements. *See, e.g.,* Dewberry v. George, 62 P.3d 525, 528–530 (Wash. App. 2003) (allowing the enforcement of an oral premarital agreement under the part performance exception to the Statute of Frauds).

12. Many states allow the disclosure requirement to be overcome by an express waiver by the other party, or by a showing that the other party had actual knowledge of the assets.

a majority of states look only to the procedural and substantive fairness of premarital agreements relative to the time the agreement was entered, a sizeable minority of jurisdictions also tests the "fairness" or "reasonableness" of the agreement relative to the time of enforcement.[13] Of course, premarital agreements are also subject to challenge under the doctrines that apply to all contracts, including, along with claims based on unconscionability (at the time the agreement is entered), duress, misrepresentation, undue influence, and mutual mistake.[14]

"Fairness" (and its many cognates) is a vague standard at the best of times, and with premarital agreements a key inquiry is the question, "relative to what?" An agreement could be seen, on one hand, to give comfortable provision to a former spouse, but could simultaneously be seen as quite stingy relative to what that former spouse enjoyed during the marriage or what that spouse would have received under the default statutory guidelines. Are the latter criteria relevant?[15] Courts disagree.[16]

---

13. *See, e.g.*, DeMatteo v. DeMatteo, 762 N.E.2d 797, 805 (Mass. 2002) (summarizing Massachusetts law, that premarital agreements must be "fair and reasonable" at the time of enforcement).

14. For a case applying a conventional contract law understanding of unconscionability to a wpremarital agreement, see *In re* Marriage of Drag, 762 N.E.2d 1111, 1115 (Ill. App. 2002).

15. Of course, what would be a fair provision at the time of divorce itself raises difficult questions that may be unrelated to the specific issues of premarital agreements. For example, what of a spouse who suffers severe and costly health problems during the course of the marriage, problems not directly related to the marriage or the other spouse? Should the healthy spouse be obligated to pay for the medical treatment, even after divorce? Does it matter how long the parties were married? Cf. Marriage of Wilson, 247 Cal. Rptr. 522 (App. 1988) (refusing to impose permanent alimony after short marriage where wife suffered permanent disability during the marriage). The answer to such questions will do much to determine whether one thinks the waiver of spousal support is unconscionable as applied to a spouse who has suffered severe medical problems. *See In re* Marriage of Rosendale, 15 Cal. Rptr. 3d 137 (App. 2004) (holding such a provision unconscionable at the time of enforcement).

16. *See, e.g., DeMatteo*, 762 N.E.2d at 809–813 (rejecting comparisons of premarital agreement with what party would have received under statutory standards).

There are limits to the coverage of premarital agreements: most prominently, they are not enforceable when they purport to cover child custody, child support, or visitation, and they cannot add or subtract from the grounds available for divorce.

2. Religious Agreements

One difficult but rarely discussed issue for the legal enforcement of premarital agreements involves those agreements whose terms are set by religious doctrine and practices. The prominent examples are the Jewish *ketubah* and the Islamic *mahr*.

The *ketubah* is signed as part of the Jewish marriage ceremony, but it is commonly treated in courts as a premarital agreement. Many modern *ketubah*s have terms requiring a husband, upon obtaining a civil divorce, to agree to cooperate in obtaining a religious divorce (a *get*), without which the former wife would not be allowed to marry under religious law.[17] While "separation of Church and State" concerns make some courts hesitant to enforce the terms of religious premarital agreements, other courts seem willing to enforce such agreements, including enforcing Jewish premarital agreements requiring a husband to submit the dispute to religious arbitration, to grant the wife a *get*, and to pay damages for failure to do so.[18]

---

17. *See* Avitzur v. Avitzur, 446 N.E.2d 136 (N.Y. 1983) (holding enforceable *ketubah* term requiring parties to appear before religious tribunal and accept its decision regarding a religious divorce). New York also has statutes requiring or creating strong incentives for similar cooperation. *New York Domestic Relations Law* §§ 236(B)(5)(h), 253; *see generally* Michael J. Broyde, "New York Regulation of Jewish Marriage: Covenant, Contract, or Statute?," in Joel A. Nichols (ed.), *Marriage and Divorce in a Multicultural Context* (Cambridge: Cambridge University Press, 2012), pp. 138–163.

18. *See, e.g., In re* Marriage of Goldman, 554 N.E.2d 1016 (Ill. App. 1990) (*ketubah* under which husband agreed to grant the wife a *get* enforceable); Lang v. Levi, 16 A.3d 980 (Md. App. 2011) (premarital agreement under which husband agreed to pay damages for every day in which he delayed obtaining a *get*, and agreement to give disputes about premarital agreement to rabbinical court, both enforceable).

Under Islamic law, marriage is a contract. Part of that contract is an agreement of payment by the husband to the wife—the *mahr*.

> *Mahr*, meaning "reward" (*ajr*) or "nuptial gift" (also designated *sadaqa* or *faridah*), is the expression used in Islamic family law to describe the "payment that the wife is entitled to receive from the husband in consideration of the marriage." .... *Mahr* is usually divided into two parts: that which is paid at the time of marriage is called prompt *mahr* (*muajjal*) and that which is paid only upon the dissolution of the marriage by death or divorce or other agreed events is called deferred *mahr* (*muwajjal*).[19]

At divorce, in Islamic practice, there is neither alimony nor the equitable division of property; household possessions are divided strictly according to title. The cultural understanding apparently is that a divorced wife is to be supported by her extended family, not by her ex-husband. Therefore, in Islamic societies, the *mahr* payments can be essential for a wife who has (or will have) little property under her own name.

The deferred payment is due if the husband divorces the wife by *talaq*, a unilateral form of divorce, which the husband has the right

---

19. Pascale Fournier, "Flirting with God in Western Secular Courts: Mahr in the West," 24 *International Journal of Law, Policy and the Family*, vol. 24, pp. 67–94 (2010), at p. 69. It should be noted that the Islamic world is quite large, and what the text describes are general tendencies rather than universal truths; different practices and understandings arise in different areas. *See, e.g.,* Asifa Quraishi & Frank E. Vogel, *The Islamic Marriage Contract: Case Studies in Islamic Family Law* (Cambridge, Mass.: Harvard University Press, 2008), in which separate chapters chronicle the practice of the Islamic marriage contract in Saudi Arabia, Iran, Malaysia, and Egypt. One report noted that in Saudi Arabia, in contrast to other Islamic communities, it is traditional for the full *mahr* to be paid by the second wedding ceremony. *Id.* at 205. Of course, if a couple comes from a community in which there is no "deferred *mahr* payment," then there will be nothing that need be litigated on the issue if or when the marriage dissolves.

to use and which requires no showing of cause. There are other forms of Islamic divorce, though the wife has no comparable right to divorce unilaterally without showing cause (unless that right is expressly granted to her by the husband). There is some uncertainty about the wife's right to the deferred payment for the other forms of divorce, but the majority rule appears to be that she is not due payment if she initiates the divorce *and* he is not clearly at fault for the end of the marriage. In any event, under Islamic law, the deferred *mahr* payment serves two functions: discouraging *talaq*, and compensating for the likely imbalance in titled property.[20]

Mahr provisions are like conventional premarital agreements in that they are part of agreements entered just before the marriage ceremony and because they concern payments that may be due at divorce; however, they are unlike conventional premarital agreements in that their express language does not purport to waive state default rules of property characterization, property division at divorce, or alimony. While some courts have enforced *mahr* provisions as though they were conventional premarital agreements,[21] this may have been unjustified—or at least too quick. There should be a burden on the party arguing that the agreement was meant to displace state default rules that this is the reasonable understanding of the provision language, in the context of the agreement of these particular parties (and then, but only then, would the question arise whether all relevant procedural and substantive criteria for a valid premarital agreement have been met).[22]

---

20. There may be some uncertainty or dispute as to whether or under what circumstances a wife might lose her right to the payment if she initiates a divorce. *See* Fournier, "Flirting with God in Western Secular Courts," 69–70 (explaining that rights to *mahr* depend on which of three kinds of divorce is involved); *see also In re* Marriage of Dajani, 251 Cal. Rptr. 871, 872 (Ct. App. 1988) (summarizing expert witness testimony that wife forfeits right to *mahr* payment if she initiates the divorce).

21. *See, e.g.*, Chaudry v. Chaudry, 388 A.2d 100 (N.J. Super. Ct. App. Div. 1978).

22. *See* Brian H. Bix, "*Mahr* Agreements: Contracting in the Shadow of Family Law (and Religious Law)—A Comment on Oman," 1 *Wake Forest Law Review Online* 61 (2011), available at http://wakeforestlawreview.com/.

As noted, religious premarital agreements also raise constitutional issues because of possible entanglement of the civil courts with religion.[23] However, such questions go beyond the scope of the present text.

✤ B. Marital Agreements

The category of "marital agreements" covers any agreement between the spouses entered after marriage, but where the parties still intend to stay married (that is, legal separation or divorce is not planned or imminent). The term is applied to agreements which purport to affect significantly the property rights of the spouses during the marriage, at divorce, or upon the death of the other spouse, or alimony claims at divorce. (An agreement between spouses that otherwise is a standard commercial agreement, e.g., a transfer of a piece of property from one spouse to the other, may raise distinctive legal issues, but not of the sort considered in this section.[24])

Some states apply the same principles to marital agreements that they apply to premarital agreements.[25] Other states impose

---

23. On this or similar grounds, an Ohio court recently refused to enforce a *mahr* that involved a promised payment of $25,000. *See* Meredith Heagney, "Muslims' Dowry Not Binding, Judge Says," *Columbus Dispatch*, Oct. 20, 2007. *See generally* Kent Greenawalt, "Religious Law and Civil Law: Using Secular Law to Assure Observance of Practices with Religious Significance," *Southern California Law Review*, vol. 71, pp. 781–843 (1998).

24. Among the questions here is whether the spouses intended their agreement to be legally binding or whether (because they are married) they preferred that the agreement not result in legally enforceable obligations. *See, e.g.*, Balfour v. Balfour, [1919] 2 K.B. 571 (C.A. 1919) (famous old case denying enforcement to an agreement between spouses); *see generally* E. Allan Farnsworth, *Contracts* § 3.7, at p. 119 (4th ed., New York: Aspen Publishers, 2004) (discussing the modern approach to such agreements).

25. *New York Domestic Relations* § 236, Part B(3); *North Carolina General Statutes* § 52-10(a); *Wis. Stat. Ann.* § 766.58; Bratton v. Bratton, 136 S.W.3d 595, 599–601 (Tenn. 2004); Flansburg v. Flansburg, 581 N.E.2d 430, 433 (Ind. Ct. App., 1991). This is also the approach the American Law Institute, *Principles of the Law of Dispute Resolution* (Newark: LexisNexis, 2002), and the Uniform Premarital and Marital Agreements Act.

different requirements on marital agreements than they do on pre-marital agreements.[26] The basis for this difference may be as simple as that in the jurisdiction in question (some version of) the UPAA applies to premarital agreements, but that law, by its own terms, does not apply to marital agreements,[27] or there may be a more con-textual analysis concluding that premarital agreements are more likely to be "arm's-length" negotiations[28] or that marital agreements are more likely to be coercive.[29]

Sometimes the legal treatment of these agreements turns on their factual context and the intentions with which they were entered. In particular, some jurisdictions treat "reconciliation agreements" as a special form of agreement, deserving some respect and defer-ence.[30] In such agreements, the parties agree to reconcile (and/or to resume cohabitation) conditioned on some modification of their marital or postdissolution property arrangements. These agree-ments may be enforceable in jurisdictions where other marital agreements are not, or at least be treated with less suspicion than other marital agreements, because of the state's interest in couples'

26. *See Minn. Stat.* § 519.11, subd. 1a; *La. Rev. Stat. Ann. Civil Code* § 2329; Ansin v. Craven-Ansin, 929 N.E.2d 955 (Mass. 2010); Bedrick v. Bedrick, 17 A.3d 17 (Conn. 2011).

27. *See, e.g.,* Davis v. Miller, 7 P.3d 1223, 1229–1230 (Kan. 2000) (holding that the Kansas version of the UPAA does not apply to marital agreements, but that the parties can, through express choice of law provisions, have their marital agreements judged under UPAA standards).

28. *See In re* Marriage of Grossman, 82 P.3d 1039, 1043 (Or. App. 2003).

29. *See* Pacelli v. Pacelli, 725 A.2d 56, 59 (N.J. Super. A.D. 1999).

30. *See, e.g., In re* Estate of Duggan, 639 So. 2d 1071 (Fla. Dist. Ct. App. 1994) (mari-tal agreement involving waiver of estate interests valid as reconciliation agree-ment); Nicolson v. Nicolson, 489 A.2d 1247 (N.J. Super. A.D. 1985) (establishing the standard for enforcing reconciliation agreements); *cf.* Bratton v. Bratton, 136 S.W.3d 595, 599–600 (Tenn. 2004) (in case upholding validity generally of marital agreements, court notes that reconciliation agreements had earlier been recognized as valid even when other marital agreements were not). Special treatment of reconciliation agreements, allowing their enforcement, has roots that are (in the context of this quickly changing area of law) rela-tively ancient. *See, e.g.,* Annotation, "Validity and Enforceability of Agreement Designed to Prevent Divorce, or Avoid or End Separation," 11 A.L.R. 277 (1921).

remaining married.[31] (Thus, if it turns out that one party's mani-
fested intention to reconcile was false, the resulting agreement will
not receive the same favorable treatment and may also be voidable
on grounds of fraud.[32])

As a matter of general contract law, to be enforceable agreements
must be supported by adequate legal consideration.[33] This is not a
problem with most commercial agreements (where the payment by
one party and the goods or services of the other party would constitute the necessary consideration), nor is it a problem with separation agreements (where both parties are waiving potential claims)
or premarital agreements (where the decision to marry is the consideration). However, it can potentially be a serious issue with marital agreements, at least those in which both (1) only one spouse is
waiving his or her rights (getting nothing in return), and (2) one
could not claim the decision to reconcile as consideration.[34]

With such cases, consideration is arguably not (or not merely)
a technical requirement there to trip up the unwary, but rather an
indirect way of determining whether there is a true bargain or just
a coerced transfer of goods or rights. Consideration had played a
similar role in commercial law, in trying to help determine whether
modifications of agreements were reasonable accommodations
or coerced "holdups" by parties who suddenly found themselves,
mid-performance, with bargaining leverage. Today, most of the
same work in commercial law modification doctrine is done by
direct inquiries into "good faith" and coercion ("duress").[35] Contract
law has for the most part moved beyond formalistic inquiries
into consideration in modification cases, in large part because

---

31. *See, e.g.*, Flansburg v. Flansburg, 581 N.E.2d 430, 437 (Ind. Ct. App. 1991).

32. *Cf.* Fogg v. Fogg, 567 N.E.2d 921, 923 (Mass. 1991) (where wife lied about her
motivation to reconcile, particular reconciliation agreement was properly
refused enforcement, though court did not decide the general enforceability
of reconciliation agreements).

33. *See, e.g.*, Farnsworth, *Contracts*, § 2.2, at p. 47.

34. *See, e.g.*, Bratton v. Bratton, 136 S.W.3d 595, 600 (Tenn. 2004) (refusing to enforce
marital agreement in part because of absence of consideration).

35. *See, e.g.*, Farnsworth, *Contracts*, §§ 4.21–4.22, at pp. 267–274.

modifications of commercial agreements are considered a normal part of daily business, with the understanding that such "one-sided changes" are frequently grounded in good reasons and good faith.[36] Accommodations are needed for unexpected changes in supply, costs of resources, and difficulty in completion. However, in the marital context, at least outside the context of reconciliation agreements, it is harder to think of good-faith reasons for mid-"performance" adjustments of terms.[37] Thus, the test for consideration might serve a useful purpose for marital agreements (at least for courts unwilling to apply a more amorphous "good-faith" test), but it is important to note that not all jurisdictions now require it.[38]

Additionally, neither the formality of consideration, nor the focus on a general structure of "reconciliation," can distinguish, in a foolproof way, the wronged or disenchanted spouse who is reluctantly persuaded (in part with a property offer) to reconcile, from the bad-faith spouse who uses a false claim of estrangement and a threat of divorce to coerce a favorable property settlement from the other spouse.[39]

This is a good place to revisit the question of whether marital agreements should be treated the same as premarital agreements. Some commentators would have less trouble with a one-sided premarital agreement than similar terms being presented to a spouse

---

36. *See, e.g.,* UCC §2-209(1) (no consideration required for a binding modification for sales of goods).

37. Some might speculate that it might be sufficient justification for an "adjustment" that one spouse turns out to be less of a hard worker or more of a hard drinker than the other spouse (or perhaps both spouses) expected. Is that sufficient, or would one simply say that such developments would already be taken into account in the broad equitable standards the state uses (e.g.) for deciding property division and alimony at divorce?

38. *See, e.g., Fla. Stat.* § 732.702(3) (expressly rejecting a consideration requirement for either marital or premarital agreements). It should be noted that both the American Law Institute, *Principles of the Law of Family Dissolution* (§ 7.01(4)), and the Uniform Premarital and Marital Agreement Act (Section 6) do not have a consideration requirement, but instead try to protect vulnerable parties through other procedural and substantive requirements.

39. *See* Pacelli v. Pacelli, 725 A.2d 56, 58 (N.J. Super. A.D. 1999) (husband used threat of divorce to coerce a favorable marital agreement).

as a part of a marital agreement. The argument is that a "take it or leave it" offer to marry on certain terms is usually less coercive than a "take it or leave it" offer to stay married—especially where the divorce would be perceived as harming the children or might leave the "offeree spouse" in a precarious social or financial condition.[40] No one has to marry, and one certainly does not have to marry the particular person who is presenting one with a proposed premarital agreement.

At the same time, marital agreements can raise special factors arguing either for or against their enforcement, depending on the context in which they are entered. On one hand, if enforceability of a marital agreement can make such an agreement instrumental to reconciling parties who might otherwise divorce, this would (at least in most cases) seem like a good thing. On the other hand, as noted, marital agreements create special opportunities for (sometimes hard-to-detect) coercion on one side and on the other side a sort of vulnerable sacrifice that may warrant paternalistic intervention.[41]

C. Separation Agreements

Separation agreements (sometimes called "marital settlement agreements") are agreements entered when legal separation or divorce

---

40. *See id.* at 59. The exceptional situation where a premarital agreement might be comparably coercive is where the agreement is presented on the eve of the marriage, when expensive wedding arrangements have been irrevocably made, and guests have already arrived. A number of courts have invalidated premarital agreements presented this late (under rubrics of duress or voluntariness). *E.g., In re* Marriage of Maifield, 796 N.W.2d 457 (Iowa App. 2004). However, if those same agreements had been presented months earlier (before wedding invitations had been sent or expensive parts of the wedding paid for) that coercive element would have been absent.

41. For a good discussion of these dynamics, and their repercussions for legal regulation, see Michael J. Trebilcock & Steven Elliott, "The Scope and Limits of Legal Paternalism: Altruism and Coercion in Family Financial Arrangements," in Peter Benson (ed.), *The Theory of Contract Law: New Essays* (Cambridge: Cambridge University Press, 2001), pp. 45–85.

is imminent, with the purpose of settling the financial rights and duties of the spouses. For the vast majority of divorces, the terms of divorce are settled by the parties—though, of course, in "the shadow of the law"—that is, aware of the terms a court would likely impose were the issues to be presented to a court.[42] This is, of course, not unusual for litigation, where even outside of family law disputes, many more cases end by settlement rather than litigated verdict. Settlement is favored not only because it saves party and judicial resources, but (in the context of divorce) because the parties might be more willing to live with an arrangement they themselves helped to work out, and because settlement prevents unpleasant court battles that might harm any children involved.

In most jurisdictions, the separation agreement must be presented to a court for its approval.[43] While separation agreements tend to deal with all aspects of the divorce, doctrinally courts are usually instructed to be deferential to the aspects of separation agreements dealing with financial matters between the parties, but not deferential to terms involving children (custody, visitation, and child support). One can find statutory or case-law language authorizing courts to reject or ignore separation agreements if their terms are unfair,[44] but most observers indicate that this rarely happens.[45]

---

42. *See* Robert H. Mnookin & Lewis Kornhauser, "Bargaining in the Shadow of the Law: The Case of Divorce," *Yale Law Journal*, vol. 88, pp. 950–997 (1979).

43. The parties may also ask for the terms of the separation agreement to be merged into the final divorce decree. When an agreement is merged into the divorce decree, the terms of the agreement become enforceable by contempt orders; at the same time, the terms also become subject to later modification (though a number of jurisdictions allow the parties to agree by express language to limit or forbid such modifications). Where an agreement is not merged into the decree, it is usually still enforceable by a conventional breach of contract action.

44. *See, e.g., In re* Marriage of Grossman, 82 P.3d 1039, 1042–1043 (Or. App. 2003) (quoting similar language from various Oregon cases).

45. In *In re* Marriage of Patterson, 255 P.3d 634 (Or. App. 2011), seven years passed between when a separation agreement had been signed and approved by the court and when the couple in fact divorced, and the passage of time had made the effect of the terms one-sided, but the court enforced the agreement as written, because of the strong public policy in favor of private settlement of divorce disputes.

For the terms relating directly to children, courts are to check to see that the best interests of the children are adequately protected by the agreement. However, according to many accounts, courts tend to rubber-stamp all but the most one-sided terms in such agreements, especially if neither partner objects at the time the agreement is submitted to the court.

There are some limits. While there is not a lot of case law, where the matter has been litigated courts seem reluctant to give (later) enforcement to separation agreement provisions that go to issues of custodial parents' relocation: either approving or denying the right to such relocations in advance.[46] The courts see authorizing or rejecting relocation of custodial parents as their own prerogative (ensuring the best interests of the children), while doubting that the parties could reasonably make judgments on such matters in advance.

Challenges brought to separation agreements after they have been signed but before they have been approved by a court are usually tested under standard contract law doctrines (e.g., considering defenses like duress, misrepresentation, undue influence, and mutual mistake). Attacks on the substantive fairness of the agreements are heard either under the standard contract law doctrine of "unconscionability"[47] (the standard suggested by the Uniform Marriage and Divorce Act[48]), or under a general standard of "fairness." Such substantive reviews are frequently made relative to what the parties would have received under statutory guidelines.[49]

---

46. *See, e.g.*, Delamielleure v. Belote, 704 N.W.2d 746 (Mich. Ct. App. 2005) (man's blanket waiver of right to challenge former wife's relocation does not bind the court; relocation of child governed by statute); Helton v. Helton, 2004 WL 63478 (Tenn. App., 2004) (separation agreement in which wife promised not to relocate without husband's written permission is not binding on the court; parties cannot "bargain away the court's continuing jurisdiction over the care of the child").

47. *See, e.g.*, Weber v. Weber, 589 N.W.2d 358, 361 (N.D. 1999) (rejecting a separation agreement on unconscionability grounds).

48. Uniform Marriage and Divorce Act § 306(b).

49. *See, e.g.*, Weber v. Weber, 589 N.W.2d at 361–362.

As noted, courts are also open to defenses based on irregularities in negotiation, as least those that can be restated in terms of general contract law doctrinal defenses. A difficulty here is that, in contrast to conventional commercial agreements, it is the nature of separation agreements that they are entered under extremes of emotion and pressure. Courts are, of course, aware of this and tend to be reluctant to void agreements that in another context might raise tenable claims of duress or undue influence.[50] In sufficiently extreme circumstances, however (including, in particular, where negotiations have occurred in a context of domestic abuse), courts will hold the agreements to be void or voidable.[51]

The courts' more favorable treatment of separation agreements relative to premarital and marital agreements (both historically and presently) is due in part to their different contexts: because separation agreements are entered knowing that legal separation or divorce is imminent, one can be less concerned that the parties will be too clouded by romantic feelings or optimism to protect their own interests (as with premarital agreements); and the decision to end the marriage has already been made, so dissolution is now a probable outcome, not a coercive threat (as is sometimes the case with marital agreements).

Suggested Further Reading

Premarital Agreements

Brian H. Bix, "Private Ordering and Family Law," *Journal of the American Academy of Matrimonial Lawyers*, vol. 23, pp. 249–285 (2010).

---

50. *See, e.g.*, Flynn v. Flynn, 597 N.E.2d 709, 714 (Ill. App. 1992) ("The anxiety inherent in [reaching a separation agreement] does not, by itself, constitute coercion.").

51. *See, e.g.*, Putnam v. Putnam, 689 A.2d 446, 449–450 (Vt. 1996). To connect to a topic discussed earlier, in section A, the threat by an Orthodox Jewish man not to give his former wife a religious divorce (thus leaving her unable to remarry) has been held to constitute duress, making a one-sided separation agreement voidable. Perl v. Perl, 512 N.Y.S.2d 372 (A.D. 1987).

Laura W. Morgan & Brett R. Turner, *Attacking and Defending Marital Agreements* (2nd ed., Chicago: ABA Family Law Section, 2012).

Linda J. Ravdin, *Premarital Agreements: Drafting and Negotiation* (Chicago: American Bar Association, 2011).

Marital Agreements

Sean Hannon Williams, "Postnuptial Agreements," *Wisconsin Law Review*, vol. 2007, pp. 827–887.

Separation Agreements

Robert H. Mnookin & Lewis Kornhauser, "Bargaining in the Shadow of the Law: The Case of Divorce," *Yale Law Journal*, vol. 88, pp. 950–997 (1979).

Property Division

ℳ A. Introduction

There is one set of rules for the ownership and control of property during marriage (discussed in passing in chapter 2), and another—distinct but related—set of rules for the division of property between the former spouses at divorce (and a third, related but distinct, set of rules upon the death of one of the spouses).[1] The rules of property (along with the rules for alimony and child support, discussed in chapters 12 and 14) are crucial in part because they set central incentives or disincentives for couples as they (individually and together) decide whether to split up or to stay together.

In common law property jurisdictions, property had, until recent decades, been divided at divorce according to title.[2] This meant that the husband—in traditional marriages, where he was the sole or primary breadwinner in the household and made most purchases in his own name—almost always received the vast majority of the marital property; this uneven distribution was said to be partly remedied by the imposition of an alimony award.[3]

---

1. *See, e.g.,* Laura A. Rosenbury, "Two Ways to End a Marriage: Divorce or Death," *Utah Law Review*, vol. 2005, pp. 1227–1290 (noting how spouses who are not the primary income-earner may often do significantly better if their marriages end by divorce than if they end by death).

2. Community property states might also divide by title; however, as discussed in chapter 2, section B, in community property states both spouses would have had equal title to almost all property acquired by either spouse during the marriage.

3. Under this traditional approach, the wife's protection if the marriage ended in death rather than dissolution was the legal right of dower, a claim on

Modern lawmakers and courts in common law property states have unanimously rejected title-based principles of property division upon divorce in favor of a "partnership" view of marriage—the understanding that marriage is a kind of joint venture, and the idea that spouses who work at home contribute to the other spouse's ability to earn. State rules have for that reason promulgated a combination of equitable distribution rules (property is to be divided on an "equitable" basis, with little to no consideration of title), homemaker provisions (expressly directing courts to consider work at home as one factor to consider in the division of property),[4] and, in a few states, presumptions for an equal division of property. (Community property states, as discussed in chapter 2, always had a partnership view of marriage and marital property; in those states, almost all of the property that is acquired during the marriage is owned equally by both spouses.)

🕊 B. Characterization and Payment

As noted in chapter 10, section C, in the vast majority of divorce cases, the parties agree to the financial terms in a separation agreement rather than awaiting the judicial resolution of such terms after litigation. Negotiators working out a separation agreement and

---

one-third of the deceased husband's real property (though lawyers and sympathetic judges found many ways to get around dower rights). *See, e.g.,* Ariela R. Dubler, "In the Shadow of Marriage: Single Women and the Legal Construction of the Family and the State," *Yale Law Journal,* vol. 112, pp. 1641–1715 (2003), at pp. 1660–1668. Under modern law, both spouses, under the vast majority of state laws, have a right to a "statutory share" (also called "elective share") of the other spouse's property (in alternative to whatever that spouse might have been granted in a will) upon that spouse's death. Currently, the only state where one may entirely disinherit one's spouse is Georgia; in Georgia, a spouse (along with minor children) has the right only to a limited one-year monetary allowance from the deceased's estate. *Ga. Code* § 53-3-1. (By contrast, only in one state, Louisiana, *La. Civil Code* 1493, are parents stopped from disinheriting their children—and even there, it applies only to children twenty-three years and younger, and disinheritance is allowed in some exceptional circumstances, *La. Civil Code* 1617.)

4. *E.g., W. Va. Code* § 48-7-103(2)(A).

those evaluating the financial terms either agreed by the parties or imposed by the courts need to understand the actual or potential connection between lump sum payments and payments over time. Property division usually involves the lump sum payments[5] along with or in lieu of assignment of real or personal property; and alimony usually involves the payments over time.[6] Because of the ability to borrow and lend money at interest and to invest money in safe investments at set levels of interest, economists, accountants, and courts generally consider lump sum payments to be translatable into equivalent payments over time, and vice versa (the "present value" of a guaranteed income stream). Thus, in private negotiations for separation agreements, the parties could consider various ways of "trading off" property division (immediately payment) claims for alimony (payment over time) claims. Of course, individuals may have definite preferences for one over the other (reflecting, e.g., ability to pay or current need), and these are subjective factors to consider in negotiations. Additionally, there are frequently important reasons arising from tax and bankruptcy law for labeling a payment "alimony" rather than "property division," or *vice versa* (tax and bankruptcy law issues will be discussed further in section H, below).[7]

✸ C. Doctrinal Rules and Views of Marriage

Although the rules and principles of property division and alimony discussed in this chapter and chapter 12 are applied at the dissolution of a marriage, they reflect the state's view of marriage and have

---

5. Although sometimes one party agrees or is ordered to pay the other in a number of installments due to practical difficulties in paying the full amount immediately.

6. Although courts in a few states will on some occasions order a single "lump sum alimony" payment.

7. Most prominently, under current law, alimony payments are usually deductible to the payor and treated as income to the recipient, while property division payments are not taxable events to either payor or recipient.

significant implications for the choices couples make regarding marriage. For example: to what extent is marriage an equal partnership, where the spouses will share equally in benefits and burdens, regardless of their role within the marriage? This is a question for which the rules of property division and alimony may be a significant part of the answer. Usually, the connection between doctrinal rules and a view about the nature of marriage is intended—and expressly stated in the relevant legislative history or in court opinions applying the rules and principles. However, even if the rules developed for reasons unrelated to a conscious view about the nature of marriage, the fact remains that these rules have significant consequences for how marriage is perceived and for the decisions individuals make regarding, and within, marriage.

This analysis does not depend on the unlikely assumption that people make all (or nearly all) of their decisions regarding marriage and divorce with an eye to the relevant legal rules (and a detailed knowledge of them). That would obviously be unrealistic.[8] However, far less than everyone acting in a calculating way would be needed for legal rules to have a significant effect on society and social perceptions. Legal rules can have significant effects even if they alter decisions only at the margins. Additionally, while it may be likely (if perhaps unfortunate) that people about to marry do not consider the consequences of legal rules, it is far more likely that spouses contemplating divorce, especially after consulting lawyers about this possibility, *will* make decisions whether or not to divorce with a clear eye to the likely financial and legal consequences of dissolving the marriage as contrasted to carrying on with it.

---

8. *For example, see* Carl Schneider's discussion of why alimony rules might have a minimal effect on marriage-related decisions. Carl E. Schneider, "Rethinking Alimony: Marital Decisions and Moral Discourse," vol. 1991, pp. 197–257, at pp. 205–209. Additionally, when people do calculate regarding marriage or divorce, they often do so in an unrealistically optimistic way. *See* Lynn A. Baker & Robert E. Emery, "When Every Relationship Is Above Average: Perceptions and Expectations of Divorce at the Time of Marriage," *Law and Human Behavior*, vol. 17, pp. 439–450 (1993).

As mentioned in chapter 1, one ongoing concern, in this area of family law but also more generally, is that the rules or decisions that might best "do justice" between the parties might differ from the rules or decisions that would creative the optimal incentives for the future actions of other individuals and couples.

𝄢 D. General Principles of Property Division

One could view a marriage abstractly as two people who have, among many other things, commingled their funds and possessions over an extended period of time, and when the partners go their separate ways some means must be found to disentangle the property. The couple could do it themselves—and through separation agreements, most couples in fact effectively do just that (usually subject to some minimal court review). However, where there are disputes, a court can be asked to set and enforce a division. This is no different from the members of a partnership or other commercial commingling of funds seeking a similar equitable division upon dissolution.[9] Of course, most people consider marriage to be something more than a mere commingling of funds. However, whether that "something more" requires a different approach to the division of property upon dissolution remains a matter of dispute.[10]

To review the basic starting point: not only in the United States but in Western nations generally, marital property regimes have divided into roughly two types: one ("common law" property) in

---

9. The connection may be clearest in the "intermediate" case of couples who had been in a long-term nonmarital cohabitation. Many jurisdictions have recognized claims for restitution or equitable partition arising from the dissolution of such relationships. *See, e.g.,* Watts v. Watts, 405 N.W.2d 303 (Wis. 1987).

10. Of course, in a broader sense, the question should be not merely how marriage affects the division of household property upon divorce but also how it affects the control (and ability to alienate) such property during the marriage and the rules regarding and restricting inheritance after the death of one of the partners. These topics, however, take us too far from the focus of this chapter.

which property is presumptively owned separately (though joint ownership is an option), and one ("community property") in which all marital property is owned jointly.[11] These two different types of regimes set the rules for ownership and control during the marriage; however, the rules for the division of property upon divorce can be, and are, distinct. In the vast majority of states (both community property states and common law property states), judges have the authority as part of a property division to give property titled to one spouse to the other spouse.[12] However, the influence of the marital property rules on the outcomes for divorce divisions is predictably large. Even when judges are given the power to transfer property from one partner to the other in the course of a dissolution procedure, it is natural to see the parties' initial property rights as the "starting point," with divisions radically different from that baseline requiring more by way of justification than a division closer to that baseline.

Certain property that the individual partners either brought to the marriage (that is, it was their property prior to marriage), or that they received as gifts or by inheritance during the marriage, is called "separate property."[13] In most states (either community property or common law property), such property is not subject to division at divorce (that is, such property automatically stays with its original owners); even in the small number of states where such property can be transferred at divorce (sometimes called "hotchpot"

---

11. For an interesting history of the two approaches, with insightful analysis regarding why they diverged in the way they did, see Charles Donahue, Jr., "What Causes Fundamental Legal Ideas? Marital Property in England and France in the Thirteenth Century," *Michigan Law Review*, vol. 78, pp. 59–88 (1979).

12. One exception is California, a community property state (thus the parties come to a divorce procedure with equal property claims to almost all property acquired by the household during the marriage) where judges are required to divide the marital property equally (that is, the division already set by the community property regime).

13. Additionally, most states will treat as separate property profits or increases in value of separate property, or property received in exchange for separate property.

states[14]), there is generally a strong presumption that all or most of such property will stay with its original owner.[15]

As earlier noted, division of marital property at divorce was once based entirely on title—on who was the named owner of the various assets. This tended to leave a fairly even split in community property states and a highly uneven split (almost always favoring the husband) in common law property states. (Alimony was the occasional equitable compensation for former wives who left the marriage with little property.) As discussed, all states have now abandoned title theories of division, in most cases for an "equitable" division of the marital property upon divorce. Property titled in one spouse can be given to the other at divorce, to allow the division to represent better a fair outcome. Many common law states have statutory or case-law-based rules defining "fairness" for this purpose in terms of a long list of factors, usually including the parties' needs and their monetary and nonmonetary contributions[16] during the marriage.

Earlier property division principles—ones that either focused entirely on title, or that downplayed nonmonetary contributions— had the effect of (unintentionally) creating incentives that were probably contrary to the best interests of most couples and of society generally. One can distinguish actions that are effectively "investments" in human capital that will have benefits for the person "investing" even if the marriage ends, from actions that may have long-term value within the relationship or the household but have limited value if the marriage ends. Thus, using one's time to

---

14. By one count, as many as sixteen states do not limit court division of property to marital/community property, but allow the transfer of separate property under at least some circumstances. Linda D. Elrod. & Robert G. Spector, "A Review of the Year in Family Law: Numbers of Disputes Increase," *Family Law Quarterly*, vol. 45, pp. 443–511 (2012), at pp. 504–506 (Chart 5).

15. *See, e.g., N.H. Stat.* § 458:16-a(II)(m), (n) (all property subject to equitable division, but value of property acquired prior to marriage or through gift, devise, or descent a factor the court must take into account).

16. Most states, by statute or case law, have expressly included efforts to take care of children or the home as a contribution that must be considered and valued in determining a fair division of property.

get a professional degree, career training, seniority at one's firm, and the like, will likely "pay dividends" over the long term, and will do so whether or not one's marriage continues. By contrast, spending time learning one's partner's likes and dislikes, being a good social host, caring for the children, or caring for the home, while all have value for an ongoing marriage, have limited monetary value if the marriage ends.[17]

Where title is in the name of the spouse who earns the money, and where a spouse who contributes to the household in nonfinancial ways is not compensated, the obvious effect of the division of property principles is to reward (and thus to encourage) investment in one's own human capital, but to punish (and thus to discourage) investment in the relationship, in caretaking, and in housework.[18] Thus, the move in common law property states[19] to value nonmonetary contributions will have the benefit of encouraging (or at least not discouraging) sacrifices of career made for the marriage and the family.

Over time, courts and legislatures have included more and more items in the category of "property" to be divided, including, most prominently, pensions, but also goodwill, earned bonuses, and workers' compensation awards. (There are also rules for the division of marital debts and for the special consideration of actions by one spouse that could be said to have "dissipated" marital assets.[20]) These additions are significant, as many long-term marriages end with little tangible property to be divided, but with one of the spouses having significant nontraditional property, like a pension

---

17. This of course is not to deny that caring for children will have (nonmonetary) "dividends" for *the children* over the long term, whatever happens to the marriage.

18. *See, e.g.*, Martha Minow, "Consider the Consequences" (book review), *Michigan Law Review*, vol. 84, pp. 900–918 (1986), at p. 915.

19. Since community property states start from an equal division of property obtained by the household, there was always less of a problem in those states of improper incentives.

20. *See* Margaret M. Mahoney, "The Equitable Division of Marital Debts," *University of Missouri-Kansas City Law Review*, vol. 79, pp. 445–475 (2010).

at his or her workplace.[21] As noted, some states have created a presumption of equal division as the starting point for the "equitable" division of property. Even in those states where there is no such formal presumption, there may be an informal understanding that divisions should be nearly equal.

Even with the modern equitable approach to property division, where significant efforts are made to compensate spouses in the property division for nonmonetary contributions, problems arise if the marriage terminates at a point where the marital household has accumulated few assets, but one of the spouses has, during the marriage, significantly increased his or her earning capacity (by obtaining a professional degree or in some other way). New York is the only jurisdiction that responds by treating a professional degree (and some other increases in earning capacity) as itself being property, subject to division.[22] A New York court must determine (with the help of expert testimony) the present value of the increased earning capacity that derives from the degree, and award an equitable portion of it to the other spouse. The award will usually be payable over many years, with the practical effect that the degree-holding spouse will be constrained in the choice of his or her career path. An award based on what most doctors or lawyers earn will thus constrain individual doctors or lawyers from devoting their life to charitable or public interest work.[23]

All jurisdictions other than New York, while refusing to treat a professional degree or increased earning capacity as property subject to division, frequently urge courts to award alimony that

---

21. It is also important to note that where a marriage has lasted more than ten years, a divorced spouse (who has not remarried) has a right to Social Security benefits that are up to 50 percent of the payment the beneficiary spouse receives. 42 U.S.C. § 402(b)(1); 20 C.F.R. § 404.331. (However, as with all spousal benefits, the married or divorced spouse must forego Social Security benefits based on his or her own past employment if that person wishes to claim benefits based on current or past marital status. *See id.*, 402(b)(1)(D), (c)(1)(D), (e)(1)(D), (f)(1)(D)).

22. O'Brien v. O'Brien, 489 N.E.2d 712 (N.Y. 1985).

23. For a detailed critique of the reasoning and consequences of *O'Brien v. O'Brien*, see Ira Mark Ellman, "*O'Brien v. O'Brien*: A Failed Reform, Unlikely Reformers," in Carol Sanger (ed.), *Family Law Stories* (New York: Foundation Press, 2008), pp. 269–294.

recognizes a spouse's contribution to the other spouse's increased earning capacity, or treats the contribution as an equitable factor to be taken into account, along with many other factors, in setting the "equitable" division of property. If the New York approach has the disadvantage of requiring courts to speculate (with expert assistance) about earnings well into the future, and burdening the degree-holding spouse, other approaches have the disadvantage of offering the other spouse only meager (restitutionary) or discretionary compensation (alimony, that is also usually subject to later modification) for that spouse's sacrifices during the marriage.

There may be something basically incoherent or untenable about "equitable division" (though one should not expect it to disappear any time soon!). The problem is exemplified by the issue of how to justify one's conclusion regarding the "contribution" or "equitable portion" of a spouse who works in the household. If one focuses on the market value of work done in the home, the chances are that the result will be an amount that seems unfairly low. This, in turn, is likely partly a product of the way the market undervalues such work, because it is associated with women, and because it is often done without financial compensation by wives and mothers.

However, if the "contribution" is not based on the market value of the services provided, what can it be based on? Courts will often recite all the work done, the emotional support offered, the career prospects sacrificed, the companionship offered, and so forth, and then announce that the ex-spouse should receive 35 percent or 40 percent or 55 percent of the marital property. This may be the judge's sincere judgment, but one doubts that any sort of articulated justification could be offered for how *this* set of facts led to *that* number (or how a different set of facts would lead to a different number). It seems inevitable that these divisions are ultimately either entirely arbitrary (a sort of nearly-random number generator), or some combination of bias and preconception disguised as judgment.[24]

---

24. There are, of course, many other areas of the law where the valuation is similarly subjective or arbitrary: e.g., awards for "pain and suffering" in tort law suits.

The alternative would be either an absolute rule of equal division or a strong presumption of equal division. A number of jurisdictions have such an official rule or presumption, and it is quite possible that many judges who purport to be applying "equitable distribution" are using equal distribution at least as a rough starting point. Where equal distribution is an official or unofficial starting point, but not the absolute rule, the courts (or the legislature) must still determine what would justify deviation from a fully equal division. Here, courts may point to special sacrifices made by one spouse, or the needs caused by a disability, or there may simply be an effort to compensate for the other spouse's greater earning capacity (especially if that earning capacity was developed during the marriage and through the first spouse's sacrifices).

While all states now have a no-fault option as a ground for divorce, many states have retained fault grounds as alternatives and, relevant to the current discussion, have retained some role for fault in the financial terms of divorce.[25] The role of fault in the decision of whether to award alimony in discussed in chapter 12. As regards property division, there are a range of roles fault might play (where it is allowed to play a role at all). In New York, fault can be a factor only in the most egregious cases.[26] Other courts create a lower threshold for bringing fault in as a factor in dividing property.[27]

---

25. Ira Mark Ellman, "The Place of Fault in Modern Divorce Law," *Arizona State Law Review*, vol. 28, pp. 773–837 (1996).

26. *See* Howard S. v. Lillian S., 62 A.D.3d 187, 876 N.Y.S.2d 351 (2009) (infidelity and concealment of parentage of a child not sufficiently egregious to be used as a factor affecting the equitable division of property).

27. *See* Sparks v. Sparks, 485 N.W.2d 893 (Mich. 1992) (fault is a legitimate factor, but only one factor among many others; lower court reversed for disproportionate weight given to fault factor); *N.H. Stat.* § 458:16-a(II)(l) (fault a factor to be considered in the equitable division of property, if the fault caused the breakdown in the marriage *and* either caused "substantial physical or mental pain and suffering" or caused "substantial economic loss"). The ALI *Principles* counted fifteen states that authorized their courts to take fault into account in dividing property. American Law Institute, *Principles of the Law of Family Dissolution* (Newark: LexisNexis, 2002), pp. 43–49, 68, 77–82.

Courts tend to be more comfortable taking into account faulty behavior that relates more directly to spending: this is the notion of "dissipation of assets"; even states that nominally exclude fault considerations from the decision about an equitable division of property will look at financial misconduct that affects the amount or property available for allocation. The clearest example of "dissipation" is where one spouse has spent significant marital funds giving gifts to an adulterous lover;[28] in such cases, courts will often compensate the innocent spouse in the division of property. However, one can also find dissipation cases based on types of spending less directly connected with marital misbehavior: large sums spent on gambling, stock speculation, or a drug addiction, especially if these expenses were incurred after it became clear that the marriage was ending.[29]

E. Conflict of Laws

A complicating factor in the division of property after divorce is the fact that couples move during the marriage and may be even more likely to move after the marriage breaks down, and this movement can lead to difficult questions about which state's laws should be applied to the division of the couple's property.[30] In principle, the state in which a couple was domiciled when property was acquired affects the legal rules about its control and disposition, such that a single couple could in principle have both community property and property subject to common law property rules. However, the

---

28. *E.g.*, Noll v. Noll, 375 S.E.2d 338 (S.C. App. 1988) (wife spent joint funds on cruise with boyfriend).
29. Siegel v. Siegel, 574 A.2d 54 (N.J. Super. Ct. Ch. Div. 1990) (husband's $227,000 gambling losses incurred after marriage "irreparably fractured" treated as dissipation).
30. For an excellent overview of the current complications of doctrine and practice (both across American jurisdictions and when crossing international borders), see J. Thomas Oldham, "What if the Beckhams Move to L.A. and Divorce? Marital Property Rights of Mobile Spouses When They Divorce in the United States," *Family Law Quarterly*, vol. 42, pp. 263–293 (2008).

reality is that neither divorcing parties nor family court judges (or, for that matter, appellate court judges) seem eager to enter this level of complexity, so divorce court rulings tend to ignore whatever conflict of laws rules might apply, generally just applying the forum state's rules regarding the characterization and division of property.[31]

✼ F. Short-Duration Marriages

In many states, if a marriage has ended after a relatively short duration, and with little commingling of funds, the courts have the discretion to divide property on the basis of title (or in some other way try to return the parties to approximately the same financial situation they were in prior to the marriage), rather than making an equitable division that disregards title.[32] This does not reflect any high principle (and certainly not a rejection of the general idea of "equitable division") but is simply a reflection of practical considerations: that neither the judge nor the parties want to go to the trouble and expense of equitable division of all the household's property, if a title-based division is likely to be much quicker, without creating significant injustice.

The sort of considerations that would discourage a simple title-based approach to dividing property at divorce—such as where one partner may have sacrificed in his or her job to help the household during the marriage, or there had been a substantial commingling of funds—are often absent in very short marriages. (In any event, by statute or case law, judges are usually only authorized to grant a title-based, former "status quo" division if it is shown that those sorts of factors are not present.)

---

31. *See id.*

32. *See, e.g.*, Rose v. Rose, 755 P.2d 1121 (Alaska 1988). California has a special "summary dissolution" procedure for marriages that lasted five years or less, there are no children to the marriage, the spouses have limited assets and liabilities, and both spouses waive any claim to alimony. *Cal. Fam. Code* §§ 2400–2406.

⁂ G. High-Income and High-Wealth Divorces

As noted in section D, above, property division tends toward fifty-fifty splits in most cases. However, there is one category of cases where the divisions (at least in reported cases) seem always to be fairly one-sided: those involving one high-earning spouse (a corporate executive, star athlete, or celebrity actor). In such cases, common law states tend to order an unequal division favoring the primary earner.[33] In these cases the differing property heritage of common law property states and community property states has a very clear impact. The estate's size has no effect on the foundational premise of equal ownership from which community property courts reason. The courts in common law states, by contrast, seem to have great difficulty justifying the transfer of so much property, for they have difficulty concluding that the homemaker's "contribution" was worth many millions of dollars, no matter how fine the homemaking job.

However, if conclusions regarding different levels of "contribution" are the basis of the unequal divisions in high-asset cases, then it is far from persuasive (and is, in some ways, self-refuting—for even a small percentage of a multi-million dollar estate will dwarf what is granted to comparable homemaking services in other marriages). If the basic idea of marriage is that the spouses are "in it together," for better and for worse, then a presumption of equal division is the logical starting point, and an exceptional ability to earn money is no more a justification for deviation than a particular facility at raising children. Any deviation from rough equality would seem to require justification. However, justification is rarely offered—and, where the courts start from a general order "to do equity" with no requirement or presumption of equal division, it is unusual to see

---

33. In community property states, the parties would come to the court each with an equal share of property obtained during the marriage, and it is unlikely, even with a higher-earning spouse, for a court to deviate significantly from that fifty-fifty split in its property division order, even in those jurisdictions where it is authorized to do so.

even fairly one-sided divisions overturned on appeal, especially when the spouse who gets the smaller portion of the household wealth is still being awarded many millions of dollars.[34]

⅏ H. Tax and Bankruptcy

It is important for parties going through a divorce (and, of course, for the lawyers counseling them) to understand the potential tax and bankruptcy implications of the financial terms of divorce. In a separation agreement, the parties come to some agreement regarding the division of household wealth, and one-time or periodic payments of one spouse to the other, where the periodic payments may be over a short period of time, a long period of time, indefinite, or ending upon some contingency. These are the descriptions that would matter to the payor and payee—how much, how often, and for how long—but for the purposes of family law doctrine and tax liability, labels matter. For family law purposes, child support and alimony are usually modifiable, property division is (with few exceptions) final. And alimony is treated as deductible to the payor for tax purposes, and income to the payee; property division and child support are not similarly deductible.

It is estimated that divorce plays a significant role in about a quarter of all bankruptcy filings, so the question of whether divorce-related obligations can be discharged in bankruptcy is crucial (and determining which sorts of debts can be discharged would also naturally affect parties' approaches to the negotiation of separation agreements). The federal Bankruptcy Abuse and Consumer Protection Act of 2005 (BAPCPA) has made it significantly harder for

---

34. *See* Ira Mark Ellman, Paul M. Kurtz, Lois A. Weithorn, Brian H. Bix, Karen Czapanskiy, & Maxine Eichner, *Family Law: Cases, Text, Problems* (5th ed., LexisNexis, 2010), pp. 342–343 (discussing the Wendt divorce case, in which a wife who was primarily a homemaker was granted $20 million of a $52 million estate). One can also see this trend in other countries: *see, e.g.,* Jack Shenker, "Biggest Divorce Settlement in British Legal History as Wife Gets £48m," *The Guardian,* Aug. 5, 2006 (against a context in which English courts had increasingly imposed fifty-fifty splits, homemaker wife received 37 percent of couples' property valued at £130 million).

ex-spouses to use bankruptcy procedures to avoid divorce-related obligations.[35] Even prior to the 2005 reforms, almost all support obligations (both child support and alimony) were nondischargeable in bankruptcy, allowing bankruptcy discharge only for a small subset of obligations relating to the division of property.

BAPCPA makes it much more difficult for consumers to discharge debts in Bankruptcy Chapter 7 (liquidation); debtors who have the means to repay a significant portion of their debt are forced into a repayment plan under Bankruptcy Chapter 13 (reorganization). However, if a consumer is in Chapter 7, both support and nonsupport debts arising from a divorce or separation are nondischargeable. BAPCPA has created a new broad category of "domestic support obligations," which includes not only child and spousal support obligations arising from a divorce but also obligations of unmarried parents to their children.

Suggested Further Reading

Division of Property

American Law Institute, *Principles of the Law of Family Dissolution: Analysis and Recommendations* (Newark: LexisNexis, 2002), chs. 4 and 5.

Charles Donahue, Jr., "What Causes Fundamental Legal Ideas? Marital Property in England and France in the Thirteenth Century," *Michigan Law Review*, vol. 78, pp. 59–88 (1979).

Carolyn J. Frantz & Hanoch Dagan, "Properties of Marriage," *Columbia Law Review*, vol. 104, pp. 75–133 (2004).

J. Thomas Oldham, *Divorce, Separation and the Distribution of Property* (Looseleaf Service; New York: Law Journal Press, 1987 & updates through 2012).

Tax

Pearlene Anklesaria, "Child Related Tax Breaks for Divorced Parents," *Journal of the American Academy of Matrimonial Lawyers*, vol. 22, pp. 425–435 (2009).

---

35. *See* Janet Leach Richards, "A Guide to Spousal Support and Property Division Claims Under the Bankruptcy Abuse Prevention and Consumer Protection Act of 2005," *Family Law Quarterly*, vol. 41, pp. 227–248 (2007).

Stephen P. Comeau, "An Overview of the Federal Income Tax Provisions Related to Alimony Payments," *Family Law Quarterly*, vol. 38, pp. 111–126 (2004).

Joanne Ross Wilder, "Divorce and Taxes: Fifty Years of Changes," *Journal of the American Academy of Matrimonial Lawyers*, vol. 24, pp. 489–504 (2012).

Richard J. Wood, *Family Tax Law* (Lake Mary, Fla.: Vandeplas Publishing, 2010).

Bankruptcy

Janet Leach Richards, "A Guide to Spousal Support and Property Division Claims Under the Bankruptcy Abuse Prevention and Consumer Protection Act of 2005," *Family Law Quarterly*, vol. 41, pp. 227–248 (2007).

Shayna M. Steinfeld, "The Impact of Changes Under the Bankruptcy Abuse Prevention and Consumer Protection Act of 2005 on Family Obligations," *Journal of the American Academy of Matrimonial Lawyers*, vol. 20, pp. 251–283 (2007).

Shayna M. Steinfeld & Bruce R. Steinfeld, *The Family Lawyer's Guide to Bankruptcy: Forms, Tips, and Strategies* (2nd ed., Chicago: ABA Publishing, 2008).

TWELVE

Alimony

※ A. History and General Principles

Alimony[1] is an award courts can make at divorce, that one ex-spouse make periodic payments to the other, payments that may be for a term of years ("temporary" or "rehabilitative" alimony) or may be indefinite ("permanent alimony"). It appears that alimony originated, in Roman law and as later developed in canon law, as a provisional award to a woman who was in litigation regarding her marital status.[2] First in the English ecclesiastical courts and later in the common law courts, alimony awards were expanded to include permanent awards to wives who no longer had husbands due to an award of a judicial separation.[3]

Historically, alimony was simply the obligation a husband had to support his wife, continuing even after the end of the marriage. The continuing obligation was justified, sometimes on the basis that it was the husband's fault that marriage had ended (alimony, like divorce, was a reward for the innocent and victimized spouse; even

---

1. Some states now prefer the label "maintenance," "spousal maintenance," or "spousal support" for what has traditionally been labeled "alimony." The text will use the traditional label.
2. R. H. Helmholz, "Canonical Remedies in Medieval Marriage Law: the Contributions of Legal Practice," *University of St. Thomas Law Journal*, vol. 1, pp. 647–655 (2003), at p. 653.
3. *Id.; see also* John Eekelaar & Mavis Maclean, *Maintenance After Divorce* (Oxford: Clarendon Press, 1986), pp. 1–18; Chester G. Vernier & John B. Hurlbut, "The Historical Background of Alimony Law and Its Present Statutory Structure," *Law & Contemporary Problems*, vol. 6, pp. 197–212 (1939).

today, there are some jurisdictions where adulterous spouses are legally prohibited from receiving alimony⁴), or because a combination of marital laws and social circumstances made it economically difficult for an ex-wife to support herself. When true divorce was not available, but only a kind of legal separation ("divorce *a mensa et thoro*," divorce "from bed and board"), the husband's continuing obligation to support his wife (who likely would have no means to support herself) made sense. And in the development of English divorce law, alimony was in part a central aspect of a compromise that led to the introduction of full legal divorce: spouses (in particular, husbands) would be allowed a complete divorce under certain circumstances, as long as it was understood that a husband's obligation to support his wife would often survive the dissolution of the marriage.

Though alimony is only awarded (or agreed to in a separation agreement) in a small fraction of divorce cases,⁵ it remains an important focus for debate regarding the proper understanding of marriage and divorce. It reflects our society's ideas about what the function of marriage is, what obligations spouses have to one another, the connection between those obligations and marital (mis-)behavior, and so forth.

There have been some significant changes in alimony in recent decades, in particular (1) the diminished role of marital fault;⁶

---

4. *E.g., Ga. Code* 19-6-1(a) ("A party shall not be entitled to alimony if it is established by a preponderance of the evidence that the separation between the parties was caused by that party's adultery or desertion."). Some courts would even terminate alimony based on "misconduct" that occurred after the divorce. *See, e.g.,* Weber v. Weber, 140 N.W.2d 1052 (Wis. 1913) (terminating support due to recipient's having chosen "a life of shame and dishonor").

5. For example, a study of Maryland divorces found that alimony was awarded (both in 1999 and 2003) in under 10 percent of the cases. The Women's Law Center of Maryland, Inc., *Families in Transition: A Follow-Up Study Exploring Family Law Issues in Maryland* (2006), pp. 16–17, available at http://www.wlcmd.org/publications.html.

6. A recent survey found that twenty-eight states and the District of Columbia still make marital fault a factor in the award of alimony. Linda D. Elrod & Robert G. Spector, "A Review of the Year in Family Law: Numbers of Disputes Increase," *Family Law Quarterly,* vol. 45, pp. 443–511 (2012), at pp. 492–493. However, in

(2) its availability to men as well as women; and (3) the availability of, and in some jurisdictions the preference for, short-term "reha-bilitative" alimony (in contrast to the traditional "permanent" ali-mony). Traditionally, permanent alimony was mandated for an indefinite period—though subject to modification for changed cir-cumstances and terminable upon the remarriage of the recipient or the death of either party. By contrast, rehabilitative alimony is meant to support a former spouse only long enough for that person to obtain the training or credentials required for self-support at a reasonable level.

Alimony awards have always been infrequent, relative to the number of marriages that end in divorce, though this infrequency may merely reflect the fact that many marriages end without sig-nificant marital assets, without children, or after only a few years of marriage, while alimony tends to be awarded only after long-term marriages, with a wealthy obligor former spouse, and a much less wealthy recipient former spouse whose income-earning has been harmed by many years working at home and perhaps having ongo-ing child-care obligations.

Both legislative and judicial pronouncements of the justifica-tions for alimony make frequent reference to "need," though here the term means a variety of things, most of which differ from the conventional use of that term. One meaning of "need" in the ali-mony context *does* track conventional usage, in that courts will frequently impose an award of alimony if not imposing an award would leave a former spouse below some minimum level of subsis-tence and perhaps dependent on state support (this, in turn reflects a persistent theme of American family law: the transfer of support awards from the state to the family where possible[7]). Some states

---

most of those jurisdictions, fault is simply one factor among a long list of fac-tors a court is directed to consider in determining the appropriate award.
7. This theme may be even more evident in the law of child support (the topic of chapter 14)—e.g., where many mechanisms have been developed to impose and enforce child support orders against unwed and absent fathers, even in situations where the mother is not seeking support from the father, and even

also create an express exception to the enforcement of premarital agreements in this area—refusing to enforce agreements waiving alimony rights where the absence of an alimony award would leave a former spouse on state support.[8]

Commonly, however, "need" in this context is understood to mean something like "the style of living to which a spouse had become accustomed in the marriage" (some jurisdictions and commentators refer to this argument not as one of "need" but as one of "status").[9] Especially after long-term marriages where a spouse (almost always the wife) has taken up the traditional homemaker role, courts will grant an alimony award that brings the recipient to or near the standard of living the recipient experienced during the marriage. The question is: what is the justification for such an award? It is not that courts think marriage automatically gives one the right to the marital standard of living, for alimony is rarely granted after a short marriage. Also, one must take into account the traditional rule (still followed in most but not all jurisdictions) that alimony ends upon the remarriage of the recipient.[10] This again recalls the older idea of a woman as being under the care (and the

---

where the unwed father's connection to the child would otherwise be sufficiently attenuated that he would lack standing to challenge adoptive placement of the child (under the standard of *Lehr v. Robertson*, 463 U.S. 248 (1983)).On the theme, generally, of viewing family law as about the privatization of care for the needy, see Martha Albertson Fineman, *The Neutered Mother, the Sexual Family, and Other Twentieth Century Tragedies* (New York: Routledge, 1995).

8. *See, e.g.*, Uniform Premarital Agreement Act, Section 6(b). Premarital agreements are discussed in chapter 10, section A.

9. According to a recent survey, all states but three direct courts to consider marital standard of living when deciding whether to award alimony. Linda D. Elrod & Robert G. Spector, "A Review of the Year in Family Law: Numbers of Disputes Increase," *Family Law Quarterly*, vol. 45, pp. 443–511 (2012), at p.492 (Chart 1).

10. As discussed in section C, *infra*, those states that do not have an automatic termination rule usually treat remarriage the same way most states treat cohabitation of the recipient: it does not automatically terminate the award, but it can justify a reduction or termination of the award if the cohabitation or remarriage has markedly improved the recipient's financial situation.

obligation of care) of a husband[11] more than it does any modern understanding of the nature of marriage and the relationship of spouses.

The practice of alimony has persisted in the United States, but its justification—and therefore also the circumstances and extent of the awards—has changed with time. One must think about alimony differently in its early context where divorce was difficult and rare (when not entirely unavailable), in a later context where divorce was available (though usually only to the "innocent and victimized spouse") but the economic opportunities for women in the workplace were limited, and in the current context where both the availability of divorce and the economic opportunities for women have increased significantly compared to prior eras.

Originally, some commentators had speculated that the combination of the moves toward no-fault divorce (discussed in chapter 9) and equitable division of property (discussed in chapter 11) would allow parties to have a "clean break" financially after divorce, with each spouse having no further financial connection or commitment after the property was divided, or perhaps a limited period of alimony was paid, allowing a stay-at-home spouse to reenter the workforce. However (even putting aside the long-term child support obligations that make true "clean breaks" unlikely for couples with minor children), it soon became clear that spouses (usually wives) who had spent decades as homemakers would have significant difficulties reentering the workforce and would likely never be able to earn an income that would make it possible to maintain anything like the lifestyle they enjoyed during their marriage.[12]

---

11. And in prior centuries, the idea was that a woman would always be under a man's care—first, under her father's care, until she was under a husband's care.

12. *See, e.g., In re* Marriage of Morrison, 573 P.2d 41 (Cal. 1978) (abuse of discretion to terminate alimony after eleven years, where there is no evidence that ex-wife, who had been homemaker during twenty-eight-year marriage, would be able to support herself).

Thus, permanent (indefinite) alimony has been retained in almost every jurisdiction[13] for situations of that kind.[14]

In either case, alimony in the modern legal and social context is not easy to justify. One modern rethinking of alimony, adopted by the American Law Institute,[15] has recharacterized it as the product of one or more compensatory payments to the recipient spouse, rather than as a discretionary form of support.[16] These payments would respond to claims relating, for example, to significant loss of earning capacity connected with a lengthy marriage or child-care obligations, and restitution of costs incurred to finance the other spouse's education (already mentioned).[17] Though rethinking alimony as more of an earned entitlement seems to have distinct theoretical and practical advantages, this view of alimony has not, to date, been adopted by any jurisdiction. Additionally, to the extent that the focus is on the losses incurred during married life (unconnected to any benefit conferred on the other spouse, which might be the basis for a kind of "restitutionary" award of alimony), the question remains why the ex-spouse (as opposed to the community generally) should have the responsibility (questions of "fault" aside) for compensating for those losses.[18]

---

13. Texas is one exception, as discussed in section F, *infra*.

14. Another fact scenario where long-term alimony seems appropriate is after a marriage of many years, in which one spouse made sacrifices while the other gained a professional degree or worked his or her way up a corporate hierarchy. The marriage might end at a point when the couple owns little, but one spouse has a future of great earning power made possible by the other spouse's sacrifices. *Cf.* DeLa Rosa v. DeLa Rosa 309 N.W.2d 755 (Minn. 1981) (award of reimbursement alimony to wife who supported husband through undergraduate and medical education).

15. This largely follows the earlier recommendations of its Chief Reporter, Ira Ellman. Ira Mark Ellman, "The Theory of Alimony," *California Law Review*, vol. 77, pp. 1–81 (1989).

16. American Law Institute, *Principles of the Law of Family Dissolution: Analysis and Recommendations* (Newark: LexisNexis, 2002), ch. 5. There are limits to the "entitlement" remaking of alimony. Unlike a true "entitlement" theory of alimony, the *ALI Principles* still presumes that awards end on the recipient's remarriage or the death of either party, *id.* at § 5.07, and allows for modification in some circumstances, *id.* at § 5.08.

17. *See id.*, §§ 5.04, 5.05, 5.12.

18. *See* Carl E. Schneider, "Rethinking Alimony: Marital Decisions and Moral Discourse," *BYU Law Review*, vol. 1991, pp. 197–257.

While property division and child support have become more predictable and uniform (within particular jurisdictions and also more homogenous across jurisdictions), alimony has remained relatively unpredictable:[19] it is not easy to foresee with any level of confidence either the duration and level of alimony that will be awarded in many cases, and it is likely that the outcome will vary significantly within a jurisdiction, depending on the vagaries of which judge hears the case. One approach to trying to make alimony more predictable, alimony guidelines, is discussed in section E, below.

One should also remember that while alimony and property division are conceptually and doctrinally distinct, parties negotiating settlement agreements, and many courts adjudicating divorce cases, will treat the two merely as alternative ways of settling the financial terms between the parties (money is money), with the differences primarily being in terms of whether payment is due all at once or over time, whether the obligation is subject to modification (for changed circumstances) or termination (e.g., upon the recipient's remarriage), the different tax consequences, and so on.

✼ B. Special Cases

One common fact scenario involves a couple where one spouse supports the other (usually, though not always, the wife supporting the husband) while the second spouse obtains an advanced educational degree or professional certification. Sometimes there is an understanding that the degree-holding spouse will then support the other spouse as that spouse works toward a degree or qualification. At other times, there is only the understanding or expectation that both spouses will benefit from the greater standard of living available once the credentials are earned.

---

19. What remains "predictable" is that alimony is granted in only a small minority of cases, and that even this modest frequency is likely to decrease with recent reforms in many states (discussed in this chapter).

Some jurisdictions have statutes or case law that speak directly to this sort of case: a sort of restitutionary alimony for the degree-holding spouse to pay back the supporting spouse for his or her support. These facts overlap a more general fact scenario: where the couple have been together a long time, and neither party has significant assets or income now, but one of them is about to start making a very high salary due to sacrifices made while the marriage was intact (e.g., medical school training, developing a new invention, or working one's way up the corporate hierarchy). There is an argument to be made that the other former spouse has a right to share in the future higher earning power, and one can find cases with facts like these where alimony is awarded.

✎ C. Remarriage or Cohabitation of the Recipient

There is a traditional rule, still followed in most jurisdictions, that alimony automatically terminates upon the recipient's remarriage. Some states have altered this slightly, to make the termination presumptive rather than automatic;[20] only a handful of states treat remarriage as cohabitation is generally treated (see below), merely as a factor indicating a potential decrease in need. However, the automatic termination rule seems to make sense only under the older model of women as inevitably dependent on some man (first father, then husband—and then second husband); it is a rule harder to justify under current social norms and social conditions.[21] If alimony is about entitlement, then that entitlement should survive remarriage.

---

20. In at least one case the "presumption" acts like a default rule that the parties can override by express agreement (or the court, by express prescription). *See, e.g., Mont. Code Ann.* § 40-4-208(4): *"Unless otherwise agreed in writing or expressly provided in the decree,* the obligation to pay future maintenance is terminated upon the death of either party or the remarriage of the party receiving maintenance" (emphasis added).

21. *See, e.g.*, Cynthia Lee Starnes, "One More Time: Alimony, Intuition, and the Remarriage-Termination Rule," *Indiana Law Journal*, vol. 81, pp. 971–999 (2006).

Even if alimony is sometimes about meeting minimal needs, and a new spouse is assumed to be a more appropriate source of support than a former spouse, that justification would hardly ground a rule of automatic (or even presumptive) termination. More appropriate would be the rule that simply looked at the recipient's marriage like any other factor (like a new job, gaining training or an academic degree, or a child's becoming self-sufficient) that may (or may not) have changed the recipient's ability to meet his or her basic needs.

The rule for nonmarital cohabitation (here we are talking about romantic cohabitation, not the cohabitation of roommates or boarders) is more mixed across jurisdictions. Some states treat such cohabitation, like remarriage, as the basis for automatic termination. The thinking here often is that, starting with the assumption that it is reasonable to terminate upon remarriage, one should not allow parties to circumvent the rule (and act contrary to the public interest in marriage) by cohabiting outside of marriage just to keep the alimony.

The modern trend is to treat cohabitation not as grounds for automatic termination but as grounds for potential reduction or termination, to the extent that the cohabitation reduces the alimony recipient's financial needs (sometimes a cohabitant brings additional resources to a household, but there are also times when what the cohabitant brings is mostly new debts).

🎚 D. Modification

Alimony (spousal support) awards, like child support awards (see chapter 14), are generally in principle modifiable in the face of substantially changed circumstances. However, unlike the case with child support, some states allow the parties, by express agreement, to make alimony nonmodifiable.[22]

---

22. *E.g., Minn. Stat.* § 518.552, subd. 5. In *Grachek v. Grachek*, 750 N.W.2d 328 (Minn. 2008), the court held that such a waiver would not preclude a recipient from seeking his or her statutory right to a cost-of-living increase in the alimony amount (*Minn. Stat.* § 518A.75).

It is important to understand how the different justifications of child support and alimony would warrant different approaches to modification in the two cases (even if one sometimes comes across cases where courts seem to have lost track of these differences). As child support is grounded on the idea that children should have (roughly) the same standard of living they would have had, had their parents still been together, and that they should share in any good fortune of their noncustodial parent, it makes sense that child support payments go up when the noncustodial parent's income goes up. And because child support is also supposed to be a function of the obligor's ability to pay and the child's need, payment obligations should go down when the obligor's income decreases and should usually increase when the custodial parent's income decreases.

The situation with alimony is less clear, for the justification for alimony has been more uncertain and contested, and one's view of the justification will naturally color one's view about modification. Traditionally, alimony was about the recipient's "need," with "need" (as already noted) understood broadly to include either, at one end of the scale, minimum requirements and, at the other end of the scale, a high standard of living to which the alimony recipient had become accustomed during a long marriage. Under this approach, an increased income for the obligor would not normally seem to be justification for increased alimony, as it does not affect either minimal needs or the standard of living during a prior marriage.[23]

A different approach would be appropriate if alimony is seen as something the recipient spouse has *earned*, though it matters in which way the alimony is thought to be an entitlement. To the extent that one sees alimony as one spouse's claim on a portion of the other spouse's increased earning power, then an increase in the

---

23. The exception would be if a court had decided that the recipient spouse merited a certain level of support, but the court imposed a lower level because the obligor spouse could not, at the time of the original order, afford to pay the merited payment level. If the obligor spouse has increased income, and now can afford the merited level, then an increase to that level would be appropriate.

obligor's income should be reflected in increased alimony. To the extent that the alimony is a reimbursement for lost income or lost earning capacity, then an increase in the obligor's income would not seem to be relevant.[24]

✂ E. Alimony Guidelines

As discussed in chapter 14, child support is now determined everywhere by guidelines. The presumptive amount of support is determined by a formula that (in almost all jurisdictions) uses the income of the obligor parent or the income of both parents. While there has been significant debate about the merits of such guidelines, there is little doubt that they have made child support determinations more consistent and predictable. Could something similar be done for and to alimony? According to one review, at least twelve states have experimented, either at a statewide level or at the county level, with guidelines for setting alimony, or alimony *pendente lite* (preliminary alimony, paid during the period between when the petition for divorce is filed and the final divorce judgment).[25] However, these guidelines tend to give only rough or "rule of thumb" guidance as to whether to order alimony, or at what level. They tend to set a minimum duration of the marriage before alimony can be awarded, a preference for rehabilitative or permanent alimony, and, occasionally, some formula for determining the level of support.

The effort of the American Academy of Matrimonial Lawyers (AAML) to make more specific and detailed alimony guidelines,

---

24. Again, unless the increase takes the obligor from a position of not being able to afford the full level of earned alimony to being able to afford it.

25. Virginia R. Dugan & Jon A. Feder, "Alimony Guidelines: Do They Work?," *Family Advocate*, vol. 25(4), pp. 20–23 (2003); *see also* Carol Rogerson & Rollie Thompson, "The Canadian Experiment with Spousal Support Guidelines," *Family Law Quarterly*, vol. 45, pp. 241–269 (2011); J. Thomas Oldham, "Changes in the Economic Consequences of Divorces, 1958–2008," *Family Law Quarterly*, vol. 42, pp. 419–447 (2008), at pp. 438–446.

promulgated in 2007,[26] has had some influence. At least one appellate court has authorized the use of these guidelines—as a factor among other factors—in the determination of the amount and duration of alimony.[27] Also, the Family Court of Maricopa County, Arizona (Phoenix), adopted guidelines, but the appellate court in that state did not approve their use.[28]

One barrier for alimony guidelines is that the varied purposes for alimony affect perceptions of the appropriate amount. For this reason, any suggested set of guidelines is unlikely to seem appropriate across the full range of cases. In the AAML guidelines, "deviation factors" are presented that would justify outcomes different from the presumptive amounts and duration set by the guidelines,[29] similar to the justifications for "deviation" one finds in child support guidelines.

✎ F. Other Limits and Reforms

A number of states have passed legislation significantly reducing, or at least constraining, the availability and award of alimony. In Texas,

26. *See* Mary Kay Kisthardt, "Rethinking Alimony: The AAML's Considerations for Calculating Alimony, Spousal Support or Maintenance," *Journal of the American Academy of Matrimonial Lawyers*, vol. 21, pp. 61–85 (2008). The guidelines are listed in the Kisthardt article and are also available at http://www.aaml.org/library/articles/considerations-when-determining-alimony/.

27. Boemio v. Boemio, 994 A.2d 911 (Md. App. 2010).

28. *See* Ira Mark Ellman, "The Maturing Law of Divorce Finances: Toward Rules and Guidelines," *Family Law Quarterly*, vol. 33, pp. 801–814 (1999); *compare* Cullum v. Cullum, 160 P.3d 231 (Ariz. App. Div. 2007) (use of spousal maintenance guidelines did not invalidate spousal award) *with* Leathers v. Leathers, 166 P.3d 929, 932 n.1 (Ariz. App. 2007) (declaring that use of guidelines is an "inappropriate analytic shortcut"). For a discussion of recent use of alimony "guidelines," see Twila Larkin, "Guidelines for Alimony: The New Mexico Experiment," *Family Law Quarterly*, vol. 38, pp. 29–68 (2004).

29. Under the AAML guidelines, the presumptive alimony amount is establishing by subtracting 20 percent of the recipient's gross income from 30 percent of the obligor's gross income—the total not to exceed 40 percent of the combined gross income of both parties. The presumptive duration is set by multiplying the length of the marriage by different multipliers: 0–3 years (0.3 multiplier); 3–10 years (0.5); 10–20 years (0.75); and permanent alimony for marriages over twenty years.

alimony beyond three years can be awarded only if the recipient, or a child in the recipient's custody, is physically or mentally disabled.[30] In Maine, there is a "rebuttable presumption" that alimony will not be awarded for marriages lasting less than ten years; and also one that alimony will not last longer than half the duration of the marriage, for marriages lasting between ten and twenty years.[31] In 2011, Massachusetts passed "alimony reform," which offered a combination of limits and guidelines: for marriages lasting five years or less, alimony may not last longer than half the number of months of the marriage; for 5–10 years, 60 percent of the number of months of the marriage; for 10–15 years, 70 percent; for 15–20 years, 80 percent; and for marriages above twenty years (only), indefinite ("permanent") alimony may be awarded. However, even for permanent alimony and for all other forms of alimony, (1) alimony will be terminated on the remarriage of the recipient; (2) it may be reduced or terminated upon the cohabitation of the recipient; and (3) alimony will terminate upon the obligor's reaching "full retirement age."[32]

Debates about limiting alimony raise in a sharp way the underlying question of what justifies alimony in the first place. It may well be that "alimony" covers a number of different and overlapping claims: long-term entitlements for spouses in long marriages who gave up a great deal during the years married; medium-term

---

30. *Tex. Fam. Code Ann.* §§ 8.051, 8.054, 8055. Texas also places a cap on the percentage of a spouse's income that he or she can be ordered to pay in alimony. *Id.*, §§ 8.054, 8.055. Prior to legislation in 1995, Texas courts had no power to order alimony at all. The Texas courts do, however, have the power to enforce alimony, even beyond these restrictions, as a contractual matter, if the parties agree to it in their separation agreement. McCollough v. McCollough, 212 S.W.3d 638 (Tex. App. 2006).

31. *Me. Rev. Stat.* tit. 19-A, § 951-A(2). The same provision names "transitional support," "reimbursement support," and "nominal support" as other types of alimony available, the last being awarded "to preserve the court's authority to grant spousal support in the future."

32. *Mass. General Laws*, Ch. 208, § 49. Some of the terms above may be changed by express agreement of the parties, or deviated from by the court based on express findings. *See id.*

rehabilitation alimony to allow spouses who have sacrificed during marriage, to allow those people to obtain the training, credentials, or degrees they need to sustain themselves; reimbursement alimony for those who supported spouses through a long degree or training process; and an indefinite alimony meant to divide up future earning capacity developed during the marriage when the payoff occurs only or mostly after divorce. Because these different types of alimony are grounded on different sorts of justifications, they may warrant different rules for whether and when they can be modified or terminated.

Suggested Further Reading

American Law Institute, *Principles of the Law of Family Dissolution: Analysis and Recommendations* (Newark: LexisNexis, 2002), ch. 5.

June Carbone, "Economics, Feminism, and the Reinvention of Alimony: A Reply to Ira Ellman," *Vanderbilt Law Review*, vol. 43, pp. 1463–1501 (1990).

Ira Mark Ellman, "The Theory of Alimony", *California Law Review*, vol. 77, pp. 1–81 (1989).

Gaytri Kachroo, "Mapping Alimony: From Status to Contract and Beyond," *Pierce Law Review*, vol. 5, pp. 163–270 (2007).

Carl E. Schneider, "Rethinking Alimony: Marital Decisions and Moral Discourse," *BYU Law Review*, vol. 1991, pp. 197–257.

Cynthia Lee Starnes, "One More Time: Alimony, Intuition, and the Remarriage-Termination Rule," *Indiana Law Journal*, vol. 81, pp. 971–999 (2006).

___, "Alimony Theory," *Family Law Quarterly*, vol. 45, pp. 271–291 (2011).

THIRTEEN

Custody, Modification, Relocation, Visitation

≋ A. Custody: History and General Principles

For many divorces, the most contentious disputes relate to how custodial responsibility over the children of the marriage will be divided between the parents.[1] What can make custody battles[2] especially bitter is that, unlike the division of property at divorce (though like awards of alimony or maintenance), custody issues are not put to rest with the trial court's decision. It is usually open to a parent unhappy with the court's decision not only to appeal the decision but also to ask at a later point for a modification of the custody order. Finally, a court's custody order for a child can be made more problematic if a custodial parent later decides to relocate out of state or out of the country, causing difficulties for a child's ability to maintain regular contact with the other parent. With so much at stake and the standards for decision making so amorphous and decisions so unpredictable, some scholars have, half-seriously, suggested that deciding most custody cases by a coin-flip would be a significant improvement over the status quo.[3]

---

1. It is important to note that custody battles can and do occur between parents who have never married and can also occur between a parent and a nonparent. Some issues relating to parent vs. nonparent custody disputes will be considered later in this chapter.

2. A number of states have changed terminology, not referring only to "parenting time." This text will follow the conventional terminology of "custody" and "visitation."

3. *See, e.g.*, Robert H. Mnookin, "Child-Custody Adjudication: Judicial Functions in the Face of Indeterminacy," *Law and Contemporary Problems*, vol. 39, pp. 226–293 (1975), at pp. 289–291.

Going back centuries and into the English law origins of American law, child custody decisions had once been relatively straightforward. The classical rule (not just of old English law but also of ancient Roman law) had been that children were the property of their father,[4] so it was a rare case where the mother got custody. In the eighteenth and nineteenth centuries, the states slowly moved to a strong maternal preference, at least for younger children.[5] That move coincided with a change in rhetorical/justificatory focus, from the rights of the parents to the "best interests of the children," and also coincided with a greater recognition of the property rights of married and divorced women.[6]

While modern custody standards tend to be phrased in terms of the "best interests of the child," within that amorphous, effectively discretionary standard, courts and legislatures have endorsed more specific principles, for example, favoring parents over nonparents, taking account of the child's preference, not taking account of the possible effects of racial discrimination, favoring continuity of care, and so on (this chapter will consider many of those principles in greater detail). Additionally, partly as a way of getting out of the business of judging parents on moral matters, many courts have established a "nexus test": that charges of a parent's allegedly immoral behavior (adultery, homosexuality, polygamy, etc.) will be

---

4. Though in Roman law it might have been more precise to say that children were the property of the oldest male ancestor (the *paterfamilias*), which in many households was the grandfather, not the father. Paul du Plessis, *Borkowski's Textbook on Roman Law* (4th ed., Oxford: Oxford University Press, 2010), p. 110.

5. For an excellent discussion of an 1840 case that marked and accelerated the move from a strong presumption of paternal custody to a presumption of maternal custody for children of "tender years," see Michael Grossberg, *A Judgment for Solomon: The D'Hauteville Case and Legal Experience in Antebellum America* (Cambridge: Cambridge University Press, 1996). For an overview of the changed thinking during this period about children, custody, and adoption, see Jamil S. Zainaldin, "The Emergence of a Modern American Family Law: Child Custody, Adoption, and the Courts, 1796–1851," *Northwestern University Law Review*, vol. 73, pp. 1038–1089 (1979).

6. *See* Lucy S. McGough, "Protecting the Children in Divorce: Lessons from Caroline Norton," *Maine Law Review*, vol. 57, pp. 14–37 (2005), at pp. 14–18.

relevant to custody decisions only to the extent that the behavior can be shown directly to affect the person's competence as a parent.[7] One should also note that the preference of the child will often be taken into account in custody decisions, especially if it is an older child.[8]

1. Best Interests of the Child

Under current law in the United States and in many other countries, most court decisions regarding a child—not just custody decisions—must be grounded on a judgment regarding which option would be in that child's "best interests." By its nature, this is a vague standard rather than a precise rule, more a broad delegation of authority combined with a direction to focus on the perspective of the child (rather than on the claims and interests of other parties). At the same time, this amorphous standard has the potential to hide significant bias and to either cover or encourage arbitrary and inconsistent decision making.

The traditional English law giving (married) fathers rights to their children in case of divorce changed with the Custody of Infants Act, 1839,[9] which gave mothers ("of unblemished character") the right to seek custody of children under the age of seven after a legal separation or divorce. Both the English and American courts quickly moved toward what became known as the "tender years presumption," that young children (usually understood as seven years old or

---

7. One influential source for the "nexus test" is the Uniform Marriage and Divorce Act, § 402, originally adopted in 1970. While the "nexus test" is most commonly established by court rule, one can also find it grounded in a legislative enactment. *See, e.g.*, 750 *Ill. Compiled Stat.* 5/602(b); *Minn. Stat.* § 518.17(13)(b). For its history and application in connection with gay parents, see Michael S. Wald, "Adults' Sexual Orientation and State Determinations Regarding Placement of Children," *Family Law Quarterly*, vol. 40, pp. 381–434 (2006).

8. *See, e.g., Tex. Fam. Code* § 153.009; *Minn. Stat.* § 518.17(2).

9. 2 & 3 Vict., c. 54.

younger) would go to the mother, unless she was shown to be unfit. Though the new rule could be seen as simply a change from a paternal to a maternal presumption of custody for young children, what was significant was the alteration in the underlying justification: the paternal presumption had been based on a sort of property right the father had in his children; the maternal presumption was grounded on arguments regarding what would be in the best interests of the children. Over time, the justificatory language of "best interests" turned into a standard itself: a legislative or judicial rule that custody decisions should be grounded on the best interests of the children.

Most American states have a statute directing courts to consider a long list of factors in coming to their decision regarding which custody outcome is in a child's "best interests," but the statutes usually offer little guidance as to the relative weight to be given to different factors (sometimes guidance has been added by subsequent judicial decisions, but usually significant discretion and indeterminacy remain).

In American child custody law today, "best interests" remains the ultimate touchstone, the underlying justification offered for choosing one standard for decision over another, but in many jurisdictions the actual rules may be more specific: for example, a presumption for joint legal or physical custody, a presumption for custody by the "primary caretaker," a strong preference for parents over nonparents in custody disputes, or deference to the stated custody preference of an older child.

It is interesting to note the way that the legal presumption most states have adopted for parents against nonparents in custody decisions grew out of a reaction against a particular "best interests" analysis: the Iowa Supreme Court's decision in the notorious 1966 case of *Painter v. Bannister*,[10] where the court argued that placement with more traditional grandparents in Iowa would be more

---

10. Painter v. Bannister, 140 N.W.2d 152 (1966).

conducive to a child's "best interests" than returning the child to his "bohemian" father in California. In response to that decision many states, by statute or court decision, established a standard that a nonparent should prevail against a parent in a custody case only if the nonparent meets a heightened standard (not merely that it would be in the best interests of the child to be with the nonparent, but something additional: often a requirement of showing that custody with the parent would be affirmatively harmful to the child[11]).

The focus on children's "best interests" has also been the moving and justifying force behind the "nexus test" in custody decisions adopted by a growing number of jurisdictions; this standard holds irrelevant all accusations of parental immorality (accusations of adultery, promiscuity, homosexuality, or polygamy had in earlier times been determinative in many custody battles), except in the unusual case where such alleged immoralities can be shown to affect directly the well-being of the children under care.

There are occasions when the rules regarding custody and visitation more clearly subordinate children's interests to other concerns—whether parental rights (e.g., in the way that it takes a significant show of harm to a child before a court will cut off a legal parent's right to visitation, or give custody to a nonparent in a custody fight with a parent) or societal interests (e.g., regarding when courts are allowed to take race or religion into account in their rulings regarding custody and visitation[12]—topics considered later in this chapter).

----

11. We saw in chapter 4 how this preference for parents over nonparents in custody and visitation matters has had the (unintended and unforeseen) consequence, when same-sex couples raise a child together, of frequently allowing one same-sex partner to exclude the other partner from contact with the child after the couple breaks up.

12. There have also been cases where the appellate court has directed trial courts in custody decisions not to assume that care at home would be better for a child than alternative child-care arrangements, like day care, for such an assumption would have the effect of discriminating against working mothers. *See, e.g.*, Burchard v. Garay, 42 Cal. 3d 531, 724 P.2d 486, 229 Cal. Rptr. 800 (1986). Not penalizing working mothers who use day care might be the right policy, for many reasons, but given fairly consistent social science data that day care

The "best interests" standard does not assume any particular theory of child development or child psychology, but can in fact work in tandem with or incorporate any such theory—for these are basically competing theories about what would be in the best interests of children. The "best interests" standard has also become common—now, the rule rather than the exception—in other jurisdictions and in international law. For example, the United Nations Convention on the Rights of the Child states: "In all actions concerning children, whether undertaken by public or private social welfare institutions, courts of law, administrative authorities or legislative bodies, the best interests of the child shall be a primary consideration."[13]

Those skeptical of the use of "best interests" standards raise various concerns. Some commentators are worried that the "best interests" standard gives too much discretion to judges, thus (1) creating too much disparity in outcomes among cases; (2) undermining any sense of predictability; and (3) creating too much of an opening for improper, and hidden, motives and reasons for decisions. Related to the above objections, one consequence of a relatively open-ended and discretionary decision standard, as contrasted to a standard more constrained by presumptions (e.g., a presumption for maternal custody, or a presumption for an equal split in physical custody), is that the uncertainty both encourages litigation and leads many who value custody (more often mothers than fathers) to give up property and alimony rights in order to establish their custody rights in a separation agreement. And the litigation that is encouraged is often harmful both to the children themselves, as well as to the parents, because the litigation will inevitably focus on each parent accusing the other of being unfit—or, at least, less fit—often an expensive and acrimonious process.[14]

---

tends to have less good outcomes than parental care at home, it might be better if courts were more up front about the choice to trade off some amount of "best interests of the child" for other societal interests.

13. United Nations Convention on the Rights of the Child, Article 3, point 1. That Convention was ratified in 1989.

14. There are also circumstances where a "best interests" standard risks misleading decision makers. For example, with adoption (the topic of chapter 5), the

Additionally, some commentators are troubled that a too-great focus on children's interests will lead to an undermining of the rights and interests of parents or the proper claims of certain communities (e.g., American Indian tribes, or certain racial and ethnic groups) to which the children belong.[15] Finally, some have argued that the standards and procedures developed to protect "the best interests of the child" in fact work only to protect the interests of a certain class of adults, often in conflict with children's real interests.[16]

2. Race, Gender, Religion

One of the most contentious issues in American family law is the proper role of race in placement decisions regarding children—adoption, foster care, and also custody decisions (see chapter 5, section E).

In the 1984 case of *Palmore v. Sidoti*, the U.S. Supreme Court held that a custody decision could not be grounded on the fact that the mother resided in a mixed-race household and the negative consequences this could have for the child.[17] The Court held that while racial prejudice is a fact of life, and may affect the welfare of

---

language of "best interests" seems to direct decision makers to find the best possible placement for a child, rejecting all others. However, this could lead an agency or court to reject quite adequate placement options, on the basis that a better placement might be available at a later time. The effect, however, would be to let children languish in foster or institutional care when loving homes are available. The better understanding of "best interests" in such cases would be to inquire whether the placement in question is in the best interests of the child, taking into account the current alternatives and those likely available in the near future (where a suboptimal but clearly loving home placement would arguably almost always be preferable to current institutional care combined with uncertain long-term prospects).

15. See the discussion of race-matching in adoption (chapter 5, section E), and the Indian Child Welfare Act (chapter 5, section F).

16. A trenchant critique of both "best interests" and "children's rights" analyses can be found in Martin Guggenheim, *What's Wrong with Children's Rights* (Cambridge, Mass.: Harvard University Press, 2005).

17. Palmore v. Sidoti, 466 U.S. 429 (1984).

children, courts are constitutionally forbidden to use other people's racist beliefs as a basis for custody decisions.

The question remains whether race can be used in other ways in custody decisions. On one side are those who argue that in our racially sensitive society, one is labeled under a racial category and will often suffer discrimination and stereotyping under that category, whether one accepts the racial label or not; therefore, it is valuable for a child be raised by a family who shares the racial category the child will carry. Additionally, as mentioned in chapter 5, some commentators and advocates have argued that the placement of minority children in white households is itself a form of racism, or a kind of attack on minority communities.[18] On the other side, there are moral and constitutional arguments that race should never be used in the placement of a child (either for race-matching purposes or otherwise).[19] Additionally, the argument is made that attempts at race-matching often have the practical effect that children are kept from loving parents and are left in foster care or institutional care longer than they otherwise would be.[20] Federal statutes now clearly favor the second position: federal legislation denies federal funding to any institution that uses race as a basis for denying or delaying the placement of a child.[21]

However, one must keep in mind that adoption decisions (the placement of a child into a new home) are distinctly different from custody decisions (usually a choice between two legal parents).

---

18. National Association of Black Social Workers, "Preserving Families of African Ancestry" (2003), available at http://www.nabsw.org/mserver/PreservingFamilies.aspx; *see also* Ruth-Arlene W. Howe, "Race Matters in Adoption," *Family Law Quarterly*, vol. 42, pp. 465–479 (2008).

19. *See, e.g.,* Ralph Richard Banks, "The Multiethnic Placement Act and the Troubling Persistence of Race Matching," *Capital University Law Review*, vol. 38, pp. 271–290 (2009).

20. *See* Elizabeth Bartholet, "Where Do Black Children Belong? The Politics of Race Matching in Adoption," *University of Pennsylvania Law Review*, vol. 139, pp. 1163–1256 (1991).

21. Removal of Barriers to Interethnic Adoption Act of 1996, Pub. L. No. 104-188, 110 Stat. 1904, codified at 42 U.S.C. § 622.

In this context, the courts have been less hostile to the use of race as a factor, at least when this use is tightly constrained. In particular, appellate courts have regularly approved decisions that appear to be using race in a *positive* way rather than a negative way (the value of having a custodial parent with the same racial identification, rather than responding to racial prejudice, as occurred in *Palmore v. Sidoti*), and using race as merely one factor among many and not as an overwhelming factor.[22]

Many observers believe that gender plays a large role in the biases and predilections of family court judges. As already discussed, there is a long tradition in Anglo-American family law of the gender of the parent seeking custody being the major factor in custody decisions. As already discussed, early English family law, perhaps borrowing from ancient Roman law,[23] held that in the case of divorce, the father should have custody of the children based on a kind of property right. However, beginning in the nineteenth century, English and American courts developed the view that it was "contrary to nature" and against the best interests of the children involved for younger children, at least, to be separated from their mothers. This "tender years doctrine" created a strong presumption of maternal custody for young children.

While express gender biases are no longer allowed,[24] there is strong anecdotal evidence, and some social science evidence, that many judges tend to favor mothers over fathers in custody matters, especially for younger children. (Courts who do not want to

---

22. Courts will sometimes go further and state that race can never be the "deciding factor." However, if race is ever a legitimate factor, one that carries *any* weight, then there will (potentially) be times, when, because all other factors are equal, race *will* be the deciding factor.

23. Where the eldest living male ancestor, the *paterfamilias*, was head of the household and had power over all of his descendants. *See, e.g.*, Paul du Plessis, *Borkowski's Textbook on Roman Law* (4th ed., Oxford: Oxford University Press, 2010), p. 110.

24. They would be contrary to the current understanding of the Constitution's equal protection norm. *See* Devine v. Devine, 398 So.2d 686 (Ala. 1981) (invalidating "tender years" presumption on constitutional sex equality grounds); *cf.* Orr v. Orr, 440 U.S. 268 (1979) (invalidating law that allowed women to be awarded alimony but not men).

be reversed would never state that the decision was based solely on the gender of the parent; however, almost any outcome can be justified under the vague prescriptions of "best interests of the child" and the long list of relevant factors given by state custody statutes.) And in a social situation where mothers remain far more likely than fathers to do most of the parenting prior to the custody decision, there are likely, in any event, to be ample reasons of experience, competence, and continuity of care, for frequently favoring mothers over fathers.

Additionally, one sometimes comes across cases where it is the gender of the child, rather than the gender of the parent, that seems salient to the court. There are occasional cases where a court seems inclined to place adolescent children with parents of the same sex.

As regards religion, family court judges never like to deal with those issues in custody debates because such issues create tensions between two strong prescriptions. The First Amendment to the U.S. Constitution requires that the government neither interfere with religious freedom nor establish a favored religion, and a custody decision grounded on one parent's religious belief could arguably be seen as doing one or both of those prohibited actions (by implying that one religion was better than another—or that religious belief in one parent was better than its absence in the other—or that one religion's practices were subject to civil sanction). On the other hand, religious beliefs often lead to religious practices, including practices that could be said to affect the best interests of children (questions of religious truth aside). These religion-connected practices could include alienating the child from its other parent (telling a child that the other parent is "evil" or "going to hell" because that other parent does not share the religious beliefs of the first parent); isolating the child from other children (perhaps encouraging a distance from nonbelievers); preventing the child from taking part in parties, dancing, or Halloween (because they are considered immoral); or refusing various forms of medical care on religious grounds (as occurs with Christian Science believers and Jehovah's Witnesses).

The working compromise is that courts will usually ignore or discount parenting practices to the extent that those practices reflect sincere religious beliefs, but practices that cause current (and not just potential) and significant harm to the child *can* be the basis for a custody decision in favor of the other parent. Sometimes, the custody decision might be split, with one parent having authority over (for example) health-care matters if the court is concerned about the other parent's (religiously motivated or otherwise) health-care decision making.[25]

The most difficult questions, perhaps, involve religiously motivated medical decision making. In all religious matters, courts will attempt to distinguish evaluating sincere religious beliefs and evaluating actions (including actions motivated by those sincere religious beliefs). As noted, courts feel more comfortable making custody decisions based on how a parent's actions (whatever his or her motivation) affect the best interests of the child, and courts will often go to some length to avoid any appearance of basing a custody decision on a religious belief. For example, in *Harrison v. Tauheed*,[26] the court refused to deny custody to the mother, who was a Jehovah's Witness, based either on her religious belief regarding refusal of medical treatment or on "speculation" about potential religiously motivated medical decisions in the future (that Jehovah's Witnesses refuse blood transfusions on religious grounds).

In the same case, the trial court had considered arguments that the mother's religious beliefs were alienating the child from his father, were isolating the child from his peers, and were making the child anxious. The Kansas Supreme Court (largely endorsing the approach of the trial court) noted on one hand that certain effects on a child may be due to society's disapproval of nonmajority religions, and the court could not indirectly endorse such views by

---

25. *See, e.g.*, Winters v. Brown, 51 So.3d 656 (Fla. Ct. App. 2011), review denied, 67 So.3d 201 (Fla. 2011) (father granted custody over health-care matters due to mother's religiously motivated refusal to give the child immunizations).
26. 256 P.3d 851 (Kan. 2011).

basing custody decisions upon them.[27] On the other hand, the court also noted that alienation of a child from the other parent could not be allowed or endorsed even when it has religious roots (e.g., a belief that nonbelievers in the faith are evil or will be damned).[28] The role of religion in family court decisions are considered further in chapter 16.

3. Jurisdiction

As discussed in chapter 9, the constitutional requirements for a court to have jurisdiction to grant a divorce and set the financial terms of a divorce are well settled (the divorce can be granted in a state where either partner is domiciled; personal jurisdiction over the defendant is required for financial orders). By contrast, the constitutional requirements for jurisdiction for custody orders are confused and (strangely) largely ignored—with all of the focus going to statutory rules.

The only Supreme Court decision on custody jurisdiction, the 1953 case of *May v. Anderson*,[29] held by a plurality opinion that where a child custody decision was made by a court that did not have personal jurisdiction over the child (in the case in question, the other spouse had moved with the children to another state), courts in other states are not constitutionally required (by the Constitution's Full Faith and Credit Clause[30]) to enforce those judgments. Justice Felix Frankfurter, the necessary fifth vote in *May*, held that personal jurisdiction is required for "full faith and credit" status, but decrees made without personal jurisdiction over the child did not offend

---

27. Note the parallel with the race case of *Palmore v. Sidoti*, discussed earlier in this chapter, and note how, once again, the court is (at least potentially) subordinating the best interests of the child to parental rights or social policy, but the court does not characterize what it is doing that way.
28. *Harrison v. Tauheed*, 256 P.3d at 866–867.
29. 345 U.S. 528 (1953).
30. U.S. Const., art. IV, § 1.

constitutional "due process" requirements (and thus would remain enforceable in the state of the decree).

One does occasionally come across a case that takes *May* seriously (while also usually ignoring Frankfurter's concurrence),[31] but these are quite rare relative to the vast number of cases deciding custody, almost always with little regard to personal jurisdiction.[32] "Full faith and credit," in any event, would have been of limited use, as that provision requires other states to give a judgment as much force as it had in the state where it was given, and custody decisions are almost always subject to modification. Therefore, a second state could give "full faith and credit" to the original custody order and still give a different custody outcome (on the basis, e.g., that there had been some substantial change in circumstances).

The focus, instead, is on the criteria set by statutes. Traditionally, state laws had required that the child subject to the custody dispute be in the jurisdiction, with no focus on whether the court had personal jurisdiction over the other parent. Modern federal statutes (like the Parental Kidnapping Prevention Act[33]) and uniform state laws (like the Uniform Child Custody Jurisdiction and Enforcement Act) relating to child custody decision require that there be sufficient connections between the state hearing the dispute and the custody issue, without any specific finding of personal jurisdiction over either the child or the other parent (these rules will be discussed further in sections B and C, below).

---

31. *See, e.g.*, Pasqualone v. Pasqualone, 406 N.E.2d 1121 (Ohio 1980); *In re* Dean, 447 So. 2d 733 (Ala. 1984).

32. *See generally* Russell M. Coombs, "Interstate Child Custody: Jurisdiction, Recognition, and Enforcement," *Minnesota Law Review*, vol. 66, pp. 711–864 (1982); *but see* Barbara Ann Atwood, "Child Custody Jurisdiction and Territoriality," *Ohio State Law Journal*, vol. 52, pp. 369–403 (1991) (offering an intriguing argument that the UCCJA and PKPA follow the spirit of Frankfurter's concurrence in *May*).

33. 28 U.S.C. § 1738A.

4. Joint Custody

As previously mentioned, the history of Anglo-American child custody law is one of gendered presumptions: for a long time, a paternal presumption, with the father having a sort of ownership right over his children; more recently, a maternal presumption, at least for younger children.

The maternal presumption was undermined by constitutional law cases invalidating discrimination on the basis of sex and also by social norms that pushed in the same direction.[34] At least two states, West Virginia and Minnesota, briefly experimented with a gender-neutral version of the maternal presumption, the primary caretaker presumption,[35] but each abandoned the experiment. The American Law Institute has advocated for a different but related presumption: one which would reproduce, approximately, the allocation of parenting time between the parents that had occurred during the marriage.[36] This standard has been largely adopted by one state, West Virginia.[37]

The traditional gendered presumptions have disappeared; as already discussed, without a presumption, however, courts are frequently left with only an all-things-considered "best interests of the child" standard (in which "primary caretaker" or "continuity of care" may well be one of the factors expressly included, but they remain just one or two factors among many). As mentioned, this amorphous standard creates unpredictability: inviting costly litigation,

34. *See, e.g.,* Devine v. Devine, 398 So.2d 686 (Ala. 1981) (invalidating "tender years" presumption on constitutional sex equality grounds); *cf.* Orr v. Orr, 440 U.S. 268 (1979) (invalidating law that allowed women to be awarded alimony but not men).

35. *See* Garska v. McCoy, 278 S.E.2d 357 (W. Va. 1981); Pikula v. Pikula, 374 N.W.2d 705 (Minn. 1985).

36. American Law Institute, *Principles of the Law of Family Dissolution* (Newark: LexisNexis, 2002), § 2.08(1), at p. 178. The approximation idea originated with Elizabeth Scott. Elizabeth S. Scott, "Pluralism, Parental Preference, and Child Custody," *California Law Review,* vol. 80, pp. 615–672 (1992).

37. *See W. Va. Code Ann.* § 48-9-206.

and of a particularly unpleasant sort (since a premium is placed on making the other parent appear incompetent or dangerous to the child).

In recent times, there has been a lot of talk (by both commentators and courts) of "joint custody," though much of the discussion has been muddled by the conflation of two distinct notions that go under that title. Joint *legal* custody is more pervasive and less demanding: it means that the two parents have an equal say in the major decisions regarding the child (e.g., medical care and education); on its own, joint legal custody has no implications for the physical location of the child. By contrast, joint *physical* custody refers to an equal, or nearly equal, sharing of custodial time between the parents.

Joint *legal* custody is an option in nearly all states, and a presumption in many.[38] Though there has been a push (especially by fathers' rights groups) in many places for a presumption in favor of joint *physical* custody, or something like it, the experience with joint physical custody has not been entirely positive (with complaints based, in particular, on the disruption in the children's lives when they must shuttle back and forth between homes too frequently). Currently, joint physical custody is now, in most jurisdictions, simply one option among others.[39]

5. Parent vs. Nonparent

As mentioned earlier this chapter, in the aftermath of *Painter v. Bannister*,[40] almost every state, through a statute or case law, created

---

38. A recent summary states that as of 2011, "forty-seven states and the District of Columbia have statutes that specifically authorize joint or shared custody. Eleven states and D.C. declare a general presumption in favor of joint custody. Seventeen states use a presumption in favor of joint custody if both parents agree to it." Linda D. Elrod & Robert G. Spector, "A Review of the Year in Family Law: Numbers of Disputes Increase," *Family Law Quarterly*, vol. 45, pp. 443–511 (2012), at p. 468.

39. *See* Margaret F. Brinig, "Penalty Defaults in Family Law: The Case of Child Custody," *Florida State University Law Review*, vol. 33, pp. 779–824 (2006).

40. 140 N.W.2d 152 (1966).

a strong presumption in favor of legal parents when they are in a custody contest with nonparents. The preference for the parent is characterized differently in different jurisdictions, but a common formulation is to state that the nonparent may be awarded custody only if it is shown *both* that custody with the nonparents would be in the best interests of the child *and* that custody with the legal parent would harm the child.[41] This preference or presumption was reinforced by the U.S. Supreme Court decision on parental rights and grandparent visitation, *Troxel v. Granville*,[42] discussed in section E, below.

Like most general rules, there are circumstances (like those of the *Painter v. Bannister* case itself, where a parent was in a custody contest with the child's grandparents) where the standard makes eminent sense, but other circumstances where its application may seem absurd, or at least unjust. Chapter 4 displayed the problem where a same-sex couple is raising a child together in a state where neither same-sex unions nor second-parent adoption is available: the result can be a situation not only where one of the people raising the child (the nominal legal parent) has a strong advantage in a custody fight with the other partner, but one partner is often able to exclude the other from even *being heard*, from even *being considered* for visitation or custody.[43] A different problematic fact situation that comes up with some regularity involves parents who divorce, with one parent continuing to raise a child of that marriage over the years with the help of a new spouse (a step-parent), while the other parent, by choice, gradually has less and less to do with the child. Should the parent primarily raising the child die, and a custody battle ensue, then the surviving step-parent (the spouse of

---

41. *See, e.g., Ariz. Stat.* § 25-415(A)(2), (B); McDermott v. Dougherty, 869 A.2d 751, 754 (Md. 2005).

42. 530 U.S. 57 (2000).

43. *See, e.g.,* Jones v. Barlow, 154 P.3d 808 (Utah 2007); *see generally* Carlos Ball, "Rendering Children Illegitimate in Former Partner Parenting Cases: Hiding Behind the Façade of Certainty," *American University Journal of Gender, Social Policy & the Law*, vol. 20, pp. 623–668 (2012).

the deceased parent), who has also had a very large role in raising the child, would be at a significant legal disadvantage in seeking custody against the other legal parent, even though that other legal parent has played a much smaller role in raising the child.[44]

𝕸 B. Enforcement and Modification

A court that makes a custody order retains jurisdiction over the child and the order until the child reaches the age of eighteen, at least where all of the parties remain in the jurisdiction. (The complications that come when one or both parents subsequently move out of state are discussed in section C, below.) The initial order is subject to "modification," at the request of either party. That is, it is open to a party who is dissatisfied with how many days or hours he or she has with the child to challenge the award, and to keep challenging it.

There are some limits on how frequently custody questions can be relitigated, even beyond the obvious constraints that come from the cost and length of litigation. First, some jurisdictions impose a minimum amount of time that must pass before a party can request that a custody order be modified,[45] or allow the parties themselves to agree to binding limits in a separation agreement.[46] Second, and more important, almost every jurisdiction[47] requires the moving party to meet a heightened standard, that there has been a

---

44. Where the legal parent and the step-parent divorce, it is common that the step-parent will have a right only to seek limited visitation with the child they have been raising together and will have no right to even ask for (joint) custody. *See, e.g.,* Geotz v. Lewis, 203 Cal. App.3d 514, 250 Cal. Rptr. 30 (1988).

45. *See, e.g., Minn. Stat.* § 518.18(a), (b) (general rule of one year after initial custody order for first petition for modification, and two years after a modification has been heard before the next modification petition can be sought).

46. *E.g., Minn. Stat.* § 518.18(a), (b), (e) (allowing parties to agree in writing to alter when petitions for modification can be brought, and what standard will be applied).

47. Pennsylvania is an exception. 23 *Pa. Consolidated Stat.* § 5338 ("best interests of the child" standard for modification).

"substantial change in circumstances," before the court will modify the custody order.[48]

🖉 C. Interjurisdictional Enforcement

The interaction of federalism, jurisdictional rules, and custody rules created an incentive for parents unhappy with a custody decision in one state to take the child to another state seeking a more favorable ruling (or simply to avoid the jurisdiction of the first court). At the height of the problem, in the 1970s and early 1980s, experts estimated the frequency of such "parental kidnapping" in the tens of thousands, and some estimates went into the hundreds of thousands.[49]

A combination of federal and state laws has significantly reduced "forum shopping" for custody decisions, without having to impose any uniformity across states in initial custody decisions. The Uniform Child Custody Jurisdiction Act (UCCJA) was promulgated in 1968, but not adopted by all states until 1981. It was superseded in 1997 by the Uniform Child Custody Jurisdiction and Enforcement Act (UCCJEA),[50] which was intended to work better with the federal legislation in the area, the 1980 Parental Kidnapping Prevention Act (PKPA).[51]

---

48. For a long time, Alabama created an even higher burden, allowing modification of custody only where the evidence in support of a change of custody was sufficient to show "an obvious and overwhelming necessity for a change." *Ex parte* Martin, 961 So.2d 83, 87 (Ala. 2006). This was subsequently reduced to merely requiring the moving party to show that a change in custody will "materially promote [the] child's welfare." *Ex parte* Cleghorn, 993 So.2d 462, 466–469 (Ala. 2008).

49. *See, e.g.*, Glenn Collins, "Study Finds Child Abduction by Parents Exceeds Estimates," *New York Times*, Oct. 23, 1983.

50. *See* Robert G. Spector, "Uniform Child-Custody Jurisdiction and Enforcement Act (with Prefatory Note and Comments by Robert G. Spector)," *Family Law Quarterly*, vol. 32, pp. 301–384 (1998); Patricia M. Hoff, "The ABC's of the UCCJEA: Interstate Child-Custody Practice Under the New Act," *Family Law Quarterly*, vol. 32, pp. 267–299 (1998).

51. 28 U.S.C. § 1738A. One question that has arisen is whether the PKPA applies to adoption cases or only to more conventional custody disputes. Most, but not all, courts have held that adoptions fall within the broad statutory language

The resulting law is complicated—intricate, full of exceptions, and not easily summarized. The basic principles are: a preference for initial custody decisions to be made in the child's "home state" (where the child has lived for the previous six months); the ability to enforce child support orders in other states; the original decree-granting state retains continuing jurisdiction under most circumstances, and there are only limited circumstances where a custody order given in one state can be modified in a second state. (The international convention meant to prevent international child kidnapping, the 1980 United Nations ("Hague") Convention on the Civil Aspects of International Child Abduction, is discussed in chapter 15.)

One recent notorious case shows both the successes and limits of the jurisdictional law in this area. Lisa Miller and Janet Jenkins were a Virginia same-sex couple who went to Vermont to obtain a civil union and later followed through on a plan to have and raise a child together. Their daughter, Isabella, was the biological child of Miller and an anonymous sperm donor. Later the same year the couple and their daughter moved to Vermont, but the parents' relationship did not last long after the move. They asked a Vermont court to dissolve their civil union; as part of the process, the court granted Miller custody of Isabella and Jenkins visitation rights. Miller moved with Isabella back to Virginia, and later stopped allowing Jenkins access to Isabella. Miller went to the Virginia courts asking them to declare her to be Isabella's only legal parent and that Jenkins should have no parental rights to Isabella. The Virginia courts ultimately refused; the Virginia Court of Appeals concluded that, under the PKPA, it was bound to enforce the Vermont custody order (granting Jenkins visitation rights).[52] However, there was no "happy ending";

---

of the PKPA (and the UCCJA and UCCJEA)—"any proceeding for a custody determination." *See In re* Adoption of E.Z., 266 P.3d 702, 708–709 & n.4 (Utah 2011) (citing cases).

52. Miller-Jenkins v. Miller-Jenkins, 637 S.E.2d 330 (Va. App. 2006); *see also* Miller-Jenkins v. Miller-Jenkins, 661 S.E.2d 822 (Va. 2008) (affirming outcome after remand); Miller v. Jenkins, No. 0705-09-4, 2010 WL 605737 (Va. App. 2010) (reaffirming decision after subsequent legal challenge by Miller).

despite the court orders, Miller continued to keep Isabella from Jenkins and eventually left the country with the child. At the time of writing, Miller and Isabella were thought to be hiding out somewhere in Nicaragua, sought by the FBI.[53]

✺ D. Relocation

We live in a mobile world, with predictable consequences for keeping children of divorce in the same location as both of their parents when those parents do not (or no longer) live together. A parent with primary custodial responsibility may wish to move to follow a better job, live near relatives, go to where a new partner has a job opportunity, or simply leave an area that carries bad memories. However, such relocation often works to undermine a standard objective of divorce courts: maintaining regular contact and good relationships between children and both of their parents.[54]

States vary significantly in how they treat the question of relocation. In earlier times, it was common to find states where parents were not allowed to relocate with their children unless "exceptional" circumstances were shown. A series of landmark cases in the 1990s in important states led to a general relaxation of that standard.[55] While the growing (judicial, and to some extent, legislative) trend

---

53. Erik Eckholm, "Which Mother for Isabella: Civil Union Ends in an Abduction and Questions," *New York Times*, July 28, 2012.

54. Only one state, Wyoming, has accepted the argument that the constitutional right to interstate travel gives the custodial parent a legal right to relocate without court consent. Watt v. Watt, 971 P.2d 608 (Wyo. 1999). Other courts facing the argument have concluded that whatever right the custodial parent has to travel must be balanced against the noncustodial parent's right to contact with the child and the court's duty to protect the best interests of the child.

55. *See, e.g.*, Tropea v. Tropea, 665 N.E.2d 146 (N.Y. 1996) (rejecting prior "exceptional circumstances" test for a best interests of the child test); *In re* Marriage of Burgess, 913 P.2d 473 (Cal. 1996) (rejecting old test that relocating parent must establish that move is "necessary"). The *Burgess* standard was expressly affirmed in legislation, *Cal. Fam. Code* § 7501(b).

seems to have been toward a presumption in favor of allowing a custodial parent to relocate (as long as that parent can offer a legitimate
reason for the relocation and it does not appear to be motivated by a
desire to cut off contact between the child and the noncustodial parent), a survey of reported relocation cases indicated that relocation
is denied as frequently as (or perhaps even slightly more frequently
than) it is granted,[56] and a handful of recent important decisions
seem to indicate a possible trend moving back toward greater hesi-
tation in authorizing relocation.[57] (There is some indication that this
greater reluctance may reflect both pressure from "fathers' rights"
groups, and some social science evidence indicating harm to children from relocation.[58])

Few states now have a strong presumption against relocation;[59]
a small number of states give the custodial parent plenary authority

---

56. Theresa Glennon, "Still Partners? Examining the Consequences of
Post-Dissolution Parenting," *Family Law Quarterly*, vol. 41, pp. 105–144 (2007).
There is ample room to speculate on causes. The same study showed that 90
percent of the published decisions on relocation involved a father challenging a mother's right to relocate. The percentage of challenges to relocations
upheld could be affected by a bias toward men, or could derive from the fact
that noncustodial parents often have greater resources than custodial parents
and thus more money to put into litigation.

One might also note simply that whatever the standard in an area of law (in this
case, whether favorable or unfavorable to a custodial parent's right to relocate),
in clear cases under the standard, no legal challenge will be brought, or the suit
will settle out, and the unclear cases are likely to divide roughly evenly. So even
in a pro-relocation jurisdiction, where 95 percent of the time hypothetical relocation requests would be granted by the courts, the litigated cases would likely
split more or less fifty-fifty. *See* George L. Priest & Benjamin Klein, "The Selection
of Disputes for Litigation," *Journal of Legal Studies*, vol. 13, pp. 1–55 (1984), at
pp. 17–24.

57. *See, e.g., In re* Marriage of LaMusga, 32 Cal.4th 1072, 88 P.3d 81 (2004).

58. *See, e.g.,* Sanford L. Braver, Ira M. Ellman, & William V. Fabricius, "Relocation of
Children After Divorce and Children's Best Interests: New Evidence and Legal
Considerations," *Journal of Family Psychology*, vol. 17, pp. 206–219 (2003); *but
see* Carol S. Bruch, "Sound Research or Wishful Thinking in Child Custody
Cases? Lessons from Relocation Law," *Family Law Quarterly*, vol. 40, pp. 281–
314 (2006) (raising questions about the anti-relocation studies).

59. Examples are Alabama (*Ala. Code* § 30-3-163); Louisiana (*La. Rev. Stat. Ann.*
§ 9:355.12); and South Carolina (*S.C. Code Ann.* § 20-3-160).

to relocate;[60] most statutes are neutral or presumptively favor relocation.[61] A handful of states treat relocation under the same standard as change of custody, and a few states, by court decision, have stated that change of custody is what must be proven by a parent wishing to relocate if the parents were previously awarded joint custody (and both parents had significant regular parenting time)— because the relocation of the parent with primary physical custody will have the effect of making the shared physical custody arrangement unworkable.[62]

In relocation cases, courts sometimes focus on the availability of alternative visitation arrangements but usually conclude that a schedule that allows the noncustodial parent some holidays and a large stretch of time in the summer is an adequate substitute for regular weekly or every-other-week contact. It may also be that the developing options for "virtual visitation" (Skype or similar ways for an absent parent to have extended communications and visual contact with a child living far away, without great expense) may also make courts more willing to assent to a custodial parent's leaving the jurisdiction with a child.

Relocation rules are one-sided, in the sense that they restrict (or potentially restrict) the movements of the custodial parent, but not

---

60. *See, e.g.,* Mahmoodjanloo v. Mahmoodjanloo, 160 P.3d 951 (Okla., 2007) (Oklahoma relocation laws have been interpreted to give the custodial parent the presumptive right to relocate out of state with his or her child, and objecting parent must meet same burden of proof required to change a custody award—material change of circumstances, showing that the move would prejudice the child's welfare).

61. *See, e.g., Cal. Fam. Code* § 7501(a) ("A parent entitled to the custody of a child has a right to change the residence of the child, subject to the power of the court to restrain a removal that would prejudice the rights or welfare of the child"); *cf.* Bodne v. Bodne, 605 S.E.2d 842 (Ga. App. 2004) (abrogating presumption in favor of custodial parent in relocation cases).

62. *See, e.g.,* Potter v. Potter (Eveleigh), 119 P.3d 1246 (Nev. 2005) (where there is joint physical custody, a parent wanting to move out of state should not file under the state relocation statute but under the criteria for change of custody); Maynard v. McNett (Maynard), 710 N.W.2d 369 (N.D. 2006) (with a joint legal and physical custody arrangement, relocation by either parent requires a court decision whether to modify custody to make the petitioning parent the custodial parent).

that of the noncustodial parent. While courts and legislators bring up the (generally accepted) importance of keeping a child in contact with both of its parents, that same reasoning is rarely invoked to place limits on a noncustodial parent's ability to move out of town, despite the fact that a noncustodial parent's move can make a child's ongoing contact with both parents as difficult as a custodial parent's move.

Relocation is also distinctive among postdissolution disputes, in that it is not especially amenable to resolution through mediation or collaborative discussions. It is too much of a zero-sum game: either a parent is allowed to relocate with the child or he or she is not. Of course, there are matters to negotiate at the margins (if relocation is allowed, how often will the child travel to be with the other parent, and will the relocating parent help to defray expenses; or what compensations could be given to a parent who agrees not to relocate, etc.), but the main issue, whether the custodial parent may relocate, is not as easy to negotiate to mutual satisfaction as are (for example) postdissolution financial terms.

ℳ E. Visitation

1. General Principles

When parents divorce (or, if unmarried, stop cohabiting and cooperating), the parties must agree on some way of dividing parenting time; absent such agreement, the court will impose such a division on the parents. Traditionally, the division used to be between a "custodial parent" and a parent with "visitation," who would normally see the child for much more limited periods of time (e.g., every other weekend, plus half of the major holidays, plus a large period during the summer). As of 2009, in roughly one out of every six cases, the custodial parent was the father.[63] While most of this chapter has

---

63. U.S. Census Bureau, *Custodial Fathers and Mothers and Their Child Support: 2009* (December 2011), available at http://www.census.gov/prod/2011pubs/p60-240.pdf.

focused on the decision of which parent should have primary custody, this section focuses on aspects of visitation.[64]

A right to visitation (plus a duty for child support) is, in a sense, a minimum that comes with being recognized as a legal parent to a child (though, as will be discussed, nonparents can also, on occasion, be granted visitation). Even if a court is convinced that visitation with a particular parent is not in the best interests of a child, it is rare to deny visitation altogether unless and until the harm to the child from this parent is sufficiently severe to justify terminating (or suspending) parental rights.

A small but growing number of courts have been willing to impose monetary judgments against parents who do fail to take their court-awarded visitation time; this is sometimes called "respite care." The argument is that custodial parents need a break occasionally from full-time custodial care, which should come when the other parent has visitation. When the other parent fails to take the visitation time, the courts may order that parent to pay the custodial parent for child-care or babysitting expenses for the relevant period.[65]

2. Conditions on Visitation

When courts award visitation, they sometimes place restrictions on what the parent may do during the period of the visitation. It was once common for judges to place restrictions on having romantic partners present when the children were there for visitation, or at least restrictions on the parent's partner being present overnight.[66]

---

64. It should be noted, though, that courts are increasingly moving toward a more equal division of parenting time and toward a change in terminology that reflects that move (often referring to "shared parenting" and "parenting time" rather than the sharper division and clear hierarchy of "custodial parent" and parent with "visitation").

65. *See, e.g.*, McIntosh v. Landrum, 377 S.W.3d 574 (Ky. App. 2012).

66. Judges seemed especially willing to impose such restrictions when the romantic partner was of the same sex.

Such visitation restrictions effectively made noncustodial parents have to choose between their romantic life and their children, and this was an unwelcome dilemma, especially given the reality that as a general matter noncustodial parents (generally fathers) often see their children less and less as the years go on.[67] However, as extra-marital cohabitation has become more common and more accepted socially, and as courts generally moved away from "morality" standards in child custody matters (the "nexus" test, discussed earlier, requiring that a factor be considered in custody and visitation only if there is a direct connection with parental competence and the best interests of the child[68]), "paramour restrictions" have become far less common.[69]

As with decisions affecting custody (discussed in section A, above), courts are very cautious when asked to restrict visitation rights relating to visitation parents' religious activities. The constitutional concerns arise from a variety of sources: the visitation parent's right to free exercise of his or her religion, the state's refusal to act in ways that would seem to endorse one religion or group of religions over others, the need to avoid state entanglement with religion, and visitation parents' constitutional rights to raise their children as they think best.

Courts have consistently found that the mere fact that the religious practices or beliefs of the visitation parent (including bringing the children to religious services and activities) may cause the

67. *See, e.g.*, David D. Meyer, "The Constitutional Rights of Non-Custodial Parents," *Hofstra Law Review*, vol. 35, pp. 1461–1494 (2006), at pp. 1469–1470 ("Within a year of the breakup, most children see their fathers only a few times a year, and contact drops off sharply after that" (footnote omitted)).

68. *See, e.g.*, Uniform Marriage and Divorce Act § 402; *Minn. Stat. Ann.* § 518.17(13)(b) ("The court shall not consider conduct of a proposed custodian that does not affect the custodian's relationship to the child"). There is a clear *trend* toward excluding or minimizing moral judgments of parental behavior, but there remain courts that will make custody or modification decisions based on their moral condemnation of extramarital cohabitation, promiscuity, homosexuality, polygamy, and the like (or uphold such decisions on appeal).

69. *See, e.g.*, Barker v. Chandler, No. W2010-01151-COA-R3-CV, 2010 WL 2593810 (Tenn. App. 2010) (reversing a "paramour provision").

children discomfort or stress (because their custodial parent is raising them within a different religious tradition) is not sufficient grounds for a court to restrict the visitation parent's religious activities.[70] However, there are extremes of perceived harm to the child when courts will finally (if reluctantly) conclude that the interests in protecting the children override the parents' interests in free exercise of their own religion and their right as a parent to raise their children (religiously) as they see fit.[71]

An increasingly common restriction on visitation involves noncustodial parents who smoke and children who are medically vulnerable, due to asthma or other medical conditions.[72] It may be that such restrictions on a noncustodial parent will place a hard choice on that parent (between that parent's smoking and spending time with his or her child), who may well be severely addicted, perhaps even harder for some than the restrictions on overnight visitors or religious observance discussed earlier. However, if there is clear

---

70. One of the main cases is *Zummo v. Zummo*, 574 A.2d 1130 (Pa. Super. 1990) (reversing trial court's limitation on father's visitation religious practices with child; showing that different religious practices create stress insufficient showing for limitation; must show harm). *See also In re* Marriage of McSoud, 131 P.3d 1208 (Colo. App. 2006) (refusing to restrict visitation father's religious practices or his right to try to raise the children in his faith); Finnerty v. Clutter, 917 N.E.2d 154 (Ind. 2009) (court refuses to order father to bring child to Mass when father has visitation).

71. One well-known example is *Kendall v. Kendall*, 687 N.E.2d 1228 (Mass. 1997), where the noncustodial father had cut off a son's religious clothing and hair and had taken the son and his siblings to religious meetings where it was claimed that nonbelievers, like the children and their mother, were damned to Hell; these activities had caused the children significant anxiety. The court concluded that on those facts restrictions on the father's religious actions when the children were with him was justified. *See also* Meyer v. Meyer, 789 A.2d 921 (Vt. 2001) (upholding decision prohibiting father from exposing children to religious observances or trying to raise them as Jehovah's Witnesses based on evidence of harm to children).

72. One commentator suggested judges ordering restrictions on parental smoking around children even when the children are not medically vulnerable, to avoid the health dangers of second-hand smoke. William F. Chinnock, "No Smoking Around Children: The Family Courts' Mandatory Duty to Restrain Parents and Other Persons from Smoking Around Children," *Arizona Law Review*, vol. 45, pp. 801–821 (2003).

CUSTODY, MODIFICATION, RELOCATION, VISITATION

evidence that exposing the child to smoking is medically dangerous, the court may have little choice.

3. Grandparent (and Other Third-Party) Visitation

At the time the U.S. Supreme Court decided *Troxel v. Granville*,[73] every
state had statutes authorizing grandparent (or other third-party) visitation. *Troxel* involved a constitutional challenge to one such statute
from the state of Washington, a particularly broadly worded third-party
visitation statute that allowed a court to grant visitation to a nonparent when it was in the best interests of the child to do so. The Supreme
Court decided that this standard was insufficiently respectful of the
constitutional right of legal parents to choose how to raise their children. The *Troxel* decision was not as clear as it might have been regarding what was required for grandparent or other third-party visitation,
but most states have, in the face of *Troxel*, created additional requirements: usually a presumption against granting visitation to a nonparent if the parents object, and/or a burden of showing that the children
will suffer significant harm if the visitation is denied.[74]

Where the dispute turns on the rights and prerogatives of parents in the raising of their children, perhaps it is not strange that the
courts will divide the world into "parents" and "nonparents," even
including grandparents and other nonparent relatives as "strangers
to the family." This is in sharp contrast to the Supreme Court's language in an earlier case, *Moore v. City of East Cleveland*.[75] In that case,
the Court invalidated a land-use regulation that defined "family" in
such a way that a grandmother was not allowed to live with her two

---

73. 530 U.S. 57 (2000).

74. *See generally* Daniel R. Victor & Keri L. Middleditch, "Grandparent Visitation:
    A Survey of History, Jurisprudence, and Legislative Trends Across the United
    States in the Past Decade," *Journal of the American Academy of Matrimonial
    Lawyers*, vol. 22, pp. 391–409 (2009).

75. 431 U.S. 494 (1977).

grandchildren, when those two children were cousins rather than siblings. The Court, in a plurality opinion,[76] held that the substantive Due Process Clause of the Constitution includes the extended family, not just the nuclear family, as our society's traditional valuing of family extends to this broader understanding of family. However, in the area of custody and visitation, the U.S. Supreme Court in *Troxel* clearly stated that extended family members have no special legal or constitutional status.

Suggested Further Reading

Best Interests

Philip Alston (ed.), *The Best Interests of the Child: Reconciling Culture and Human Rights* (Oxford: Clarendon Press, 1994).

Claire Breen, *The Standard of the Best Interests of the Child: A Western Tradition in International and Comparative Law* (The Hague: Martinus Nijhoff Publishers, 2002).

Martin Guggenheim, *What's Wrong with Children's Rights* (Cambridge, Mass.: Harvard University Press, 2005).

Nancy E. Walker, Catherine M. Brooks, & Lawrence S. Wrightsman, *Children's Rights in the United States: In Search of a National Policy* (Thousand Oaks, Calif.: Sage Publications, 1999).

Relocation

Carol S. Bruch, "Sound Research or Wishful Thinking in Child Custody Cases? Lessons from Relocation Law," *Family Law Quarterly*, vol. 40, pp. 281–314 (2006).

Theresa Glennon, "Still Partners? Examining the Consequences of Post-Dissolution Parenting," *Family Law Quarterly*, vol. 41, pp. 105–144 (2007).

Merle H. Weiner, "Inertia and Inequality: Reconceptualizing Disputes Over Parental Relocation," *U.C. Davis Law Review*, vol. 40, pp. 1747–1834 (2007).

Custody

Douglas W. Allen & Margaret Brinig, "Do Joint Parenting Laws Make Any Difference?," *Journal of Empirical Legal Studies*, vol. 8, pp. 304–324 (2011).

---

76. The necessary fifth vote, Justice Stevens, concurred in the judgment, on a related but somewhat different ground.

Scott Altman, "Should Child Custody Rules Be Fair?," *University of Louisville Journal of Family Law*, vol. 35, pp. 325–354 (1996–1997).

Kent Greenawalt, "Child Custody, Religious Practices, and Conscience," *University of Colorado Law Review*, vol. 76, pp. 965–988 (2005).

Jurisdiction

Barbara Ann Atwood, "Child Custody Jurisdiction and Territoriality," *Ohio State Law Journal*, vol. 52, pp. 369–403 (1991).

Robert G. Spector, The New Uniform Law with Regard to Jurisdiction Rules in Child Custody Cases in the United States," in *Yearbook of Private International Law*, vol. 2, pp. 75–98 (2000).

Visitation

Daniel R. Victor & Keri L. Middleditch, "Grandparent Visitation: A Survey of History, Jurisprudence, and Legislative Trends Across the United States in the Past Decade," *Journal of the American Academy of Matrimonial Lawyers*, vol. 22, pp. 391–409 (2009).

Judith T. Younger, "Post-Divorce Visitation for Infants and Young Children— The Myths and the Psychological Unknowns," *Family Law Quarterly*, vol. 36, pp. 195–210 (2002).

FOURTEEN

Child Support

※ A. Introduction and General Principles

Parents have obligations to support their children, at least until those children reach the age of majority.[1] They have this obligation whether they are married to one another or not (the history and current legal treatment of nonmarital children is considered in chapter 4, section A). The support obligation is most commonly enforced at divorce; though a support action can also be brought at legal separation, between nonmarried parents who are not living together, or against an unmarried father (on behalf of the mother) by the state, seeking to recover state benefits paid to the mother. In an intact married household, the support obligation generally only becomes relevant if the level of support goes so far below the required minimum that the child is removed for neglect (a topic discussed in chapter 7).

The basic principle of the modern child support rules is that children should do as well as they would have done if their parents were (still) together, or, to put the matter another way, children have the right to benefit from the good fortune of a noncustodial parent. This is, of course, more ideal or objective than likely reality—inevitably, the cost of maintaining two households rather than one will make some diminishment of lifestyle probable—but it still focuses the courts' attention on allowing children to share in whatever

---

1. Parental obligations to support children can go past the age of majority when the child suffers from a severe physical or mental disability. Additionally, in some states, court-ordered child support can include postmajority support for educational costs.

earnings or good fortune a noncustodial parent may receive. This basic principle is instantiated different ways in different states.

For many decades, child support had been a matter of great discretion placed in the court. Courts set the support award they considered appropriate, in the best interests of the child, given all the circumstances. The objection was that this approach entailed too much uncertainty, unpredictability, and inequality, with support awards turning on the arbitrary assignment of a generous or less generous judge (or what mood the judge might be in that day). Under pressure from the commentators, critics, and eventually the federal government (which backed up its views with a threat to withhold federal monies from states that did not establish child support guidelines[2]), all states eventually established support guidelines, with deviations allowed only when special circumstances were found. Advocates applaud the greater predictability and consistency of the current system; critics point to occasional fact situations where the guidelines produce absurd outcomes and look back nostalgically to when family court judges could individualize support orders for the needs and circumstances of the parties before the court.

As noted, the federal government has played an important role in child support,[3] by requiring the states to create and follow child support guidelines which set presumptive support levels. A second way in which the federal government has significantly changed child support is in enforcement matters: in offering its own enforcement

---

2. Much of Congress's action in this area was thus done under the Spending Clause of the U.S. Constitution. A recent U.S. Supreme Court decision indicated (seemingly for the first time) that there are constitutional limits on Congress's spending power. National Federation of Independent Business v. Sebelius, 132 S. Ct. 2566 (2012). However, as this part of the Court's decision was split between two opinions offering different limits and justifications, one will likely have to await future cases to ascertain what the limits are and the extent to which they will constrain the sort of action Congress has taken in the child support area.

3. A good overview of the federal role in child support law is given in Laura W. Morgan, "Child Support Fifty Years Later," *Family Law Quarterly*, vol. 41, pp. 365–380 (2008), at pp. 366–370.

mechanisms (e.g., income-withholding, garnishment of tax refunds, federal benefits, and blocking of passport availability[4]), by clarifying the enforceability of child support orders in sister states,[5] and in creating strong financial incentives for the states to create their own enforcement mechanisms. A third federal intervention is the creation of federal criminal liability for extreme cases of willful failure of support (that cross state boundaries).[6]

The child support guidelines usually state that (presumptively) a certain percentage of the obligor's income is to be paid in support.[7] Where the obligor's income is temporarily very high (e.g., with professional athletes and other celebrities) or high indefinitely (as with corporate executives, hedge fund managers, some medical specialists, etc.), the presumptive support figure that may come from the guideline percentage may seem indefensibly large. Some states (e.g., Kansas[8]) have responded to the problem of high-income obligors by making the guideline figures discretionary for above a certain income level, while other states (like Texas[9]) set a maximum presumptive support award, which does not increase even for extremely high obligor incomes.[10]

---

4. Additionally, the granting of Temporary Assistance for Needy Families (TANF) benefits has been made conditional on unwed mothers naming the fathers of their children at birth. This then makes it easier for the government to go after the fathers for child support.

5. *See* The Full Faith and Credit for Child Support Orders Act, codified at 28 U.S.C. § 1738B.

6. *See* The Federal Child Support Recovery Act of 1992 (as amended in 1998), 18 U.S.C. § 228.

7. The guidelines of thirty-eight states and the District of Columbia are based on the income of both parents; the guidelines from nine states are based on the income of the obligor parent only; the remaining three states follow the "Melson formula," which divides available net income based on the needs of both the parents and the children. *See* Linda D. Elrod & Robert G. Spector, "A Review of the Year in Family Law: Numbers of Disputes Increase," *Family Law Quarterly*, vol. 45, pp. 443–511 (2012), at pp. 498–499 (Chart 3).

8. *Kansas Child Support Guidelines* III(B)(3) (as amended, 2009).

9. *Tex. Fam. Code* § 154.126. Under that statute, the court retains discretion to award more than the presumptive amount where the children's needs warrant it.

10. *See, e.g.*, Lori W. Nelson, "High-Income Child Support," *Family Law Quarterly*, vol. 45, pp. 191–218 (2011).

✻ B. What Counts as Income?

Because child support orders are generally derived from formulas which use as inputs (along with number of children supported and, perhaps, division of parenting time) either the obligor's income alone, or the obligor's and recipient's incomes combined, how one measures income becomes crucial. There is often extensive statutory language and case law in each state on the subject. Here is language from a Kentucky statute:

> "Gross income" includes income from any source, ... and includes but is not limited to income from salaries, wages, retirement and pension funds, commissions, bonuses, dividends, severance pay, pensions, interest, trust income, annuities, capital gains, Social Security benefits, workers' compensation benefits, unemployment insurance benefits, disability insurance benefits, Supplemental Security Income (SSI), gifts, prizes, and alimony or maintenance received. Specifically excluded are benefits received from means-tested public assistance programs, including but not limited to public assistance as defined under Title IV-A of the Federal Social Security Act, and food stamps. For income from self-employment, rent, royalties, proprietorship of a business, or joint ownership of a partnership or closely held corporation, "gross income" means gross receipts minus ordinary and necessary expenses required for self-employment or business operation.... Expense reimbursement or in-kind payments received by a parent in the course of employment, self-employment, or operation of a business or personal use of business property or payments of expenses by a business, shall be counted as income if they are significant and reduce personal living expenses such as a company or business car, free housing, reimbursed meals, or club dues.[11]

---

11. *Ky. Rev. Stat.* § 403.212.

As the statute exemplifies, states err on the side of including someone as income if it could be colorably characterized that way.

There are certain standard difficult cases. One-time payments from an employer or from litigation or a state compensation agency could arguably be classified as either income or nonincome wealth (where only income counts in calculating child support payments). If the litigation or state compensation award is either to be paid periodically or is meant to compensate for lost (past or future) wages, it will likely be treated as income.

When a parent receives stock options as part of that parent's compensation at work, should that count as income for child support? Stock options give the recipient the right to purchase a certain amount of stock at a set price, usually from some date a year or more in the future. The idea is that this gives corporate executives an incentive to work for improved economic performance of the company, as a better-performing company will have a higher stock price, and if that price is much higher than the price set by the options, this could give the option-holder a significant profit. However, there is no requirement that the options be exercised (the stock purchased). So in any given year the options might yield no actual money. The growing consensus[12] is that stock options are income for the purposes of determining child support, even when they are not exercised. This conclusion is grounded on the fact that stock options are generally perceived as being part of the income of those who receive them, and to treat them as income only when they are exercised is to give stock-option holders a means (and an incentive) to hide significant wealth from their children.[13]

---

12. Beginning probably with *Murray v. Murray*, 716 N.E.2d 288 (Ohio App. 1999).
13. In the *Murray* case, the difference between counting the options and not counting them was the difference between a child support obligation of $2,700 a month and one of $6,300 a month. *See* Debra Baker, "New $upplement for Kids of Divorce," *ABA Journal*, p. 32 (October 1999). Stock options raise intricate questions regarding how they are to be valued (either for child support or property division purposes). *See, e.g.,* Diana Richmond, "The Challenges of Stock Options," *Family Law Quarterly*, vol. 35, pp. 251–262 (2001); David S. Rosettenstein, "Exploring the Use of the Time Rule in the Distribution of Stock

🏵 C. Imputing Income

Where child support payments are set as a formula based in part on a parent's income (as they are in almost every state), there is a natural temptation for parents with child support obligations, especially those who may be angry with their former spouses (in general, about the divorce, or perhaps specifically relating to disputes about visitation with the child) to reduce their income as a way of reducing their support payments. In part to deter such strategic behavior, courts are authorized to "impute income" to child support obligors: to base the support obligation on what the court concludes the parent *could have been* earning rather than what he or she actually earns.[14]

Even if the obligor parent acts in good faith (e.g., in the decision to take one job rather than another, to retire early, or to work part-time or not at all in order to spend more time with this or another child), there is still the question of whether he or she should be free to make job and career choices that lead to less money being paid for the support of the children. Questions about imputation of income are also central when the obligor parent has gone back to school to get additional training or has been fired from a job.[15] There are some other technical issues that sometimes go under the topic of "imputing income." For example, courts have sometimes been willing to impute a higher rate of return for stocks than the stocks

---

Options at Divorce," *Family Law Quarterly*, vol. 35, pp. 262–303 (2001); Susan Isard, "Stock Options and Child Support: The Price of Accuracy," *Hastings Women's Law Journal*, vol. 14, pp. 215–248 (2003).

14. *See generally* Elizabeth Trainor, "Basis for Imputing Income for Purpose of Determining Child Support Where Obligor Spouse is Voluntarily Unemployed or Underemployed," 76 A.L.R.5th 191 (2000).

15. *See, e.g.*, Metz v. Metz, 711 S.E.2d 737 (N.C. App. 2011) (income imputed to obligor father fired from job due to sexual abuse conviction); *In re* Applegate, No. 10-1606, 801 N.W.2d 627 (Table), 2011 WL 2042049 (Iowa App. 2011) (income imputed to obligor father fired from job for misconduct, action treated as "voluntary"); *but see* Douglas v. State, 954 N.E.2d 1090 (Ind. 2011) (man incarcerated for nonpayment of support entitled to reduction of support).

actually achieved.[16] Imputation issues also arise when an obligor has the power to determine whether money earned by a company the obligor controls goes to the obligor's salary or is reinvested in the company.

To be clear: courts do not actually order obligor parents not to retire, not to take the lower paying job, or not to give up their job to go back to school, or the like. The courts simply make the child support award based on the higher earning capacity, and the practical effect of that will usually be to constrain the obligor's choice.[17]

Of course, courts never (directly or indirectly) tell parents in *intact* families which jobs to take, how much money to spend on their children, or whether to pay their children's college expenses for them. In part this is in part a matter of general noninterference with the internal workings of a household ("family privacy," discussed in chapter 1), and in part a respect for the moral (and constitutional) right of parents to raise their children as they see fit. However, when a marriage splits up, or an unmarried couple bring their parenting disputes to the court, the view of American courts is that the court's *parens patriae* obligation to protect the interests of minor children trumps the liberty and autonomy claims of the adults involved.

🌾 D. The Process: Modification and Enforcement

As child support is often understood as grounded in the principle that children's levels of support should not suffer just because their parents are not or no longer together, and as child support guidelines

---

16. *In re* Marriage of Schlafly, 149 Cal. App. 4th 747, 57 Cal. Rptr. 3d 274 (2007) (imputing 3 percent rate of return on father's $2.9 million portfolio, rather than the actual 1.6 percent return).

17. A similar practical constraint was seen in chapter 11, section D, in New York, when a professional degree is "divided" based on its full earning capacity, effectively preventing obligors there from choosing a lower-paying public interest career path.

are usually based on the income of the obligor parent or the income of both parents, it follows naturally that parents will be able to seek a modification of child support when parental means increase or decrease. In a state that pegs child support to the income of both parents, then an increase or decrease in *either* parent's income can justify a modification. An extraordinary and unexpected change in the child's financial needs (e.g., due to an illness or disability) could also justify a modification.

Enforcement of child support awards is a serious and ongoing problem. As of 2009, almost 30 percent of the custodial parents due child support received no payments at all, and only slightly more than 40 percent received the full amount due.[18] And this is with the use of a large panoply of state, interstate, and federal enforcement processes and remedies. The most important interstate process is the Uniform Interstate Family Support Act (UIFSA),[19] which was promulgated in 1992 and enacted in all states (under federal governmental pressure) by 1998. Combined with the federal Full Faith and Credit for Child Support Orders,[20] the law allows the enforcement of

---

18. U.S. Census Bureau, *Custodial Fathers and Mothers and Their Child Support: 2009* (December 2011), p. 9, available at http://www.census.gov/prod/2011pubs/p60-240.pdf.

19. Clarificatory amendments were added to UIFSA in 1996 and 2001. *See* John J. Sampson, "Uniform Interstate Family Support Act (1996) (with More Unofficial Annotations by John J. Sampson)," *Family Law Quarterly*, vol. 32, pp. 390–520 (1998); John J. Sampson with Barry J. Brooks, "Uniform Interstate Family Support Act (2001) With Prefatory Note and Comments (With Still More Unofficial Annotations)," *Family Law Quarterly*, vol. 36, pp. 329–447 (2002). Further amendments were made in 2008 to help facilitate implementation of the Hague Convention on the International Recovery of Child Support and Other Forms of Family Maintenance. Eric M. Fish, "The Uniform Interstate Family Support Act (UIFSA) 2008: Enforcing International Obligations Through Cooperative Federalism," *Journal of the American Academy of Matrimonial Lawyers*, vol. 24, pp. 33–56 (2011).

20. 28 U.S.C. § 1738B. There remain some complications in the interactions of the two laws, especially regarding the modification of one state's order in a second state. *See* Steven K. Berenson, "Home Court Advantage Revisited: Interstate Modification of Child Support Orders Under UIFSA and FFCCSOA," *Gonzaga Law Review*, vol. 45, pp. 479–498 (2009–2010).

one state's child support order in another state, while sharply limiting the ability of a parent dissatisfied with the support order in one state to obtain an entirely new or modified order in a second state.

Within a jurisdiction, failure to comply with a child support court order can subject the obligor to contempt of court, including the threat of prison. Using the threat of prison to encourage payment of support remains highly controversial. On one hand, it has proven to be effective in increasing the rate of compliance and thus increases the money that goes to needy children and families. On the other hand, there are indications that it also speeds the estrangement of noncustodial parents from their children, while introducing harsh penalties in what is likely to already be an emotionally complex conflict.[21]

Suggested Further Reading

Douglas W. Allen & Margaret F. Brinig, "Child Support Guidelines: The Good, the Bad and the Ugly," *Family Law Quarterly*, vol. 45, pp. 135–156 (2011).

Scott Altman, "A Theory of Child Support," *International Journal of Law, Policy, and the Family*, vol. 17, pp. 173–210 (2003).

Ira Mark Ellman, "A Case Study in Failed Law Reform: Arizona's Child Support Guidelines," *Arizona Law Review*, vol. 54, pp. 137–196 (2012).

Laura W. Morgan, "Child Support Fifty Years Later," *Family Law Quarterly*, vol. 42, pp. 365–380 (2008).

John J. Sampson & Paul M. Kurtz, "UIFSA: An Interstate Support Act for the 21st Century," *Family Law Quarterly*, vol. 27, pp. 85–90 (1993).

---

21. For an excellent overview of the issue, see David L. Chambers, *Making Fathers Pay: The Enforcement of Child Support* (Chicago: University of Chicago Press, 1979), pp. 241–253.

PART FIVE

Other Topics in Family Law

IT IS HARD for any short book to come close to offering a comprehensive overview of American family law. The final chapters will offer brief discussions of three of the prominent topics of modern family law that did not fit neatly into the larger categories of the prior parts of this book: international aspects of family law, the relationship of family law and religion, and domestic violence.

International Aspects of Family Law

FAMILY LAW PRACTICE in the United States (and elsewhere) increasingly requires consideration of international issues, as increasing numbers of couples live married lives in more than one country, or seek a divorce in a country different from the one in which the couple had lived. There are disputes about one parent bringing a child to another country against the other parent's wishes or contrary to a judicial order in another country. And parents seek to adopt children from another country.[1]

In earlier chapters, we have seen the rules and procedures that have been put into place to respond to the combination of a mobile society and a federalist government structure: where (semi)sovereign states within the union must learn how to apply or modify the family court rules (relating to marriage, divorce, child custody, and child support) of other states. A comparable problem occurs on an international scale, with rules and procedures starting to be offered to deal with the problem of family law issues across nations. This chapter will look at some of those rules and procedures. Some solutions come from international conventions and treaties, where

---

1. International adoption was discussed briefly in chapter 5. On whether international adoption is generally good or bad for the children involved, see the contrasting views in Elizabeth Bartholet, "International Adoption: Thoughts on the Human Rights Issues," *Buffalo Human Rights Law Review*, vol. 13, pp. 151–203 (2007); and Johanna Oreskovic & Trish Maskew, "Red Thread or Slender Reed: Deconstructing Prof. Bartholet's Mythology of International Adoption," *Buffalo Human Rights Law Review*, vol. 14, pp. 71–128 (2008).

these have been adopted by the United States. At other times, the legal response is based simply on general principles of comity.

"Comity" is the basic principle of respect for other jurisdictions' laws, procedures, and judgments. Generally, these laws, procedures, and judgments are to be treated as valid and subject to enforcement in this country, unless either (1) the foreign legal process did not meet minimal standards of due process, or (2) the applicable law is contrary to a fundamental public policy of the forum state or country.

✐ A.   International Recognition of Marriages, Family-Related Decrees

The recognition of marriages and divorces follows basic rules of conflict of laws and comity. Parallel to the *interstate* recognition of marriages (discussed in chapter 2, section H), marriages performed in another country will generally be recognized in the United States if they were valid where celebrated and if they are not contrary to the fundamental public policy of the state being asked to recognize it.[2]

The comity treatment of foreign divorces and divorce-related decrees similarly requires a state to recognize the judgment from another country if, but only if, the procedure in that other country met basic principles of due process, and if the applicable law is not contrary to the fundamental policy of the state being asked to recognize it. This may seem a minimal test, but in recent years, a number of state courts applying that test have refused to recognize certain foreign judgments in this area.[3]

---

2. *See, e.g., In re* Marriage of Akon, 248 P.3d 94 (Wash. App. 2011) (treating Sudanese marriage as valid after determining that it was a valid "cultural marriage" under the norms of Sudan).

3. *See, e.g.*, Aleem v. Aleem, 947 A.2d 489 (Md. 2008) (Islamic *talaq* divorce not afforded comity in Maryland); Tarikonda v. Pinjari, No. 287403, 2009 WL 930007 (Mich. App. 2009) (refusing to recognize *talaq* divorce); *In re* Custody of R., 947 P.2d 745 (Wash. App. 1997) (if mother can show that foreign child support decree

With adoptions, the Hague Convention on the Protection of Children and Co-operation in Respect of Intercountry Adoption 1993[4] governs the adoption of children in one country by parents from another country.[5] This Convention was adopted in the United States under the Intercountry Adoption Act,[6] an Act which gives the federal government significant regulatory power over those individuals or agencies which provide international adoption services.

※ B. The Hague Convention on Child Abduction

The Hague Convention on the Civil Aspects of International Child Abduction (often referred to simply as "the Hague Convention," though there are actually a number of different Hague Conventions dealing with family law[7]) was concluded in 1980 and entered into force in 1983.[8] As of early 2011, eighty-four countries had signed this

---

was based on proceedings not consistent with strong state public policy favoring the best interests of children, then decree would not warrant recognition).

4. Available at http://hcch.e-vision.nl/index_en.php?act=conventions.text&cid=69.

5. Within Europe there is also a European Convention on Recognition and Enforcement of Decisions Concerning Custody of Children and the Restoration of Custody of Children (Luxembourg, May 20, 1980), http://conventions.coe.int.

6. 42 U.S.C. §§ 14901–14954.

7. E.g., The Hague Convention on Protection of Children and Cooperation in Respect of Intercountry Adoption, the Hague Convention on the International Enforcement of Child Support and Other Forms of Family Maintenance, and the Hague Convention on the Protection of Children. Linda D. Elrod & Robert G. Spector, "A Review of the Year in Family Law: Numbers of Disputes Increase," *Family Law Quarterly*, vol. 45, pp. 443–511 (2012), at p. 448.

8. Information about the Convention, as well as the full text, is available at http://www.hcch.net. The Convention was implemented in American law by The International Child Abduction Remedies Act (ICARA), 42 U.S.C. § 11601 *et seq.* A different federal law, the International Parental Kidnapping Crime Act of 1993, 18 U.S.C. § 1204, makes it a crime to remove a child from the country for the purpose of obstructing another person's exercise of parental rights.

Convention. The basic purpose of the Convention is to discourage international "child kidnapping" and forum shopping across nations for favorable child custody adjudications. Thus, where a child has been wrongfully removed or wrongfully retained in a country other than the country that is the child's habitual residence, that child is to be returned to that habitual residence, barring extraordinary circumstances.[9] The point of a Hague Convention proceeding is not to adjudicate which parent (or other guardian) should have custody, but to return the child to the proper forum for making such determinations, though courts are often accused of misunderstanding their role in this way.[10]

Unsurprisingly, there has been significant litigation over the basic terms of this relatively straightforward Convention: how does one determine "habitual residence,"[11] what constitutes "wrongful removal" or "wrongful retention,"[12] what counts as a "right to custody,"[13] and what would qualify as "extraordinary circumstances"?[14]

There is a long list of other international and regional conventions that affect family law, many of which may have growing importance as they become more established in American and

9. Under Article 12 of the Convention, if the Hague proceedings are commenced more than a year after the child's wrongful removal, the court must consider whether the child in question has become settled in the new environment. *See, e.g.*, *Re M (Abduction: Zimbabwe)* [2007] UKHL 55.

10. *See, e.g.*, Kirk Semple, "Custody Case Tests Abduction Laws and U.S.-Brazil Ties," *New York Times*, Feb. 25, 2009 (claim that Brazilian court responded to Hague Convention petition by inappropriately making a substantive custody determination).

11. *E.g.*, Robert v. Tesson, 507 F.3d 981 (6th Cir. 2007) (preferring the 6th Circuit's "acclimatization" test for "habitual residence" to the "shared intent" test of the 9th Circuit); *cf.* Mozes v. Mozes, 239 F.3d 1067 (9th Cir. 2001) (shared intent test).

12. *See, e.g.*, Pielage v. McConnell, 516 F.3d 1282 (11th Cir. 2008) (state court's *ne exeat* order did not constitute a "retention" for the purpose of the Hague Convention).

13. *See, e.g.*, Abbott v. Abbott, 130 S. Ct. 1983 (2010) (father's *ne exeat* right was a "right of custody" for the purpose of the Hague Convention).

14. *See, e.g.*, Walsh v. Walsh, 221 F.3d 204 (1st Cir. 2000) (discussing and narrowly interpreting the "grave risk of harm" exception to the obligation to return a child wrongfully removed).

international practice,[15] but their discussion must be left to texts devoted to that topic.[16]

Suggested Further Reading

D. Marianne Blair & Merle H. Weiner (eds.), *International Family Law: Conventions, Statutes, and Regulatory Materials* (2nd ed., Durham, N.C.: Carolina Academic Press, 2010).

Ann Laquer Estin, "Families Across Borders: The Hague Children's Convention and the Case for International Family Law in the United States," *Florida Law Review*, vol. 62, pp. 47–108 (2010).

___, "International Divorce: Litigating Marital Property and Support Rights," *Family Law Quarterly*, vol. 45, pp. 293–327 (2011).

Nigel V. Lowe & Victoria Stephens, "Global Trends in the Operation of the 1980 Hague Abduction Convention," *Family Law Quarterly*, vol. 46, pp. 41–85 (2012).

Jeremy D. Morley, *The Hague Abduction Convention: Practical Issues and Procedures for the Family Lawyer* (Chicago: American Bar Association, Section on Family Law, 2012).

Barbara Stark, *International Family Law: An Introduction* (Aldershot, England: Ashgate, 2005).

___, "The Internationalization of American Family Law," *Journal of the American Academy of Matrimonial Lawyers*, vol. 24, pp. 467–487 (2012).

---

15. *See, e.g.,* William Duncan, "The New Hague Child Support Convention: Goals and Outcomes of the Negotiations," *Family Law Quarterly*, vol. 43, pp. 1–20 (2009).

16. *See, e.g.,* D. Marianne Blair & Merle H. Weiner, *International Family Law: Conventions, Statutes and Regulatory Materials* (Durham, N.C.: Carolina Academic Press, 2010) (almost 800 pages of relevant documents).

SIXTEEN

Family Law and Religion

AS RELIGION IS an integral part of most people's lives, it inevitably plays a regular role in family life and family law. The interaction of religion and family law doctrine and practice has already been seen sporadically in earlier chapters: relating to religion as a factor in adoption (chapter 5), child custody and visitation (chapter 13), and premarital agreements (chapter 10). This chapter will review some of those topics and consider some additional areas where religion and family law intersect.

✺ A. Religious Marriage

Under old English law, from which the American legal system derives, the law of domestic relations was left to the ecclesiastical courts (a matter that was not changed until the Divorce and Matrimonial Causes Act of 1857), with the occasional and difficult exception of private acts of divorce through Parliament. The United States, with its separation of Church and State, would not delegate family law wholesale to religious courts, but such delegation continues in a number of other countries.

While religious authorities and religious courts do not have initial authority as a matter of American law, complicated questions arise when private parties try to *give* such institutions power over domestic matters. For example, what happens when a couple enters a premarital agreement stating that they will present marital disputes to a religious court or arbitrator? Is such an agreement enforceable? If the parties in fact go to a religious decision-maker, is that decision-maker's resolution enforceable in an American court (and should it be)?

Mary Anne Case has argued that much of the fervor of the current debate over same-sex marriage has come from the fact of secularization and centralization of marriage in the United States: that if certain family issues were delegated to religious communities, issues of the right or best way to form and dissolve families would no longer end up as public disputes about legislation (and constitutional interpretation).[1]

✎ B. Religious Premarital Agreements

Both Judaism and Islam have agreements to be entered on the eve of marriage. As discussed in chapter 10, section A, the enforceability of the Jewish *ketubah* and the Islamic *mahr* have generally been treated no differently than nonreligious premarital agreements, often being enforced,[2] and occasionally having terms deemed unenforceable because the court considered the terms either insufficiently protective of one of the spouses[3] or unduly encouraging of divorce.[4] Additionally, courts have occasionally balked when they concluded that enforcement would unduly entangle the courts in religious matters.[5]

---

1. Mary Anne Case, "Marriage Licenses," *Minnesota Law Review*, vol. 89, pp. 1758–1797 (2005).
2. *See, e.g.*, Aziz v. Aziz, 488 N.Y.S.2d 123 (N.Y. Sup. Ct. 1985) (enforcing deferred *mahr* payment); Akileh v. Elchahal, 666 So.2d 246 (Fla. App. 1996) (same).
3. Ahmad v. Ahmad, No. L-00-1391, 2001 WL 1518116 (Ohio App. 2001) (refusing to enforce *mahr* provision because of procedural and substantive unfairness of the agreement).
4. *See, e.g.*, *In re* Marriage of Dajani, 251 Cal. Rptr. 871 (Ct. App. 1988) (deferred payment agreement in *mahr* held unenforceable for encouraging divorce).
5. *See* "Judge: Dowry not a Prenup," Associated Press, Oct. 22, 2007 (describing trial court decision). On appeal, the appellate court affirmed the refusal to enforce the agreement, relying primarily on the conclusion that the agreement

🕮 C. Religious Divorce

In Judaism, a divorce occurs when the husband presents the wife with a *get*. Without a *get*, the wife is not allowed to remarry, and any child she would have with another man would be a *mamzer* (illegitimate) and could be shunned from orthodox religious communities. As the husband has control over whether a religious divorce is granted, he has significant leverage over a wife who wishes to remarry and stay a member of the religious community.

New York has passed two laws, both strongly supported by the local Orthodox Jewish community, to try to remove some of the problems that can arise from the inequality, in particular, to prevent a husband from using the threat of not giving his wife a *get* as a means to coerce a one-sided separation agreement from her. The first *get* statute states that in situations where a religious divorce is required, to obtain a civil divorce the husband must submit an affidavit stating that he has done everything he can to make a religious divorce available.[6] Under the second statute, a civil court has the authority to take a husband's unwillingness to obtain a religious divorce as a factor in setting financial orders (including temporary support orders).[7]

As mentioned in chapter 15, section A, a few American courts have refused to recognize *talaq* divorces from the Islamic tradition, at least where the divorce becomes final with no official participation by the wife.[8]

---

did not meet the legal requirements for enforceability. Zawahiri v. Alwattar, No. 07AP-925, 2008 WL 2698679 (Ohio App. 2008), appeal denied, 900 N.E.2d 198 (Table) (Ohio 2009).

6. *New York Domestic Relations* § 253.

7. *New York Domestic Relations* § 236 Part B(5)(h).

8. *See, e.g.,* Aleem v. Aleem, 947 A.2d 489 (Md. 2008) (Islamic *talaq* divorce not afforded comity in Maryland); Tarikonda v. Pinjari, No. 287403, 2009 WL 930007 (Mich. App. 2009) (refusing to recognize *talaq* divorce); *but see* Chaudry v. Chaudry, 388 A.2d 1000 (N.J. Super. 1978) (reversing trial court's refusal to grant comity to *talaq* divorce).

✺ D. Religion in Child Placement

Religion comes up regularly in child placement issues and has been discussed in earlier parts of this book: in chapter 5 (section E, religion and adoption) and in chapter 13 (section A, custody, and section E, visitation).

As noted, courts are reluctant to act in ways in which they might be seen as favoring one religion over another, or in any way commenting on the truth or value of particular religions. (Courts will, however, sometimes make decisions that, in passing, claim or imply that religious parents are superior to parents who do not practice a religion.[9])

While courts are very reluctant to restrict the religious practices and comments of visitation parents when children are with them,[10] they may do so when the evidence of harm is sufficiently clear and the harm sufficiently severe.[11]

---

9. *See* Stavig v. Stavig, No. 05-0464 (S.D. Cir. Ct. 2008), *aff'd*, 774 N.W.2d 454 (S.D., 2009) (custody granted to father over primary caretaker mother, in part because father was more religious); Buck v. Buck, 4 Pa. D. & C. 5th 238 (Pa. Ct. Com. Pl. 2008) (child's "spiritual well-being" better served by being with religious father rather than nonreligious mother, as factor in custody decision); *but see* Jackson v. Jackson, No. 1 CA-CV 06-0527, 2007 WL 5446673 (Ariz. App. 2007) (rejecting on First Amendment grounds argument that trial court should have considered it in mother's favor in custody decisions that she was more religious).

10. Zummo v. Zummo, 574 A.2d 1130 (Pa. Super. 1990) (reversing trial court's limitation on father's visitation religious practices with child); *In re* Marriage of McSoud, 131 P.3d 1208 (Colo. App. 2006) (refusing to restrict visitation father's religious practices with children or his right to try to raise the children in his faith); Finnerty v. Clutter, 917 N.E.2d 154 (Ind. 2009) (court refuses to order father to bring child to Mass when he has visitation).

11. Kendall v. Kendall, 687 N.E.2d 1228 (Mass. 1997) (restricting bringing children to religious meetings where it was claimed that nonbelievers, like children and their mother, were damned to hell); Meyer v. Meyer, 789 A.2d 921 (Vt. 2001) (upholding decision prohibiting father from exposing children to religious observances or trying to raise them as Jehovah's Witnesses based on evidence of harm to children).

🎢 E. Religiously Grounded Medical Decisions

While competent adults generally have plenary power to refuse medical treatment for themselves on whatever grounds, including religious grounds (or, given First Amendment protections for the free exercise of religion and against a state establishment of religion, *especially* on religious grounds), the question becomes more complicated when adults are making decisions on behalf of their minor children.

As discussed in chapter 7, a failure to provide medical care for a child can be labeled "neglect," and be a basis for suspending or terminating parental rights. However, when parents refuse medical care, or choose unconventional forms of treatment (e.g., "spiritual healing") for religious reasons, this choice is often given express statutory protection.[12] At the same time, some courts have ruled that an exemption within abuse or neglect statutes for religious-based refusals of treatment or alternative may not necessarily immunize such decisions from potential criminal liability should the child in question die.[13]

Suggested Further Reading

Eugene Volokh, "Parent-Child Speech and Child Custody Speech Restrictions," *New York University Law Review*, vol. 81, pp. 631–733 (2006).
Joanne Ross Wilder, "Resolving Religious Disputes in Custody Cases: It's Really Not About Best Interests," *Journal of the American Academy of Matrimonial Lawyers*, vol. 22, pp. 411–423 (2009).

---

12. *See, e.g., California Welfare and Institutions Code* § 300(b).
13. *See* Walker v. Superior Court, 763 P.2d 852 (Cal. 1988); *cf.* Commonwealth v. Twitchell, 617 N.E.2d 609 (Mass. 1993); *cf.* Hermanson v. State, 604 So.2d 775 (Fla. 1992) (given accommodation for religious treatment in abuse statute, criminal prosecution barred because of lack of adequate notice).

SEVENTEEN

Domestic Violence

EXPERTS HAVE ESTIMATED the level of domestic violence in the United States to include as many as twelve million victims each year.[1] Domestic violence is obviously a central moral and policy concern, a social problem with pervasive effects on the well-being of individuals and families in this country.

There was a time, not that very long ago, when violence within the family was considered a private matter, not the business of other people, or the business of the state (and this view has by no means entirely disappeared). In 1864, the North Carolina Supreme Court responded to an assault-and-battery charge a wife had brought against her husband, as follows:

> A husband is responsible for the acts of his wife, and he is required to govern his household, and for that purpose the law permits him to use toward his wife such a degree of force as is necessary to control an unruly temper and make her behave herself; and unless some permanent injury be inflicted, or there be an excess of violence, or such a degree of cruelty as shows that it is inflicted to gratify his own bad passions, the law will not invade the domestic forum or go

---

1. "Between 600,000 and 6 million women are victims of domestic violence each year, and between 100,000 and 6 million men, depending on the type of survey used to obtain the data." Domestic Violence Resource Center, "Domestic Violence Statistics" (2012), available at http://www.dvrc-or.org/domestic/violence/resources/C61/.

behind the curtain. It prefers to leave the parties to themselves, as the best mode of inducing them to make the matter up and live together as man and wife should.[2]

American society has moved a great distance from those earlier assumptions. Today, violence against partners (and against children) is universally and publicly condemned as unacceptable, and not merely a private concern. Every jurisdiction has protective statutes and procedures to give the victims of domestic violence recourse against their attackers.[3] Still, domestic violence remains a serious social problem, and the proper response of courts, legislatures, and police forces remains a matter of controversy and debate.

There are state and federal laws creating remedies for victims of domestic violence, including protective orders and orders allowing victims to stay in a home even if that home is titled in the name of the perpetrator of the violence.

Domestic violence has legal repercussions throughout family law. Consider the following examples.

1. In marriage and divorce law, domestic violence would constitute a ground for divorce in those states that still have fault grounds. Similarly, it would be relevant where fault is a factor courts can or should take into account in determining the division of property or the setting of alimony.

2. In a number of states, domestic violence (against the child, against other children in the household, or against the other parent) is a factor a court must consider in determining child custody, and may create a strong presumption against custody in the party guilty of such violence.[4]

---

2. State v. Black, 60 N.C. 252, 1 Win. 255 (1864). This is not an isolated case. *See, e.g.*, State v. Rhodes, 61 N.C. 453 (1868) (charges against husband of assault and battery against his wife dismissed on the grounds that the state should not "interfere with family government").

3. *See, e.g., Massachusetts General Laws* Chapter 209A.

4. *Miss. Code Ann.* § 93-5-24(9). While a presumption of this sort may create an unfortunate incentive for a parent seeking custody to make a false accusation

3. Domestic violence can also be the basis for a claim that an agreement—premarital agreement, marital agreement, or separation agreement—was voidable because it was reached through duress.

4. Many statutes and international law conventions create exceptions to the normal rules where domestic violence or child abuse is present.[5]

The proper response to domestic violence is a necessary concern for all people, but perhaps a special concern for lawyers, judges, and other officials who may be in a position to report such violence or to make sure that the negative effects of such abuse are not exacerbated by the outcomes in family law disputes.

Suggested Further Reading

Martha Albertson Fineman, "Domestic Violence, Custody, and Visitation," *Family Law Quarterly*, vol. 36, pp. 211–225 (2002).

Martha R. Mahoney, "Legal Images of Battered Women: Redefining the Issue of Separation," *Michigan Law Review*, vol. 90, pp. 1–94 (1991).

Emily J. Sack, "Battered Women and the State: The Struggle for the Future of Domestic Violence Policy," *Wisconsin Law Review*, vol. 2004, pp. 1657–1740.

Reva B. Siegel, "'The Rule of Love': Wife Beating as Prerogative and Privacy," *Yale Law Journal*, vol. 105, pp. 2117–2207 (1996).

---

of domestic violence against the other parent, and such false accusations have occurred, they are probably no more common than other false accusations (of drug use, mental instability, child abuse, etc.) put forward to gain a custody litigation advantage.

5. *See, e.g., La. Rev. Stat.* §§ 9: 307(4) (domestic violence or child abuse ground for divorce, even in a covenant marriage); *Minn. Stat.* § 518.18(c) (waiting period for motion seeking modification of custody does not apply in cases of child abuse); *The Hague Convention on the Civil Aspects of International Child Abduction Article* 13b (return of child need not be ordered if the return would subject the child to physical or psychological harm).

Conclusion and Overview

IN CHAPTER 1, I offered an overview of the principles and core tensions that run throughout family law, and I hope that the remainder of the book has in part served to illustrate those principles and tensions.

American family law remains an unsettled area of law. This reflects in part the way that the legal rules here express a wide variety of values and objectives. Law everywhere is a product of different views about the best way to live and to structure society. Sometimes the conflict of perspectives leads to compromise in legislation, as fault divorce (see chapter 9) was a compromise between those who wanted divorce made freely available and those who wanted no divorce; and "civil unions" and "domestic partnership" (see chapter 2, section E) are a compromise between those who want same-sex couples to be able to marry and those who want no legal recognition for same-sex unions. And sometimes the conflicting force of different principles leads to different compromises in judicial decisions: as the tension between parental rights, children's rights, the best interests of the child, family privacy, and arguments for the common good are worked out in different (and inconsistent) ways across the rules for decision making for children and child placement determinations. Society wants to protect the best interests of children and other vulnerable parties, strengthen marriages (at least the kind of marriages which contribute to the common good), make sure that individual parties are treated fairly and justly, and use state resources efficiently and sparingly, and so on, but these different objectives often conflict.

Family law has been, and likely will remain, unsettled in the straight-forward sense that its rules—whether these come from legislatures, administrative agencies, or courts—change at a faster rate than is the case in almost any other area of law. This state of deep and pervasive change ultimately reflects changes in society, both changes in social norms and new facts presented by changing circumstances and technologies (especially the reproductive technologies discussed in chapter 6), combined with a greater willingness of legal officials (including judges) to question settled rules and reopen old doctrinal disputes.

Family law involves matters that we care about deeply, so individual disputes and policy questions evoke an intensity not generally found when we are talking about (for example) zoning variances, breaches of contract, trespass, or the rule against perpetuities. Family law is ultimately about our own lives, our own views about the right way to live, the right way to treat others, and the right way to build a good society. There will always be disagreements about such matters; it can only be hoped that through our discussions and our experiments that we are learning, and doing better at getting things right.

Bibliography

Ali, Lorraine & Kelley, Raina, "The Curious Lives of Surrogates," *Newsweek*, Apr. 7, 2008.

Allen, Douglas W. & Brinig, Margaret F., "Child Support Guidelines: The Good, the Bad and the Ugly," *Family Law Quarterly*, vol. 45, pp. 135–156 (2011).

___, "Do Joint Parenting Laws Make Any Difference?," *Journal of Empirical Legal Studies*, vol. 8, pp. 304–324 (2011).

Altman, Scott, "Should Child Custody Rules Be Fair?," *University of Louisville Journal of Family Law*, vol. 35, pp. 325–354 (1996–1997).

___, "A Theory of Child Support," *International Journal of Law, Policy, and the Family*, vol. 17, pp. 173–210 (2003).

American Bar Association, "Model Act Governing Assisted Reproductive Technology February 2008," *Family Law Quarterly*, vol. 42, pp. 171–202 (2008).

American Law Institute, *Principles of the Law of Family Dissolution: Analysis and Recommendations* (Newark: LexisNexis, 2002).

Anklesaria, Pearlene, "Child-Related Tax Breaks for Divorced Parents," *Journal of the American Academy of Matrimonial Lawyers*, vol. 22, pp. 425–435 (2009).

Annotation, "Validity and Enforceability of Agreement Designed to Prevent Divorce, or Avoid or End Separation," 11 A.L.R. 277 (1921).

Appell, Annette Ruth, "The Move Toward Legally Sanctioned Cooperative Adoption: Can It Survive the Uniform Adoption Act?," *Family Law Quarterly*, vol. 30, pp. 483–518 (1996).

___, "Reflections on the Movement Toward a More Child-Centered Adoption," *Western New England Law Review*, vol. 31, pp. 1–32 (2010).

Appleton, Susan Frelich, "Illegitimacy and Sex, Old and New," *American University Journal of Gender, Social Policy, and Law*, vol. 20, pp. 347–384 (2012).

___, "Parentage by the Numbers: Should Only Two Always Do?," *Hofstra Law Review*, vol. 37, pp. 11–69 (2008).

___, "Presuming Women: Revisiting the Presumption of Legitimacy in the Same-Sex Couples Era," *Boston University Law Review*, vol. 86, pp. 227–294 (2006).

Appleton, Susan Frelich & Weisberg, D. Kelly, *Adoption and Assisted Reproduction: Families Under Construction*. New York: Aspen Publishers, 2009.

Archard, David William, "Children's Rights" (2010), *Stanford Encyclopedia of Philosophy*, http://plato.stanford.edu/entries/rights-children/.

Associated Press, "Judge: Dowry not a Prenup," Oct. 22, 2007.

___, "New Federal Report Shows Drop in Child Abuse Rates," Apr. 1, 2010.

Atwood, Barbara Ann, "Child Custody Jurisdiction and Territoriality," *Ohio State Law Journal*, vol. 52, pp. 369–403 (1991).

___, *Children, Tribes, and States: Adoption and Custody Conflicts over American Indian Children* (Durham, N.C.: Carolina Academic Press, 2010).

___, "Tribal Jurisprudence and Cultural Meanings of Family," *Nebraska Law Journal*, vol. 79, pp. 577–656 (2000).

Baker, Debra, "New $upplement for Kids of Divorce," *ABA Journal*, p. 32, (October 1999).

Baker, Katharine K., "Homogenous Rules for Heterogeneous Families: The Standardization of Family Law When There Is No Standard Family," *University of Illinois Law Review*, vol. 2012, pp. 319–371.

Baker, Lynn A., "'I Think I Do': Another Perspective on Consent and the Law," *Law, Medicine & Health Care*, vol. 16, pp. 256–260 (1988).

Baker, Lynn A. & Emery, Robert E., "When Every Relationship Is Above Average: Perceptions and Expectations of Divorce at the Time of Marriage," *Law and Human Behavior*, vol. 17, pp. 439–450 (1993).

Ball, Carlos, "Rendering Children Illegitimate in Former Partner Parenting Cases: Hiding Behind the Façade of Certainty," *American University Journal of Gender, Social Policy & the Law*, vol. 20, pp. 623–668 (2012).

Banks, Ralph Richard, "The Multiethnic Placement Act and the Troubling Persistence of Race Matching," *Capital University Law Review*, vol. 38, pp. 271–290 (2009).

Barry, Dan, "Trading Vows in Montana, No Couple Required," *New York Times*, Mar. 10, 2008.

Bartholet, Elizabeth, "International Adoption: Thoughts on the Human Rights Issues," *Buffalo Human Rights Law Review*, vol. 13, pp. 151–203 (2007).

___, *Nobody's Children: Abuse and Neglect, Foster Drift, and the Adoption Alternative* (Boston: Beacon Press, 2000).

___, "Where Do Black Children Belong? The Politics of Race Matching in Adoption," *University of Pennsylvania Law Review*, vol. 139, pp. 1163–1256 (1991).

Basch, Norma, *Framing American Divorce: From the Revolutionary Generation to the Victorians* (Berkeley: University of California Press, 1999).

Benson, Peter (ed.), *The Theory of Contract Law* (Cambridge: Cambridge University Press, 2001).

Berenson, Steven K., "Home Court Advantage Revisited: Interstate Modification of Child Support Orders Under UIFSA and FFCCSOA," *Gonzaga Law Review*, vol. 45, pp. 479–498 (2009–2010).

Bernstein, Nina, "In Secret, Polygamy Follows Africans to N.Y.," *New York Times*, Mar. 23, 2007.

Beschle, Donald L., "God Bless the Child? The Use of Religion as a Factor in Child Custody and Adoption Proceedings," *Fordham Law Review*, vol. 58, pp. 383–426 (1989).

Bix, Brian H., "Bargaining in the Shadow of Love: The Enforcement of Premarital Agreements and How We Think About Marriage," *William & Mary Law Review*, vol. 40, pp. 145–207 (1998).

___, *Contract Law: Rules, Theory, and Context* (Cambridge: Cambridge University Press, 2012).

___, "Private Ordering and Family Law," *Journal of the American Academy of Matrimonial Lawyers*, vol. 23, pp. 249–285 (2010).

___, "The Role of Contract: Stewart Macaulay's Lessons from Practice," in Jean Braucher, John Kidwell, & William Whitford (eds.), *Revisiting the Contracts Scholarship of Stewart Macaulay: On the Empirical and the Lyrical* (Hart Publishing, 2013), pp. 241–255.

Blair, D. Marianne & Weiner, Merle H. (eds.), *International Family Law: Conventions, Statutes, and Regulatory Materials* (2nd ed., Durham, N.C.: Carolina Academic Press, 2010).

Bodin, Jean, *The Six Books of a Commonwealth* (Kenneth Douglas McRae ed., Cambridge, Mass.: Harvard University Press, 1962) (first published in 1606).

Borchers, Patrick, "The Essential Irrelevance of the Full Faith and Credit Clause to the Same-Sex Marriage Debate," *Creighton Law Review*, vol. 38, pp. 353–363 (2005).

Bowman, Cynthia Grant, "A Feminist Proposal to Bring Back Common Law Marriage," *Oregon Law Review*, vol. 75, pp. 709–780 (1996).

___, "Social Science and Legal Policy: The Case of Heterosexual Cohabitation," *Journal of Law & Family Studies*, vol. 9, pp. 1–52 (2007).

Braver, Sanford L.; Ellman, Ira M. & Fabricius, William V., "Relocation of Children After Divorce and Children's Best Interests: New Evidence and

Legal Considerations," *Journal of Family Psychology*, vol. 17, pp. 206–219 (2003).

Brinig, Margaret F., "Penalty Defaults in Family Law: The Case of Child Custody," *Florida State University Law Review*, vol. 33, pp. 779–824 (2006).

Browning, Don S. & Witte, John, Jr., *From Private Order to Public Covenant: What Christianity Offers to Modern Marriage Law* (forthcoming, Cambridge: Cambridge University Press, 2013).

Broyde, Michael J., "New York Regulation of Jewish Marriage: Covenant, Contract, or Statute?," in Joel A. Nichols (ed.), *Marriage and Divorce in a Multicultural Context* (Cambridge: Cambridge University Press, 2012), pp. 138–163.

Bruch, Carol S., "Sound Research or Wishful Thinking in Child Custody Cases? Lessons from Relocation Law," *Family Law Quarterly*, vol. 40, pp. 281–314 (2006).

Burke, Edmund, *Reflections on the Revolution in France* (New Haven: Yale University Press, 2003) (first published 1790).

Cahn, Naomi R., "Perfect Substitutes or the Real Thing?," *Duke Law Journal*, vol. 52, pp. 1077–1166 (2003).

___, *Test Tube Families: Why the Fertility Market Needs Legal Regulation* (New York: New York University Press, 2009).

Cahn, Naomi & Carbone, June, *Red Families v. Blue Families: Legal Polarization and the Creation of Culture* (Oxford: Oxford University Press, 2010).

Cahn, Naomi & the Evan B. Donaldson Adoption Institute, "Old Lessons for a New World: Applying Adoption Research and Experience to ART," *Journal of the American Academy of Matrimonial Law*, vol. 24, pp. 1–32 (2011).

Cahn, Naomi R. & Hollinger, Joan Heifetz (eds.), *Families by Law: An Adoption Reader* (New York: New York University Press, 2004).

Carbone, June, "Economics, Feminism and the Reinvention of Alimony: A Reply to Ira Ellman," *Vanderbilt Law Review*, vol. 43, pp. 1463–1501 (1990).

___, "The Legal Definition of Parenthood: Uncertainty at the Core of Family Identity," *Louisiana Law Review*, vol. 65, pp. 1295–1344 (2005).

Carbone, June & Cahn, Naomi, "Marriage, Parentage, and Child Support," *Family Law Quarterly*, vol. 45, pp. 219–240 (2011).

___, "Which Ties Bind? Redefining the Parent-Child Relationship in an Age of Genetic Certainty," *William & Mary Bill of Rights Journal*, vol. 11, pp. 1011–1070 (2003).

Carpenter, Benjamin C., "A Chip Off the Old Iceblock: How Cryopreservation Has Changed Estate Law, Why Attempts to Address the Issue Have Fallen Short, and How to Fix It," *Cornell Journal of Law and Public Policy*, vol. 21, pp. 347–430 (2011).

Case, Mary Anne, "Marriage Licenses," *Minnesota Law Review*, vol. 89, pp. 1758–1797 (2005).

Chambers, David L., *Making Fathers Pay: The Enforcement of Child Support* (Chicago: University of Chicago Press, 1979).

Chinook, William F., "No Smoking Around Children: The Family Courts' Mandatory Duty to Restrain Parents and Other Persons from Smoking Around Children," *Arizona Law Review*, vol. 45, pp. 801–821 (2003).

Chused, Richard H., "Married Women's Property Law: 1800–1850," *Georgetown Law Journal*, vol. 71, pp. 1359–1425 (1983).

Cody, Edward, "Straight Couples in France Are Choosing Civil Unions Meant for Gays," *Washington Post*, Feb. 14, 2009.

Cohen, I. Glenn, "Response: Rethinking Sperm-Donor Anonymity: Of Changed Selves, Non-Identity, and One-Night Stands," *Georgetown Law Journal*, vol. 100, pp. 431–447 (2012).

Collins, Glenn, "Study Finds Child Abduction by Parents Exceeds Estimates," *New York Times*, Oct. 23, 1983.

Comeau, Stephen P., "An Overview of the Federal Income Tax Provisions Related to Alimony Payments," *Family Law Quarterly*, vol. 38, pp. 111–126 (2004).

Coombs, Russell M., "Interstate Child Custody: Jurisdiction, Recognition, and Enforcement," *Minnesota Law Review*, vol. 66, pp. 711–864 (1982).

Coontz, Stephanie, *Marriage, a History* (New York: Viking, 2005).

Corvino, John, "Are Gay Parents Really Worse for Children? How a New Study Gets Everything Wrong," *The New Republic*, June 11, 2012, http://www.tnr.com.

Cott, Nancy F., *Public Vows: A History of Marriage and the Nation* (Cambridge, Mass.: Harvard University Press, 2000).

Coupet, Sacha M., "'Ain't I a Parent?': The Exclusion of Kinship Caregivers from the Debate Over Expansions of Parenthood," *New York University Review of Law & Social Change*, vol. 34, pp. 595–656 (2010).

Culhane, John & Marquardt, Elizabeth, "California Should Not Pass 'Multiple Parents' Bill," *Huffington Post*, Aug. 17, 2012, http://www.huffingtonpost.com.

Curry, Amberlynn, Comment, "The Uniform Premarital Agreement Act and Its Variations throughout the States," *Journal of the American Academy of Matrimonial Lawyers*, vol. 23, pp. 355–383 (2010).

Daar, Judith F., "Accessing Reproductive Technologies: Invisible Barriers, Indelible Harms," *Berkeley Journal of Gender Law & Justice*, vol. 23, pp. 18–82 (2008).

Dan-Cohen, Meir, "Decision Rules and Conduct Rules: An Acoustic Separation in Criminal Law," *Harvard Law Review*, vol. 97, pp. 625–677 (1984).

Darrin, Ellen, "Marriage and Law Reform: Lessons from Nineteenth Century Married Women's Property Acts," *Texas Journal of Women and the Law*, vol. 20, pp. 1–53 (2010).

DiFonzo, J. Herbie & Stern, Ruth C., "The Children of Baby M.," *Capital University Law Review*, vol. 39, pp. 345–411 (2011).

Domestic Violence Resource Center, "Domestic Violence Statistics" (2012), available at http://www.dvrc-or.org/domestic/violence/resources/C61/.

Donahue, Charles, Jr., "'Clandestine' Marriage in the Later Middle Ages: A Reply," *Law & History Review*, vol. 10, pp. 315–322 (1992).

___, *Law, Marriage, and Society in the Later Middle Ages: Arguments About Marriage in Five Courts* (Cambridge: Cambridge University Press, 2007).

___, "The Western Canon Law of Marriage: A Doctrinal Introduction," in Asifa Quraishi & Frank E. Vogel (eds.), *The Islamic Marriage Contract: Case Studies in Islamic Family Law* (Cambridge, Mass.: Harvard University Press, 2008), pp. 46–56.

___, "What Causes Fundamental Legal Ideas? Marital Property in England and France in the Thirteenth Century," *Michigan Law Review*, vol. 78, pp. 59–88 (1979).

Douthat, Ross, "The Birds and the Bees (via the Fertility Clinic)," *New York Times*, May 30, 2010.

Dubler, Ariela R., "In the Shadow of Marriage: Single Women and the Legal Construction of the Family and the State," *Yale Law Journal*, vol. 112, pp. 1641–1715 (2003).

Dugan, Virginia R. & Feder, Jon A., "Alimony Guidelines: Do They Work?," *Family Advocate*, vol. 25(4), pp. 20–23 (2003).

Duncan, William, "The New Hague Child Support Convention: Goals and Outcomes of the Negotiations," *Family Law Quarterly*, vol. 43, pp. 1–20 (2009).

Dworkin, Ronald, *Taking Rights Seriously* (rev. ed., Cambridge, Mass.: Harvard University Press, 1978).

Eckholm, Erik, "Which Mother for Isabella: Civil Union Ends in an Abduction and Questions," *New York Times*, July 28, 2012.

Eekelaar, John, *Family Law and Personal Life* (Oxford: Oxford University Press, 2006).

Eekelaar, John & Maclean, Mavis, *Maintenance After Divorce* (Oxford: Clarendon Press, 1986).

Eisenberg, Theodore & Lanvers, Charlotte, "What Is the Settlement Rate and Why Should We Care?," *Journal of Empirical Legal Studies*, vol. 6, pp. 111–146 (2009), also available at http://ssrn.com/abstract=1276383.

Ellman, Ira Mark, "The Maturing Law of Divorce Finances: Toward Rules and Guidelines," *Family Law Quarterly*, vol. 33, pp. 801–814 (1999).

____, "*O'Brien v. O'Brien*: A Failed Reform, Unlikely Reformers," in Carol Sanger (ed.), *Family Law Stories* (New York: Foundation Press, 2008), pp. 269–294.

____, "The Place of Fault in Modern Divorce Law," *Arizona State Law Review*, vol. 28, pp. 773–837 (1996).

Ellman, Ira Mark; Kurtz, Paul M.; Weithorn, Lois A.; Bix, Brian H.; Czapanskiy, Karen; & Eichner, Maxine, *Family Law: Cases, Text, Problems* (5th ed., Charlottesville, Va.: LexisNexis, 2010).

Ellman, Ira Mark & Lohr, Sharon, "Marriage as Contracts, Opportunistic Violence, and Other Bad Arguments for Fault Divorce," *University of Illinois Law Review*, vol. 1997, pp. 719–772.

Elrod, Linda D. & Spector, Robert G., "A Review of the Year in Family Law: Numbers of Disputes Increase," *Family Law Quarterly*, vol. 45, pp. 443–511 (2012).

Empire State Pride Agenda Foundation & The New York City Bar Association, *1,324 Reasons for Marriage Equality in New York State* (2007), available at http://www.nycbar.org/pdf/report/marriage_v7d21.pdf.

Erickson, Theresa M. & Erickson, Megan T. "What Happens to Embryos When a Marriage Dissolves? Embryo Disposition and Divorce," *William Mitchell Law Review*, vol. 35, pp. 469–488 (2009).

Estin, Ann Laquer, "Families Across Borders: The Hague Children's Convention and the Case for International Family Law in the United States," *Florida Law Review*, vol. 62, pp. 47–108 (2010).

____, "International Divorce: Litigating Marital Property and Support Rights," *Family Law Quarterly*, vol. 45, pp. 293–327 (2011).

Ezer, Nicole Lawrence, "The Intersection of Immigration Law and Family Law," *Family Law Quarterly*, vol. 40, pp. 339–366 (2006).

Farnsworth, E. Allan, *Contracts* (4th ed., New York: Aspen Publishers, 2004).

Fernandez, Jennifer, "The Price of an Affair? $9 Million," *Greensboro News & Record*, Mar. 18, 2010.

Fineman, Martha Albertson, "Domestic Violence, Custody, and Visitation," *Family Law Quarterly*, vol. 36, pp. 211–225 (2002).

___, "Families and Federalism," *Washington University Journal of Law & Policy*, vol. 4, pp. 175–238 (2000).

___, *The Neutered Mother, the Sexual Family, and Other Twentieth Century Tragedies* (New York: Routledge, 1995).

Fish, Eric M., "The Uniform Interstate Family Support Act (UIFSA) 2008: Enforcing International Obligations Through Cooperative Federalism," *Journal of the American Academy of Matrimonial Lawyers*, vol. 24, pp. 33–56 (2011).

Fournier, Pascale, "Flirting with God in Western Secular Courts: Mahr in the West," *International Journal of Law, Policy and the Family*, vol. 24, pp. 67–94 (2010).

Frantz, Carolyn J. & Dagan, Hanoch, "Properties of Marriage," *Columbia Law Review*, vol. 104, pp. 75–133 (2004).

Friedman, Lawrence M., "A Dead Language: Divorce Law and Practice Before No-Fault," *Virginia Law Review*, vol. 86, pp. 1497–1536 (2000).

___, *A History of American Law* (3rd ed., New York: Simon & Schuster, 2005).

___, *Private Lives: Families, Individuals, and the Law* (Cambridge, Mass.: Harvard University Press, 2004).

___, "Rites of Passage: Divorce Law in Historical Perspective," *Oregon Law Review*, vol. 63, pp. 649–669 (1984).

Frier, Bruce W. & McGinn, Thomas A. J., *A Casebook on Roman Family Law* (Oxford: Oxford University Press, 2004).

Fuller, Lon L., "Consideration and Form," *Columbia Law Review*, vol. 41, pp. 799–824 (1941).

Gambrell, Jon, "Ark. Voters OK Unmarried Foster, Adoption Bans," Associated Press, Nov. 5, 2008.

Garrison, Marsha, "Law Making for Baby Making: An Interpretive Approach to the Determination of Legal Parentage," *Harvard Law Review*, vol. 113, pp. 835–923 (2000).

___, "Nonmarital Cohabitation: Social Revolution and Legal Regulation," *Family Law Quarterly*, vol. 42, pp. 309–331 (2008).

___, "Why Terminate Parental Rights?," *Stanford Law Review*, vol. 35, pp. 423–496 (1983).

George, Robert P. & Elsthtain, Jean Bethke (eds.), *The Meaning of Marriage: Family, State, Market & Morals* (Dallas: Spence Publishing Co., 2006).

Gilles, Stephen G., "On Educating Children: A Parentalist Manifesto," *University of Chicago Law Review*, vol. 63, pp. 937–1034 (1996).

Girgis, Sherif; George, Robert P. & Anderson, Ryan T., "What Is Marriage?," *Harvard Journal of Law & Public Policy*, vol. 34, pp. 245–287 (2011).

Glennon, Theresa, "Still Partners? Examining the Consequences of Post-Dissolution Parenting," *Family Law Quarterly*, vol. 41, pp. 105–144 (2007).

Godard, Joëlle, "Pacs Seven Years On: Is It Moving Towards Marriage?," *International Journal of Law, Policy, and the Family*, vol. 21, pp. 310–321 (2007).

Goldberg, Charlotte K., "The Schemes of Adventuresses: The Abolition and Revival of Common-Law Marriage," *William & Mary Journal of Women and the Law*, vol. 13, pp. 483–538 (2007).

Grady, Denise, "Lesley Brown, Mother of First 'Test Tube Baby', Dies at 64," *New York Times*, June 23, 2012.

Graff, E. J., *What Is Marriage For? The Strange Social History of Our Most Intimate Institution* (Boston: Beacon Press, 1999).

Greenawalt, Kent, "Child Custody, Religious Practices, and Conscience," *University of Colorado Law Review*, vol. 76, pp. 965–988 (2005).

———, "Religious Law and Civil Law: Using Secular Law to Assure Observance of Practices with Religious Significance," *Southern California Law Review*, vol. 71, pp. 781–843 (1998).

Grossberg, Michael, *A Judgment for Solomon: The D'Hauteville Case and Legal Experience in Antebellum America* (Cambridge: Cambridge University Press, 1996).

Grossman, Joanna L. & Friedman, Lawrence M., *Inside the Castle: Law and the Family in 20th Century America* (Princeton: Princeton University Press, 2011).

Gurr, Stephen, "Jury Awards Jilted Bride $150,000," *gainesvilletimes.com*, July 23, 2008, http://www.gainesvilletimes.com/news/article/7296/.

Halley, Janet, "What Is Family Law? A Genealogy," *Yale Journal of Law and the Humanities*, vol. 23, pp. 1–109 (2011).

Hamilton, Vivian, "Principles of U.S. Family Law," *Fordham Law Review*, vol. 75, pp. 31–73 (2006).

Harris, Judith Rich, *The Nurture Assumption: Why Children Turn Out the Way They Do* (New York: Free Press, 2008).

Harris Leslie Joan, "Failure to Protect From Exposure to Domestic Violence in Private Custody Contests," *Family Law Quarterly*, vol. 44, pp. 169–196 (2010).

Hartog, Hendrik, *Man and Wife in America: A History* (Cambridge, Mass: Harvard University Press, 2000).

Hasday, Jill, "Federalism and the Family Reconstructed," *UCLA Law Review*, vol. 45, pp. 1297–1400 (1998).

Hay, Peter, "The American 'Covenant Marriage' in the Conflict of Laws," in John Witte, Jr. & Eliza Ellison (eds.), *Covenant Marriage in Comparative*

Perspective (Grand Rapids, Mich.: William B. Eerdmans Publishing Co., 2005), pp. 294–316.

Hayek, Friedrich, *Law, Legislation, and Liberty* (Chicago: University of Chicago Press, 1973–1979), 3 vols.

Heagney, Meredith, "Muslims' Dowry Not Binding, Judge Says," *Columbus Dispatch*, Oct. 20, 2007.

Helmholz, R. H., "Canonical Remedies in Medieval Marriage Law: The Contributions of Legal Practice," *University of St. Thomas Law Journal*, vol. 1, pp. 647–655 (2003).

___, *Marriage Litigation in Medieval England* (Cambridge: Cambridge University Press, 1974).

___, "Support Orders, Church Courts, and the Rule of Filius Nullius: A Reassessment of the Common Law," *Virginia Law Review*, vol. 63, pp. 431–448 (1977).

Hinson, Diane S. & McBrien, Maureen, "Surrogacy Across America," *Family Advocate*, vol. 34(2), pp. 32–36 (Fall 2011).

Hirschler, Ben, "Scientists Create Three-Parent Embryos," *Reuters*, Feb. 5, 2008.

Hoff, Patricia M., "The ABC's of the UCCJEA: Interstate Child-Custody Practice Under the New Act," *Family Law Quarterly*, vol. 32, pp. 267–299 (1998).

Hollinger, Joan Heifetz & Cahn, Nancy, "Forming Families by Law: Adoption in America Today," *Human Rights*, pp. 16–19 (Summer 2009).

Holmes, Oliver Wendell, Jr., "The Path of the Law," *Harvard Law Review*, vol. 10, pp. 457–478 (1897).

Howe, Ruth-Arlene W., "Race Matters in Adoption," *Family Law Quarterly*, vol. 42, pp. 465–479 (2008).

Isard, Susan, "Stock Options and Child Support: The Price of Accuracy," *Hastings Women's Law Journal*, vol. 14, pp. 215–248 (2003).

Jacobs, Melanie B., "When Daddy Doesn't Want to Be Daddy Anymore: An Argument Against Paternity Fraud Claims," *Yale Journal of Law and Feminism*, vol. 16, pp. 193–240 (2004).

Joslin, Courtney G., "Modernizing Divorce Jurisdiction: Same-Sex Couples and Minimum Contacts," *Boston University Law Review*, vol. 91, pp. 1669–1722 (2011).

Kachroo, Gaytri, "Mapping Alimony: From Status to Contract and Beyond," *Pierce Law Review*, vol. 5, pp. 163–270 (2007).

Katz, Sanford N., *Family Law in America* (Oxford: Oxford University Press, 2011).

Kempe, C. Henry, et al., "The Battered Child Syndrome," *Journal of the American Medical Association (JAMA)*, vol. 181, pp. 17–24 (July 7, 1962).

Kennedy, Duncan, "Form and Substance in Private Law Adjudication," *Harvard Law Review*, vol. 89, pp. 1685–1778 (1976).

Kershaw, Sarah, "Shaking Off the Shame," *New York Times*, Nov. 26, 2009.

Kindregan, Charles P., Jr. & McBrien, Maureen, "Posthumous Reproduction," *Family Law Quarterly*, vol. 39, pp. 579–597 (2005).

Kindregan, Charles P., Jr. & Snyder, Steven H., "Clarifying the Law of ART: The New American Bar Association Model Act Governing Assisted Reproductive Technology," *Family Law Quarterly*, vol. 42, pp. 203–229 (2008).

Kisthardt, Mary Kay, "Rethinking Alimony: The AAML's Considerations for Calculating Alimony, Spousal Support or Maintenance," *Journal of the American Academy of Matrimonial Lawyers*, vol. 21, pp. 61–85 (2008).

Koch, Wendy, "Many States Usher in New Laws with the New Year," *USA Today*, Dec. 29, 2008.

Koppelman, Andrew, *Same Sex, Different States: When Same-Sex Marriages Crosses State Lines* (New Haven: Yale University Press, 2006).

Krause, Harry D., "On the Danger of Allowing Marital Fault to Re-Emerge in the Guise of Torts," *Notre Dame Law Review*, vol. 73, pp. 1355–1367 (1998).

Kumar, Anita, "Kaine: Gay Couples Should Be Allowed to Adopt," *Washington Post*, May 18, 2011.

Kurtz, Stanley, "Heather Has 3 Parents," *National Review Online*, Mar. 12, 2003, http://www.nationalreview.com.

Kuykendall, Mae & Candeub, Adam, "Symposium Overview: Perspectives on Innovative Marriage Procedure," *Michigan State Law Review*, vol. 2011, pp. 1–33.

Larkin, Twila, "Guidelines for Alimony: The New Mexico Experiment," *Family Law Quarterly*, vol. 38, pp. 29–68 (2004).

Larson, Jane, "'Women Understand So Little, They Call My Nature "Deceit"': A Feminist Rethinking of Seduction," *Columbia Law Review*, vol. 93, pp. 374–472 (1993).

Law, Sylvia, "Families and Federalism," *Washington University Journal of Law & Policy*, vol. 4, pp. 175–238 (2000).

___, "Rethinking Sex and the Constitution," *University of Pennsylvania Law Review*, vol. 132, pp. 955–1040 (1984).

Leeson, Peter T.; Boettke, Peter J. & Lemke, Jayme S., "Wife Sales," unpublished manuscript (2011), available at http://www.peterleeson.com.

Lettmaier, Saskia, *Broken Engagements: The Action for Breach of Promise of Marriage and the Feminine Ideal, 1800–1940* (Oxford: Oxford University Press, 2010).

Lind, Göran, *Common Law Marriage* (Oxford: Oxford University Press, 2008).

Lowe, Nigel V. & Stephens, Victoria, "Global Trends in the Operation of the 1980 Hague Abduction Convention," *Family Law Quarterly*, vol. 46, pp. 41–85 (2012).

Mahoney, Margaret M., "The Equitable Division of Marital Debts," *University of Missouri-Kansas City Law Review*, vol. 79, pp. 445–475 (2010).

___, "Permanence and Parenthood: The Case for Abolishing the Adoption Annulment Doctrine," *Indiana Law Review*, vol. 42, pp. 639–674 (2009).

___, "Stepparents as Third Parties in Relation to Their Stepchildren," *Family Law Quarterly*, vol. 40, pp. 81–108 (2006).

Mahoney, Martha R., "Legal Images of Battered Women: Redefining the Issue of Separation," *Michigan Law Review*, vol. 90, pp. 1–94 (1991).

Maine, Henry Sumner, *Ancient Law* (10th ed., London: J. Murray, 1920).

Markel, Dan; Leib, Ethan J. & Collins, Jennifer, "Rethinking Criminal Law and Family Status," *Yale Law Journal*, vol. 119, pp. 1864–1903 (2010).

Marquardt, Elizabeth, "When Three Really Is a Crowd," *New York Times*, July 16, 2007.

Marquardt, Elizabeth; Glenn, Norval D. & Clark, Karen, *My Daddy's Name Is Donor* (New York: Institute for American Values, 2010), available at http://familyscholars.org/my-daddys-name-is-donor-2/.

McClain, Linda C., *The Place of Families: Fostering Capacity, Equality, and Responsibility* (Cambridge, Mass.: Harvard University Press, 2006).

McGough, Lucy S., "Protecting Children in Divorce: Lessons from Caroline Norton," *Maine Law Review*, vol. 57, pp. 14–37 (2005).

Mehrotra, Vikas et al., "Adoptive Expectations: Rising Sons in Japanese Family Firms" (unpublished manuscript, 2010), linked at http://www.freakonomics.com/2011/08/09/the-church-of-scionology-why-adult-adoption-is-key-to-the-success-of-japanese-family-firms/.

Mertz, Elizabeth, "Translating Science into Family Law: An Overview," *DePaul Law Review*, vol. 56, pp. 799–821 (2007).

Meyer, David D., "The Constitutional Rights of Non-Custodial Parents," *Hofstra Law Review*, vol. 35, pp. 1461–1494 (2006).

Ministry of Attorney General, White Paper on *Family Relations Act*: Reform Proposals for a New Family Law Act (July 2010), available at http://www.ag.gov.bc.ca/legislation/index.htm.

Minow, Martha, "Consider the Consequences," *Michigan Law Review*, vol. 84, pp. 900–918 (1986).

Mnookin, Robert H., "Child-Custody Adjudication: Judicial Functions in the Face of Indeterminacy," *Law and Contemporary Problems*, vol. 39, pp. 226–293 (1975).

Mnookin, Robert H. & Kornhauser, Lewis, "Bargaining in the Shadow of the Law: The Case of Divorce", *Yale Law Journal*, vol. 88, pp. 950–997 (1979).

Morgan, Laura W., "Child Support Fifty Years Later," *Family Law Quarterly*, vol. 42, pp. 365–380 (2008).

Morgan, Laura W. & Turner, Brett R., *Attacking and Defending Marital Agreements* (2nd ed., Chicago: ABA Family Law Section, 2012).

Morley, Jeremy D., *The Hague Abduction Convention: Practical Issues and Procedures for the Family Lawyer* (Chicago: American Bar Association, Section on Family Law, 2012).

Morris, Anne & Nott, Sue, "Rights and Responsibilities: Contested Parenthood," *The Journal of Social Welfare & Family Law*, vol. 31, pp. 3–16 (2009).

Munzer, Stephen R., *A Theory of Property* (Cambridge: Cambridge University Press, 1990).

Murray, Melissa, "Marriage as Punishment," *Columbia Law Review*, vol. 112, pp. 1–65 (2012).

The National Archives, "Divorce Records Before 1858," http://www.nationalarchives.gov.uk/records/research-guides/divorce-before-1858.htm.

National Association of Black Social Workers, "Position Statement on Transracial Adoption" (1972), reprinted in The Adoption History Project, http://www.uoregon.edu/~adoption/archive/NabswTRA.htm.

___, "Preserving Families of African Ancestry" (2003), http://www.nabsw.org/mserver/PreservingFamilies.aspx?menuContext=757.

National Council for Adoption, *Adoption Factbook V* (Alexandria, Va.: National Council for Adoption, 2011).

Nelson, Barbara, *Making an Issue of Child Abuse* (Chicago: University of Chicago Press, 1984).

Nelson, Lori W., "High-Income Child Support," *Family Law Quarterly*, vol. 45, pp. 191–218 (2011).

Nichols, Joel A., "Louisiana's Covenant Marriage Law: A First Step toward a More Robust Pluralism in Marriage and Divorce Law?," *Emory Law Journal*, vol. 47, pp. 929–1001 (1998).

___, "Misunderstanding Marriage and Missing Religion," *Michigan State Law Review*, vol. 2011, pp. 195–208.

___, "Multi-Tiered Marriage: Ideas and Influences from New York and Louisiana to the International Community," *Vanderbilt Journal of Transnational Law*, vol. 40, pp. 135–196 (2007).

Nock, Steven L.; Sanchez, Laura Ann & Wright, James D., *Covenant Marriage: The Movement to Reclaim Tradition in America* (New Brunswick: Rutgers University Press, 2008).

Oldham, J. Thomas, "Changes in the Economic Consequences of Divorces, 1958–2008," *Family Law Quarterly*, vol. 42, pp. 419–447.

___, *Divorce, Separation and the Distribution of Property* (New York: Law Journal Seminars Press; looseleaf, 1987, updated through 2012).

___, "Everything Is Bigger in Texas, Except the Community Property Estate: Must Texas Remain a Divorce Haven for the Rich?," *Family Law Quarterly*, vol. 44, pp. 293–316 (2010).

___, "What if the Beckhams Move to L.A. and Divorce? Marital Property Rights of Mobile Spouses When They Divorce in the United States," *Family Law Quarterly*, vol. 42, pp. 263–293 (2008).

Olsen, Frances E., "The Myth of State Intervention in the Family," *University of Michigan Journal of Law Reform*, vol. 18, pp. 835–864 (1985).

Oreskovic, Johanna & Maskew, Trish, "Red Thread or Slender Reed: Deconstructing Prof. Bartholet's Mythology of International Adoption," *Buffalo Human Rights Law Review*, vol. 14, pp. 71–128 (2008).

Parness, Jeffrey A., "Lost Paternity in the Culture of Motherhood: A Different View of Safe Havens," *Valparaiso Law Review*, vol. 42, pp. 81–98 (2007).

Petrecca, Laura, "Prenuptial Agreements: Unromantic, but Important," *USA Today*, Mar. 8, 2010.

du Plessis, Paul, *Borkowski's Textbook on Roman Law* (4th ed., Oxford: Oxford University Press, 2010).

Polikoff, Nancy, *Beyond Straight and Gay Marriage: Valuing All Families Under the Law* (Boston: Beacon Press, 2008).

___, "Where Can a Child Have Three Parents?," *Beyond (Straight and Gay) Marriage* (Blog), July 14, 2012, available at http://beyondstraightandgay-marriage.blogspot.com/2012/07/where-can-child-have-three-parents.html.

Posner, Richard A., *The Problems of Jurisprudence* (Cambridge, Mass.: Harvard University Press, 1990).

Postema, Gerald J. (ed.), *Philosophy and the Law of Torts* (Cambridge: Cambridge University Press, 2001).

Presser, Stephen B., "The Historical Background of the American Law of Adoption," *Journal of Family Law*, vol. 11, pp. 443–516 (1971).

___, "Marriage and the Law: Time for a Divorce?," in Joel A. Nichols (ed.), *Marriage and Divorce in a Multicultural Context* (Cambridge: Cambridge University Press, 2012), pp. 78–91.

Priest, George L. & Klein, Benjamin, "The Selection of Disputes for Litigation," *Journal of Legal Studies*, vol. 13, pp. 1–55 (1984).

Probert, Rebecca, "Common Misunderstandings" (book review), *Family Law Quarterly*, vol. 43, pp. 587–597 (2009).

___, *Marriage Law and Practice in the Long Eighteenth Century* (Cambridge: Cambridge University Press, 2009).

___, "Why Couples Still Believe in Common-Law Marriage," *Family Law*, vol. 37, pp. 403–406 (2007).

Ramsey, Sarah H. & Abrams, Douglas E., "A Primer on Child Abuse and Neglect Law," *Juvenile and Family Court Journal*, vol. 61, pp. 1–31 (2010).

Ramsey, Sarah H. & Kelly, Robert F., "Assessing Social Science Studies: Eleven Tips for Judges and Lawyers," *Family Law Quarterly*, vol. 40, pp. 367–380 (2006).

Rauch, Jonathan, "Objections to These Unions," *Reason*, June 2004, available at http://reason.com/archives/2004/06/01/objections-to-these-unions/singlepage.

Ravdin, Linda J., *Premarital Agreements: Drafting and Negotiation* (Chicago: American Bar Association, 2011).

Reid, Charles J., Jr., "The Rights of Children in Medieval Canon Law," in Patrick Brennan (ed.), *The Vocation of the Child* (Grand Rapids, Mich.: William B. Eerdmans, 2008), pp. 243–265, also available at http://papers.ssrn.com/abstract=1015403.

Reynolds, William J. & Richman, William M., *The Full Faith and Credit Clause* (Westport, Conn.: Praeger, 2005).

Richards, Janet Leach, "A Guide to Spousal Support and Property Division Claims Under the Bankruptcy Abuse Prevention and Consumer Protection Act of 2005," *Family Law Quarterly*, vol. 41, pp. 227–248 (2007).

Richmond, Diana, "The Challenges of Stock Options," *Family Law Quarterly*, vol. 35, pp. 251–262 (2001).

Riley, Glenda, *Divorce: An American Tradition* (New York: Oxford University Press, 1991).

Roberts, Dorothy E., "Poverty, Race, and New Directions in Child Welfare Policies," *Washington University Journal of Law & Policy*, vol. 1, pp. 63–76 (1999).

Rogerson, Carol & Thompson, Rollie, "The Canadian Experiment with Spousal Support Guidelines," *Family Law Quarterly*, vol. 45, pp. 241–269 (2011).

Rosenbury, Laura A., "Two Ways to End a Marriage: Divorce or Death," *Utah Law Review*, vol. 2005, pp. 1227–1290 (2005).

Rosettenstein, David S., "Exploring the Use of the Time Rule in the Distribution of Stock Options at Divorce," *Family Law Quarterly*, vol. 35, pp. 262–303 (2001).

Ross, Allison E., "Taking Care of Our Caretakers: Using Filial Responsibility Laws to Support the Elderly Beyond the Government's Assistance," *Elder Law Journal*, vol. 16, pp. 167–209 (2008).

Ross, Kathryn G., "Justified Suits or Jilted Brides—An Analysis of the Illinois Breach of Promise Act and the Case of *Buttitta v. Salerno*" (2011), available at http://ssrn.com/abstract=1837620.

Roy, Nilanjana S., "Protecting the Rights of Surrogate Mothers in India," *New York Times*, Oct. 4, 2011.

Sack, Emily J., "Battered Women and the State: The Struggle for the Future of Domestic Violence Policy," *Wisconsin Law Review*, vol. 2004, pp. 1657–1740.

Saletan, William, "You: The Updated Owner's Manual," *New York Times Book Review*, Aug. 2, 2009, p. 23.

Sampson, John J., "Uniform Interstate Family Support Act (1996) (with More Unofficial Annotations by John J. Sampson)," *Family Law Quarterly*, vol. 32, pp. 390–520 (1998).

Sampson, John J., with Brooks, Barry J., "Uniform Interstate Family Support Act (2001) with Prefatory Note and Comments (with Still More Unofficial Annotations)," *Family Law Quarterly*, vol. 36, pp. 329–447 (2002).

Sampson, John J. & Kurtz, Paul M., "UIFSA: An Interstate Support Act for the 21st Century," *Family Law Quarterly*, vol. 27, pp. 85–90 (1993).

Sanders, Jim, "Jerry Brown Vetoes Bill Allowing More Than Two Parents," *Sacramento Bee*, Sept. 30, 2012.

Sanger, Carol, "Acquiring Children Contractually: Relational Contracts at Work at Home," in Jean Braucher, John Kidwell, & William Whitford (eds.), *Revisiting the Contracts Scholarship of Stewart Macaulay: On the Empirical and the Lyrical* (Oxford: Hart Publishing, 2013).

___, "Regulating Teenage Abortion in the United States: Politics and Policy," *International Journal of Law, Policy and the Family*, vol. 18, pp. 305–318 (2004).

Schauer, Frederick, "Precedent", *Stanford Law Review*, vol. 39, pp. 571–605 (1987).

___, *Thinking Like a Lawyer: A New Introduction to Legal Reasoning* (Cambridge, Mass: Harvard University Press, 2009).

Schneider, Carl E., "Moral Discourse and the Transformation of American Family Law," *Michigan Law Review*, vol. 83, pp. 1803–1879 (1985).

___, "Rethinking Alimony: Marital Decisions and Moral Discourse," *BYU Law Review*, vol. 1991, pp. 197–257.

Schneider, Carl E. & Brinig, Margaret F., *An Invitation to Family Law: Principles, Process and Perspectives* (3rd ed., St. Paul: West Publishing, 2006).

Scott, Elizabeth S., "Pluralism, Parental Preference, and Child Custody," *California Law Review*, vol. 80, pp. 615–672 (1992).

___, "Surrogacy and the Politics of Commodification," *Law and Contemporary Problems*, vol. 72, pp. 109–146 (2009).

Semple, Kirk, "Custody Case Tests Abduction Laws and U.S.-Brazil Ties," *New York Times*, Feb. 25, 2009.

Shaman, Jeffrey M., "Legal Aspects of Artificial Insemination," *Journal of Family Law*, vol. 18, pp 331–351 (1979–1980).

Shenker, Jack, "Biggest Divorce Settlement in British Legal History as Wife Gets £48m," *The Guardian*, Aug. 5, 2006.

Siegel, Reva B., "'The Rule of Love': Wife Beating as Prerogative and Privacy," *Yale Law Journal*, vol. 105, pp. 2117–2207 (1996).

Singer, Jana, "Marriage, Biology, and Paternity: The Case for Revitalizing the Marital Presumption," *Maryland Law Review*, vol. 65, pp. 246–270 (2006).

___, "The Privatization of Family Law," *Wisconsin Law Review*, pp. 1443–1567 (1992).

Snyder, Steven H. & Byrn, Mary Patricia, "The Use of Pre-Birth Parentage Orders in Surrogacy Proceedings," *Family Law Quarterly*, vol. 39, pp. 633–662 (2005).

Solinger, Rickie, *Wake Up Little Susie: Single Pregnancy and Race before Roe v. Wade* (New York: Routledge, 1992).

Spector, Robert G., "The New Uniform Law with Regard to Jurisdiction Rules in Child Custody Cases in the United States," in *Yearbook of Private International Law*, vol. 2, pp. 75–98 (2000).

___, "Uniform Child-Custody Jurisdiction and Enforcement Act (with Prefatory Note and Comments by Robert G. Spector)," *Family Law Quarterly*, vol. 32, pp. 301–384 (1998).

Stark, Barbara, *International Family Law: An Introduction* (Aldershot, England: Ashgate, 2005).

___, "The Internationalization of American Family Law," *Journal of the American Academy of Matrimonial Lawyers*, vol. 24, pp. 467–487 (2012).

Starnes, Cynthia Lee, "Alimony Theory," *Family Law Quarterly*, vol. 45, pp. 271–291 (2011).

___, "One More Time: Alimony, Intuition, and the Remarriage-Termination Rule," *Indiana Law Journal*, vol. 81, pp. 971–999 (2006).

Steinfeld, Shayna M., "The Impact of Changes Under the Bankruptcy Abuse Prevention and Consumer Protection Act of 2005 on Family Obligations," *Journal of the American Academy of Matrimonial Lawyers*, vol. 20, pp. 251–283 (2007).

Steinfeld, Shayna M. & Steinfeld, Bruce R., *The Family Lawyer's Guide to Bankruptcy: Forms, Tips, and Strategies* (2nd ed., Chicago: ABA Publishing, 2008).

Stephen, James Fitzjames, *Liberty, Equality, Fraternity and Three Brief Essays* (Chicago: University of Chicago Press, 1991) (first published in 1873).

Strasser, Mark P., "You Take the Embryos but I Get the House (and the Business): Recent Trends in Awards Involving Embryos upon Divorce," *Buffalo Law Review*, vol. 57, pp. 1159–1225 (2009).

Sugarman, Stephen D. & Kay, Herma Hill, eds., *Divorce Reform at the Crossroads* (New Haven: Yale University Press, 1990).

Swanson, Kara W., "Adultery by Doctor: Artificial Insemination, 1890–1945," *Chicago-Kent Law Review*, vol. 87, pp. 591–633 (2012).

Symposium, "Unmarried Partners and the Legacy of *Marvin v. Marvin*," *Notre Dame Law Review*, vol. 76, pp. 1261–1490 (2001).

Tait, Allison, "Unhappy Marriages and Unpaid Creditors: Chancery's Enforcement of a Wife's Right to Property Within Marriage in Seventeenth- and Eighteenth-Century England" (2012), http://ssrn.com/abstract=2007144.

tenBroek, Jacobus, "California's Dual System of Family Law: Its Origin, Development, and Present Status" (Parts I, II, & III), *Stanford Law Review*, vol. 16, pp. 257–317, 900–981 (1964), vol. 17, pp. 614–682 (1965).

Thomas, Jennifer, Comment, "Common Law Marriage," *Journal of the American Academy of Matrimonial Lawyers*, vol. 22, pp. 151–167 (2009).

Tingley, John & Svalina, Nicholas, Updated by McKenna, Nancy, *Marital Property Law, rev. 2d.* (St. Paul: West, 2011), 3 vols.

Trainor, Elizabeth, "Basis for Imputing Income for Purpose of Determining Child Support Where Obligor Spouse is Voluntarily Unemployed or Underemployed," 76 A.L.R.5th 191 (2000).

Trebilcock, Michael J. & Elliott, Steven, "The Scope and Limits of Legal Paternalism: Altruism and Coercion in Family Financial Arrangements," in Peter Benson (ed.), *The Theory of Contract Law: New Essays* (Cambridge: Cambridge University Press, 2001), pp. 45–85.

Turcios, Erica, "Remaining versus Removal: Preventing Premature Removal When Poverty Is Confused with Neglect," *Michigan Child Welfare Law Journal*, vol. 12(4), pp. 20–28 (Summer 2009).

Turner, Anna & Field, Michael, "Cousins Marrying No Big Problems, Say NZ Geneticists," *Press* (New Zealand), July 10, 2012.

U.S. Census Bureau, *Custodial Fathers and Mothers and Their Child Support: 2009* (December 2011), available at http://www.census.gov/prod/2011pubs/p60-240.pdf.

U.S. Commission on Civil Rights, *The Multiethnic Placement Act: Minorities in Foster Care and Adoption* (July 2010), available at http://www.usccr.gov/pubs/MEPABriefingFinal_07-01-10.pdf.

U.S. Department of Health and Human Services, *Child Maltreatment 2008* (2010), available at http://www.acf.hhs.gov/programs/cb/pubs/cm08.

U.S. Department of Health and Human Services, *Postadoption Contact Agreements Between Birth and Adoptive Families* (2011), available at http://www.childwelfare.gov/systemwide/laws_policies/statutes/cooperative.cfm.

U.S. Department of Health and Human Services, Administration for Children & Families, *Postadoption Contact Agreements Between Birth and Adoptive Families* (2011), available at http://www.childwelfare.gov/systemwide/laws_policies/statutes/cooperative.cfm.

U.S. Department of Health and Human Services, Administration for Children & Families, Children's Bureau, *Trends in Foster Care and Adoption*, FY 2002–FY 2011 (2012), available at http://archive.acf.hhs.gov/programs/cb/stats_research/afcars/trends_july2012.pdf

U.S. Department of Health and Human Services, Centers for Disease Control and Prevention, *2005 Assisted Reproductive Technology Success Rates* (2007), report available at http://www.cdc.gov/art/PDF/508PDF/2005ART508.pdf.

U.S. Department of Health and Human Services, Child Welfare Information Gateway, *Acts of Omission: An Overview of Child Neglect* (2001), available at http://www.childwelfare.gov/pubs/focus/acts/.

Ventura, Stephanie J., "Changing Patterns of Nonmarital Childbearing in the United States" (Center for Disease Control and Prevention, National Center for Health Statistics, May 2009), available at http://www.cdc.gov/nchs/data/databriefs/db18.pdf.

Vernier, Chester G. & Hurlbut, John B., "The Historical Background of Alimony Law and Its Present Statutory Structure," *Law & Contemporary Problems*, vol. 6, pp. 197–212 (1939).

Victor, Daniel R. & Middleditch, Keri L., "Grandparent Visitation: A Survey of History, Jurisprudence, and Legislative Trends Across the United States in the Past Decade," *Journal of the American Academy of Matrimonial Lawyers*, vol. 22, pp. 391–409 (2009).

Volokh, Eugene, "Parent-Child Speech and Child Custody Speech Restrictions," *New York University Law Review*, vol. 81, pp. 631–733 (2006).

Wald, Michael S., "Adults' Sexual Orientation and State Determinations Regarding Placement of Children," *Family Law Quarterly*, vol. 40, pp. 381–434 (2006).

Wallerstein, Judith S.; Lewis, Julia & Blakeslee, Sandra, *The Unexpected Legacy of Divorce: A 25 Year Landmark Study* (New York: Hyperion, 2000).

Wardle, Lynn D.; Strasser, Mark; Duncan, William C. & Coolidge, David Orgon (eds.), *Marriage and Same-Sex Unions: A Debate* (Westport, Conn.: Praeger, 2003).

Weiner, Merle H., "Inertia and Inequality: Reconceptualizing Disputes Over Parental Relocation," *U.C. Davis Law Review*, vol. 40, pp. 1747–1834 (2007).

Weintraub, Russell J., *Commentary on the Conflict of Laws* (6th ed., New York: Foundation Press, 2010).

Weitzman, Lenore J., "The Economics of Divorce: Social and Economic Consequences of Property, Alimony and Child Support," *UCLA Law Review*, vol. 28, pp. 1181–1268 (1981).

West, Robin, *Marriage, Sexuality, and Gender* (Boulder: Paradigm Publishers, 2007).

Widner, Kirsten, "Continuing the Evolution: Why California Should Amend Family Code Section 8616.5 to Allow Visitation in All Postadoption Contact Agreements," *San Diego Law Review*, vol. 44, pp. 355–386 (2007).

___, "Resolving Religious Disputes in Custody Cases: It's Really Not About Best Interests," *Journal of the American Academy of Matrimonial Lawyers*, vol. 22, pp. 411–423 (2009).

Wilder, Joanne Ross Wilder, "Divorce and Taxes: Fifty Years of Changes," *Journal of the American Academy of Matrimonial Lawyers*, vol. 24, pp. 489–504 (2012).

Williams, Sean Hannon, "Postnuptial Agreements," *Wisconsin Law Review*, vol. 2007, pp. 827–887.

Witte, John, Jr., *From Sacrament to Contract: Marriage, Religion, and Law in the Western Tradition* (Louisville: Westminster John Knox Press, 1997).

___, *The Sins of the Fathers: The Law and Theology of Illegitimacy Reconsidered* (Cambridge: Cambridge University Press, 2009).

Witte, John, Jr. & Ellison, Eliza (eds.), *Covenant Marriage in Comparative Perspective* (Grand Rapids, Mich.: William B. Eerdmans Publishing Co, 2005).

Women's Law Center of Maryland, Inc., *Families in Transition: A Follow-Up Study Exploring Family Law Issues in Maryland* (2006), available at http://www.wlcmd.org/publications.html.

Wood, Richard J., *Family Tax Law* (Lake Mary, Fla.: Vandeplas Publishing, 2010).

Woodhouse, Barbara Bennett, "Hatching the Egg: A Child-Centered Perspective on Parent's Rights," *Cardozo Law Review*, vol. 14, pp. 1746–1865 (1993).

Wright, John deP., "Wife Sale," *Green Bag 2d*, vol. 7, pp. 169–173 (2004).

Yardley, William, "A Washington State Indian Tribe Approves Same-Sex Marriage," *New York Times*, Aug., 12, 2011.

Younger, Judith T., "Lovers' Contracts in the Courts: Forsaking the Minimal Decencies," *William & Mary Journal of Women and the Law*, vol. 13, pp. 349–428 (2007).

___, "Post-Divorce Visitation for Infants and Young Children—The Myths and the Psychological Unknowns," *Family Law Quarterly*, vol. 36, pp. 195–210 (2002).

Zainaldin, Jamil S., "The Emergence of a Modern American Family Law: Child Custody, Adoption, and the Courts, 1796–1851," *Northwestern University Law Review*, vol. 73, pp. 1038–1089 (1979).

Zelinsky, Edward A., "Deregulating Marriage: The Pro-Marriage Case for Abolishing Civil Marriage," *Cardozo Law Review*, vol. 27, pp. 1161–1220 (2006).

Table of Cases

Constitution, Statutes, Uniform Laws, Regulations and Restatements

United States Constitution

Federal Statutes

Federal Regulations

Uniform Laws

State Statutes and Regulations

Indian Tribes

Restatements

282 CONSTITUTION, STATUTES, UNIFORM LAWS, REGULATIONS

Foreign and International

Index